ALL MY RELATIVES

**New Visions in Native American
and Indigenous Studies**

SERIES EDITORS

Margaret D. Jacobs
Robert Miller

"A must-read for the student of Lakota ontology, belief, and ritual. Posthumus adds to the field of collected works that capture once again the adage, 'We have much to learn from the American Indian.'"
—Maka Akan Najin Clifford, *Nebraska History*

"A work that challenges the modern West's collective memory of American Indian spiritual beliefs, a relic of nineteenth-century Christian colonialism through missionary enterprises. Most impressive is the author's use of Lakota language to offer a more accurate translation of words and phrases that the Christian missionaries defined and employed to portray Lakota religion as void of any spiritual value. To the contrary, Posthumus argues that in an animist ontology, the principle of relatedness is at the heart of Lakota spirituality."
—Lisa Barnett, *South Dakota History*

"The serious reader will be richly rewarded in working through the book given Posthumus's sophisticated explication of Lakota interspecies relations and their implications for ritual enactment. . . . His work clearly demonstrates the promise of the new animism for indigenous research, and its application to Lakota lifeways specifically, and to Native American sacred traditions in general."
—Fritz Detwiler, *Reading Religion*

"The subject of Lakota ontology, belief, and ritual has enduring value and significance for all who are interested in the Sioux, in the literature of Black Elk, and in Plains ethnohistory generally. . . . *All My Relatives* is very strong in its command of Lakota sources, notably the writings of the Delorias, of ethnohistorical records, and of relevant secondary sources."
—Jennifer S. H. Brown, professor emerita of history at the University of Winnipeg and editor of *Ojibwe Stories from the Upper Berens River: A. Irving Hallowell and Adam Bigmouth in Conversation*

All My Relatives

Exploring Lakota Ontology, Belief, and Ritual

DAVID C. POSTHUMUS

CO-PUBLISHED BY THE UNIVERSITY OF NEBRASKA PRESS
AND THE AMERICAN PHILOSOPHICAL SOCIETY

© 2018 by the Board of Regents of the University of Nebraska
All rights reserved

The University of Nebraska Press is part of a land-grant institution with campuses and programs on the past, present, and future homelands of the Pawnee, Ponca, Otoe-Missouria, Omaha, Dakota, Lakota, Kaw, Cheyenne, and Arapaho Peoples, as well as those of the relocated Ho-Chunk, Sac and Fox, and Iowa Peoples.

Library of Congress Cataloging-in-Publication Data
Names: Posthumus, David C., author.
Title: All my relatives: exploring Lakota ontology, belief, and ritual / David C. Posthumus.
Description: Lincoln: University of Nebraska Press, [2018] | Series: New visions in Native American and Indigenous studies | "Co-published with the American Philosophical Society." | Includes bibliographical references and index.
Identifiers: LCCN 2017044990
ISBN 9780803299948 (cloth: alk. paper)
ISBN 9781496230393 (paperback)
ISBN 9781496205704 (pdf)
Subjects: LCSH: Lakota philosophy. | Lakota mythology.
Classification: LCC E99.T34 P67 2018 | DDC 978.004/975244—dc23 LC record available at https://lccn.loc.gov/2017044990

CONTENTS

List of Illustrations — vii

Acknowledgments — ix

Introduction — 1

1. Hallowell, Descola, Ontology, and Phenomenology — 19

2. Situated Animism and Lakota Relational Ontology — 34

3. The Living Rock, Grandfather of All Things — 73

4. Persons and Transformation — 92

5. Spirits and Ghosts — 103

6. Nonhuman Persons in Lakota Mythology — 123

7. Nonhuman Persons in Lakota Dreams
   and Visions   136

8. Nonhuman Persons in Lakota Ritual   168

9. The Dynamics of Life Movement   206

   Glossary of Lakota Terms and Phrases   221

   Notes   231

   References   251

   Index   267

ILLUSTRATIONS

MAPS

1. Mid-nineteenth-century Lakota territory   2

2. Pine Ridge Reservation   3

3. Sioux territory, early to mid-nineteenth century   7

FIGURES

1. The Lakota model of the person   61

2. *Yuwí tapi* 'ritual supplication' and *cʿąnúpa iyáȟpeyapi* 'ceremonial pipe offering'   88

3. Depiction of the vision quest, by Amos Bad Heart Bull   182

4. Depiction of the vision quest, by
   Stephen Standing Bear   183

5. Dream or Spirit Elk   187

6. Deer and Elk dreamer ritual
   performance (*káǧa*)   190

7. *The Bear Dance, Preparing for a Bear
   Hunt* (1844), by George Catlin   192

ACKNOWLEDGMENTS

I am indebted to many people for their friendship, encouragement, criticism, patience, and support. First of all I want to thank my Lakota friends and adoptive relatives for sharing their lives and deep knowledge with me. I am very thankful for your friendship, acceptance, generosity, and enduring support, and for allowing me to tag along with you on your many adventures. I am eternally grateful to each and every one of you. Thank you to Robert Brave Heart Sr. and the entire Brave Heart family; Stanley Good Voice Elk; the late Alvin and Steve Slow Bear; Tom Cook and Loretta Afraid of Bear; Joe Giago, Richard Giago, and Tyler Lunderman; Roger White Eyes, Philomine Lakota, Gloria Two Crows, and Beverly Pipe On Head; John Gibbons and his family; Russ and the late Foster "Boomer" Cournoyer; Gene Thin Elk; Leon Leader Charge; Rich Boyd; and the entire Wase Wakpa native community in Vermillion, South Dakota. Special thanks go to Arthur Amiotte and his wife, Janet Murray, the late Wilmer "Stampede" Mesteth and his wife, Lisa, Richard Two Dogs and his wife, Ethleen, and their families. I cannot thank you all enough. Thank you to the Department of Anthropology at Indiana University Bloomington (IUB); the American Indian Studies Research Institute (AISRI) at IUB; the College of Arts & Sciences, Department of Anthropology and Sociology, and Native American Studies Program at the University of South Dakota; the American Society for Ethnohistory;

and Red Cloud Indian School for their practical support of my work. I am so grateful for my teachers, both within and beyond academia, native and nonnative, and want to thank all of you who have been instrumental not only in this project but also in my development as a scholar. Thank you to Raymond Bucko, S.J., Peter Klink, S.J., Robert McKinley, and Laura Scheiber for your advice, comments, and encouragement; Jennifer Brown and Rani-Henrik Andersson for your careful and insightful readings of this manuscript; and Douglas Parks for your kindness and support throughout the years and one-of-a-kind sense of humor. The most special thanks of all goes to my advisor and friend Raymond DeMallie, whose work originally inspired me to become an anthropologist. Without Ray's unwavering support, encouragement, generosity, and wisdom I truly would not be who I am today. He is an uncommonly kind person, a wonderful mentor, and an even better friend. His brilliant and empathetic scholarship continues to inspire me to this day, and my work has been greatly enhanced by his positive influence and steadfast guidance. Last but not least, I want to thank my wife, Emily Posthumus, for her patience and support. I sincerely hope that I have not forgotten anyone in these brief acknowledgments, and if I have, please forgive me. Finally, I am solely responsible for any errors of fact or interpretation in the work presented here.

Introduction

The Lakota or Western (Teton) Sioux, and particularly the Oglala tribe of the Pine Ridge Reservation in southwestern South Dakota (see maps 1 and 2), have captured the imagination of millions the world over and captivated countless peoples for myriad reasons.[1] *Lakota* refers generally to the seven tribes of the westernmost division of the Sioux or Dakota peoples. The Lakotas are sometimes referred to as the Tetons, Teton Sioux, Teton Dakotas, or Western Sioux, and I use these designations interchangeably. I use the term *Sioux*, rather than *Dakota*, to designate the Lakotas, Yanktons, Yanktonais, and Dakotas (Sisseton or Eastern Sioux) collectively (see Daniels 1970, 216).

Lakota warriors, political leaders, and religious practitioners of the nineteenth and early twentieth centuries such as Crazy Horse, Sitting Bull, Red Cloud, and Nicholas Black Elk remain among the most well-known, enigmatic, and romanticized figures in American history. They have become emblazoned upon our collective understandings of the past and fixtures of popular culture since their rise to prominence in the mid-nineteenth century. Their names alone evoke a multitude of powerful symbols and emotions—resistance, bravery, fortitude, balance, harmony, mysticism—that define the ways in which many contemporary people conceptualize American Indians and their histories. The Lakotas

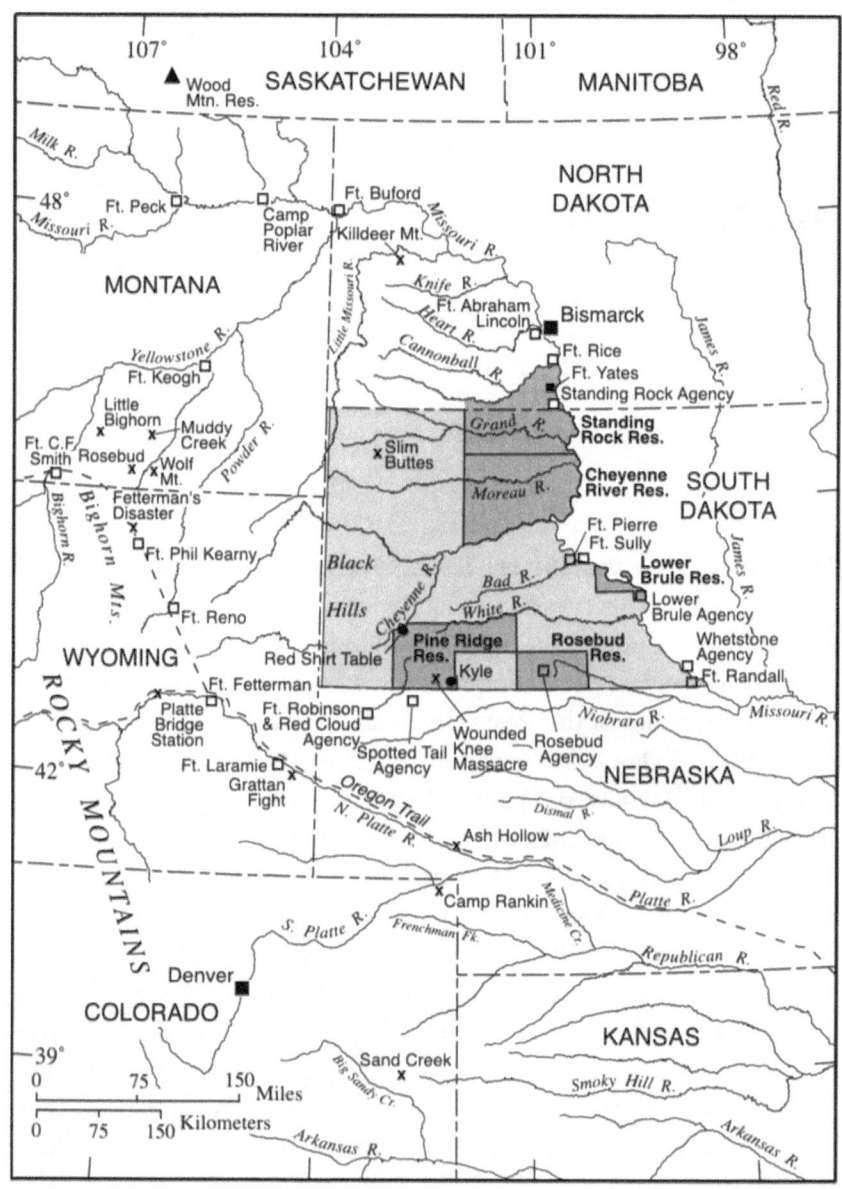

Map 1. Mid-nineteenth-century Lakota territory, with modern reservations and the former Great Sioux Reservation in light gray. Courtesy of the American Indian Studies Research Institute.

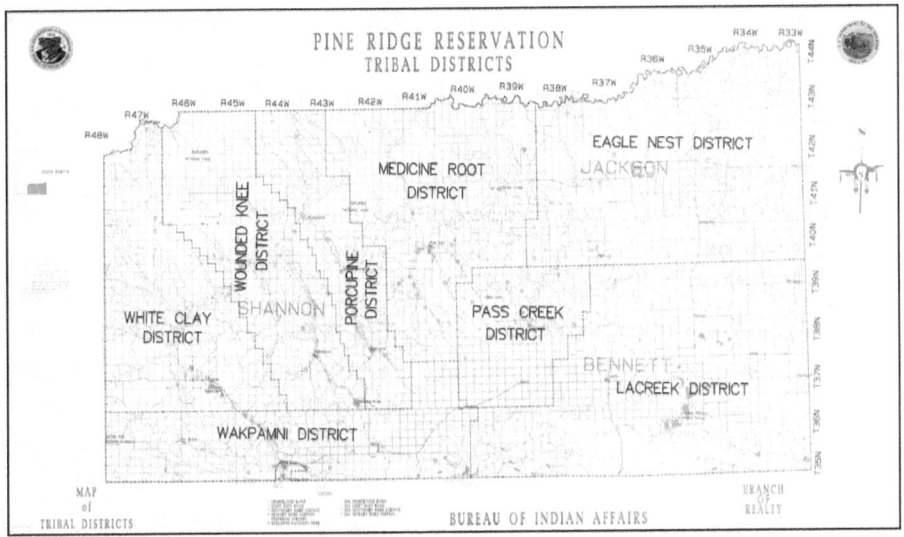

Map 2. Pine Ridge Reservation. Courtesy of the Bureau of Indian Affairs.

continue to inspire and inform people today throughout the United States and the world.

The Lakotas are especially renowned for their poignant religious philosophies and eloquent religious leaders and thinkers. Brilliant and exceptional individuals like Sitting Bull, George Sword, Horn Chips, Black Elk, Frank Good Lance, Frank Fools Crow, John Fire Lame Deer, and Peter Catches Sr. found ingenious ways, despite settler colonialism and difficult historical circumstances, to translate their spiritual beliefs and traditions in such a way as to make them accessible to all. A number of publications in the twentieth century, the most influential being the classic *Black Elk Speaks* (Neihardt 2008), and a renewed desire to (re)connect with Lakota traditions, among other things, led to a cultural and religious revitalization and renaissance in the 1960s and 1970s, the impact of which is still being felt today. Contemporary Lakota religious leaders such as Richard Two Dogs, Richard Moves Camp, Leonard Crow Dog, and the late Wilmer "Stampede" Mesteth continue to carry the torch of their ancestors, ensuring that their traditions remain strong, vibrant, and relevant in the modern world.

Various Lakota hunting camps began crossing the Missouri River circa 1750 in the vanguard of the westward migration of the Sioux and adopted (or adapted to) the Plains nomadic, bison-hunting lifestyle. In the process, culture and the Lakota religious landscape were continually evolving. Sioux religion or spirituality was never fixed, even before the transition to the Great Plains. Religion, like culture in general, conceived of as a system or web of meaningful symbols, as practice and process, is first and foremost dynamic, never static, and characterized by constant change. From the adaptation to Plains life to the centrality of the horse, from the vision quest to the sun dance to *yuwípi*,[2] Lakota religion is and always has been dynamic, characterized by adaptation, individuality, innovation, and practicality or pragmatism, notwithstanding a number of vital and significant continuities with the past. Today religion has superseded kinship and become perhaps the dominant factor in and central foundation of Sioux culture and identity (see Posthumus 2015).

It is important to note that many Lakotas and other Native Americans resist using the term *religion* in reference to their particular systems of religious belief and practice. Indeed, there is no corresponding word in most Native American languages nor anything close to the Western meaning of religion. Citing *religion*'s deep connection to and collusion with Christianity, missionization, and settler colonialism, many native people prefer the term *spirituality*, as it is less constricted and does not refer to an organized, hierarchical religion and system of beliefs rooted in Western epistemologies and philosophies. Hence, many Lakotas prefer *spirituality* to *religion* or simply refer to the spiritual domain as "a way of life," highlighting the processual aspects of belief and practice and implying the interconnectedness of the spiritual realm to all other areas of life in American Indian worldviews, cultures, and lifeways (Posthumus 2015, 2008–17). For lack of better general terms I begrudgingly use *religion* and *spirituality* interchangeably and hope that my usage, although not wholly adequate, will be acceptable as a means of classification, categorization, comparison, and discussion. One thing is clear: it is very difficult in the Lakota case to draw concrete boundaries between cultural domains involving religion, such as kinship, belief, ritual, identity, and so on. Religion is an all-encompassing total social phenomenon. In most cases many of the concepts that could be labeled religious interact continually, are discursive, and are not mutually exclusive.

Underpinning the dynamic ceremonial traditions, beliefs, and practices of the Lakotas is an ancient way of schematizing experience, an ontology or general integrating schema that structures the relations between the Sioux and their world. The constituent elements of this foundational mode of identification or cognitive schema, I argue, are shared not only by the seven tribes of the Lakotas but also by their eastern relatives, namely, the Eastern Sioux or Dakotas, Yanktons, and Yanktonais. Further, I attempt to demonstrate through comparison with the Berens River Ojibwes or Saulteaux that the basic elements of an animist ontology are shared by other hunter-gatherer tribes in North America. I do not claim that these groups are homologous. Certainly there are significant cultural differences among these diverse peoples: distinct traditions, beliefs, and practices based on distinct historical, environmental, and linguistic circumstances. That said, I attempt to demonstrate that there are commonalities or parallels in terms of a similar underlying ontological orientation, the deep and persistent ways in which (former) hunter-gatherer tribes in North America schematize and classify experience, conceptualize personhood, distribute resemblances and differences between existing entities, and structure relations between and among themselves, other humans, nonhumans, and the environment (cf. Descola 2013a, 110–11).

This work examines primarily nineteenth-century Sioux ontology as it relates to religious belief and ritual practice. It focuses mainly on the Lakotas or Western Sioux but also uses data from the Dakotas or Eastern Sioux for comparative purposes to demonstrate the common ontological assumptions inherent in Sioux culture and worldview, which transcend both time and tribal divisions. These ontological similarities likely stem from the common origins of the Sioux people. For instance, circa 1900 the aged Oglala holy man No Flesh explained, "Before the Seven Council Fires the Sioux Indians all made their winter camp together. Before then, in ancient times, there was a head chief of all the Sioux who had four sons" (in Walker 1991, 193). Around the same time Ringing Shield, another elderly Oglala shaman, explained, "The Lakota all lived together a long time ago.... That was before there were any Oglalas. All were Lakota" (in Walker 1991, 206).

Paradoxically, while the Sioux shared common culture, language, and history as one people originally, they were at the same time always composed of independent and autonomous nested social groups. Their sociopolitical organization was loose and dynamic. Hence the notion of a politically or even socially united "Sioux Nation" is a misnomer, as there was no real overarching sociopolitical organization. Sioux political leadership was fluid, more or less democratically vested in chiefs who had little coercive authority, leading by example and influence. The atom or basic element of traditional Sioux social organization was the *t'iyóšpaye* (lodge group), an extended family or group of extended families usually designated "band" or "sub-band" in English. Historically, a band averaged from ten to twenty nuclear families or fifty to one hundred people, and all its members were related to one another through genetics, marriage, or adoption. Membership in a t'iyóšpaye was largely a matter of choice, not descent, and usually based on residence. Each band was autonomous yet still united with other bands through common culture, kinship, traditions, language, history, and so on (see DeMallie 2001, 801; 2006; DeMallie in Walker 1982, 10–11; Walker 1982).

Likewise, if the idea of the "Sioux Nation" as an organized sociopolitical entity is historically inaccurate then the notion of a unified "Sioux tradition" or "Sioux spirituality" is also an untenable misnomer. Sioux religious belief and ritual practice, much like sociopolitical organization, was in constant flux and never codified. It was revelatory and inspired by direct spiritual experience: personal encounters with nonhuman spirit beings, innovation, and adaptation. Instead, then, it is better to think of multiple, dynamic Sioux traditions and ceremonial beliefs and practices evolving through interaction with other persons, tribes, and environments over time and space.

According to the ethnohistorian Raymond DeMallie, "The unity of the Sioux as a people is most fundamentally reflected in language" (DeMallie 2001, 718). Linguistic reconstruction places the homeland of the proto-western Siouans west of Lake Michigan in the area of southern Wisconsin, southeastern Minnesota, northeastern Iowa, and northern Illinois. Early

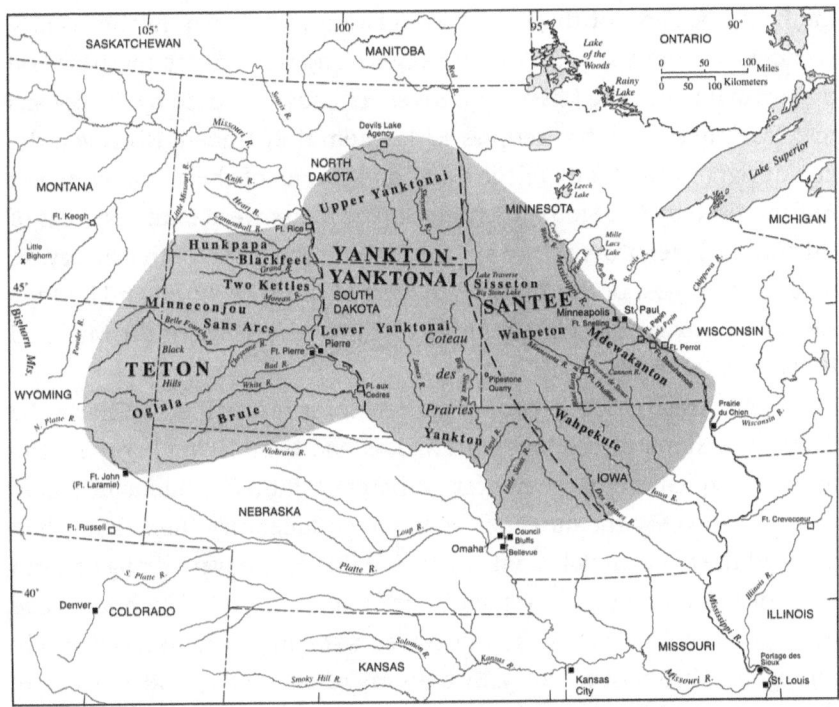

Map 3. Sioux territory, early to mid-nineteenth century. Boundaries between the divisions suggest areas of greatest use. Courtesy of the American Indian Studies Research Institute.

Sioux traditions recorded in 1839 by the French geographer and explorer Joseph N. Nicollet recount an origin near "the northern lakes east of the Mississippi" (Nicollet in DeMallie 1976, 253–54).

Europeans first encountered the Sioux in the mid-seventeenth century when Sioux territory stretched from the coniferous forests around Mille Lacs, through the deciduous forests and open grassland-forests along the Mississippi and Minnesota Rivers, and across the tallgrass prairies of present-day western Minnesota and eastern North and South Dakota to the Missouri River (DeMallie 2001, 719). Common cultural patterns centered on bison hunting are evident in the earliest written descriptions of the Sioux.[3] In 1660, for instance, the French fur trader and explorer Pierre-Esprit Radisson (1961, 134, 142) called the Sioux "the nation of the Beef" because of their close association with bison. In these early accounts the Sioux are divided into eastern and western groups, based on their proximity to the Mississippi River, a handy tool used by Europeans to classify and track the peoples with whom they traded. However, the etic designations "Sioux of the East" and "Sioux of the West" were not self-imposed by the Sioux themselves. The Sioux were in the process of shifting their territory westward throughout the eighteenth century, so that by 1736 most of the Sioux lived west of the Mississippi and by 1750 western Sioux groups were hunting on the prairies east of the Missouri River (DeMallie 2001, 718–31).

Since at least 1700, according to French fur trader Pierre-Charles Le Sueur, the Sioux of the West or Lakotas had been living "only by the hunt" in typical nomadic hunter-gatherer fashion (Le Sueur in Wedel 1974, 165–66). By the dawn of the nineteenth century the Lakotas had adopted the horse, revolutionizing their culture, and were living on both sides of the Missouri (Lewis and Clark 2002, 415–17). The horse gave them great mobility, wealth, and power, allowing them to travel freely throughout their vast territory. By the early reservation period, circa 1876, the Lakotas had followed the remnants of the great northern bison herd northwest into present-day Wyoming, North Dakota, and Montana (see White 1978; Cunfer and Waiser 2016). Throughout this period of rapid change and westward expansion a core animist ontology schematized and classified the vicissitudes of everyday experience, allowing the Lakotas to practically adapt to new environments and technologies. This innovative and pragmatic adaptability is at the heart of Lakota culture, past and present, but an underlying ontological orientation was generative and essential in unifying emergent Lakota experience and worldview.

Sioux spirituality, experiential and largely based on visions and interaction with nonhumans, has always been idiosyncratic. The ethnohistorical literature on the Sioux, not to mention more recent ethnographic accounts and the opinions of many contemporary Sioux people, consistently attests to this fact. The French-Canadian fur trader Pierre-Antoine Tabeau provides one of the earliest descriptions of the Indians of the Upper Missouri. Living among the Arikaras in 1803–4, Tabeau provided an account that is full of significant ethnographic data on the Lakotas. Tabeau recognized the idiosyncratic, nondogmatic nature of Lakota spirituality, writing that they "have no religion that is fixed or established" (Tabeau 1939, 190). Indeed, Sioux ceremonial belief and practice was never dogmatic or formulated in specific, inflexible creeds. As Oglala author Luther Standing Bear explains, "Since for the Lakota there was no wilderness; since nature was not dangerous but hospitable; not forbidding but friendly, Lakota philosophy was healthy—free from fear and dogmatism. And here I find the great distinction between the faith of the Indian and the white man. Indian faith sought the harmony of man with his surroundings; the other sought the dominance of surroundings" (Standing Bear 2006a, 196). Although Standing Bear's words are slightly idealistic—there were certainly dangerous and unknown entities lurking in the world beyond the Lakota camp circle—he nonetheless touches on an important distinction between native and Western worldviews.

But let me clarify at the outset that I am not Native American and do not claim to speak for anyone other than myself. Neither would I claim that every Sioux individual at all times firmly believed the things explored herein. Sioux people, like all others, are heterogeneous when it comes to spiritual matters, and no one speaks for everyone. Further, the beliefs and orientations I discuss in this book were interrelated sets, composed of parts or isolates, which were organized into consistent patterns of ideas and behaviors that were situated, activated, and made meaningful in specific religious and magico-ritual contexts. They cannot be understood outside the cultural milieu in which they are found or as anything other than related parts of a coherent system (cf. Evans-Pritchard 1965; Hall 1959). Although it is undeniable that traditional Sioux religious belief and ritual practice were individualistic, idiosyncratic, and contextual, useful generalizations can still be made.

But the domains of Sioux mythology, dreams and visions, and ceremony are individual and personal in many ways, making generalizations exceedingly difficult. As I have alluded to above and will explore in greater detail throughout the pages of this book, much of Sioux belief and ritual is based on direct and immediate mystical revelation or gnosis in the form of interpersonal communication with various nonhuman spirits and is thus highly resistant to dogmatization. Yet despite the idiosyncratic nature of Sioux spirituality certain common bedrock ontological assumptions emerge from in-depth study of the ethnohistorical literature and ethnographic fieldwork with contemporary Sioux people.

This study demonstrates that there are indeed basic underlying similarities that organize and integrate experience in terms of basic ontological assumptions and relational schemas that crosscut Sioux tribal divisions and are surprisingly consistent throughout history. These foundational modes of identification give rise to specific relational schemas, religious beliefs, and magico-ritual forms that are, at their core, similar among all Sioux groups. I believe that examining these issues has the potential to uncover startling parallels and telling differences that would both enrich and stimulate our studies and fields.

In recent years anthropology has taken a renewed interest in alterity and otherness, exploring divergent ontologies and the composition of alter worlds (see Jensen 2013). While I do not necessarily see myself as a proponent, per se, of the so-called ontological turn in anthropology, I have become increasingly intrigued by certain currents in this trend that seek to explore what might be called "ethno-ontologies," as opposed to ontology in the universal sense. As David Graeber points out, usage of the term *ontology* by adherents of the ontological turn is inconsistent and unclear. In philosophy, ontology commonly refers to a discourse about the nature of being (or about its essence, about being as such, or in itself, or about the constituent building blocks of reality). In contrast, ontology is variously defined in the ontological-turn literature as "way of being" or "manner of being" (Graeber 2015, 15). I prefer Michael Scott's definition of ontology as "the investigation and theorization of diverse experiences and understandings of the nature of being itself" (Scott 2013, 859), or better yet, Eduardo Kohn's minimalist definition of ontology as reality as a cultural construct: "the study of 'reality'—one that encompasses but is not limited to humanly constructed worlds" (Kohn 2015, 312).

In particular, this work draws heavily on Philippe Descola's groundbreaking *Beyond Nature and Culture* (2013a) and builds on his restoration of animism, shed of its problematic social evolutionary elements, common in late eighteenth- and early nineteenth-century scholarship. Descola isolates and describes elementary structures in the classical French tradition of Durkheim, Mauss, and Lévi-Strauss. The advantages and disadvantages of this approach have been discussed elsewhere and debated to no end. But I think Descola is onto something significant that moves anthropology in a positive and productive direction. Descola is careful to point out that his schemas are synchronic ideal types. While I incorporate historical evidence to account for cultural change in my study of Sioux animist ontology—or the relative lack thereof where ontological assumptions are concerned—it must be clearly understood that this work builds on these ideal types identified by Descola. But what is particularly interesting is the apparent resistance to change over time of the core elements of these ontological orientations.

As I read *Beyond Nature and Culture* time and again I was struck by how well Descola's animist framework could be used to articulate and unite otherwise disparate or elusive aspects of the ethnohistorical literature on the Lakotas. Later, I was struck again by how it could also illuminate similar features of Dakota culture equally well. Descolian animism is the perfect lens for revealing commonalities in terms of basic, underlying modes of identification among the Sioux, as well as other animist, hunter-gatherer tribes in North and South America and beyond.

Above all, Descola's *Beyond Nature and Culture* is anthropology in the grand or comparative sense of the word, a direction we all should consider (or reconsider) as a means for maintaining anthropology's relevance in the modern world (see Gingrich and Fox 2002). Too often today anthropology neglects its comparative or relational cofoundation, opting instead to focus only on the minute description of singularities and endless postmodern deconstruction. While cultural description is certainly valuable we must be careful not to forsake comparative theories and methods in anthropology, which render our discipline useful and relevant in terms of understanding the logic of culture as it continually emerges and evolves as part of the ongoing human experience.

Descola's project is first and foremost comparative, seeking to identify and explore the limited number of general integrating schemas that structure the relations of all people with the world in terms of both identity and relation. Through the exploration of deep, underlying ontological isolates, sets, and patterns we may come to a better understanding of the composition of alter worlds and articulate the complicated and persistent part played by religion, belief, mythology, and ritual in the ongoing drama of social life.

Before proceeding I'll say a little something about myself and how I came to be interested in Lakota culture, history, language, and spirituality. As I mentioned before, I am not Native American, but I have been fascinated with native culture and history since I was a boy, partly influenced by my grandfather, whose interest in and respect for indigenous peoples was contagious. I have always been particularly drawn to the Lakotas, and in college I first read *Black Elks Speaks* (Neihardt 2008), which drew my focus toward religion. As an undergraduate I first read *The Sixth Grandfather* (DeMallie 1984) and examined the discrepancies between what the Oglala Lakota holy man Nicholas Black Elk actually said and how it was represented by John Neihardt in *Black Elk Speaks*. This experience fueled my interest in traditional Lakota religion and the ways in which it is represented.

In graduate school I worked with Raymond DeMallie, focusing on Lakota belief and ritual. Indiana University's American Indian Studies Research Institute (AISRI) provided me with wonderful opportunities to work with and within native communities on various projects and in various capacities. In particular, I spent six years working on the Lakota Language Project, a K–12 Lakota-language curriculum development project and partnership between Red Cloud Indian School on Pine Ridge Reservation and AISRI. My work on this important project gave me valuable opportunities to visit and live on the reservation and collaborate with Lakota people. Much of the present study is informed by my fieldwork, research, and time spent working at Pine Ridge with Lakota-language speakers, educators, community leaders, and spiritual leaders, or "medicine men," as they are commonly called on the reservation.

I have spent roughly twenty-four months conducting fieldwork at Pine Ridge since 2008, during which time I have developed many reciprocal relationships with Lakota friends and adoptive relatives. As I collaborated with Oglala people on the Lakota Language Project I discovered that people at Pine Ridge were very interested and active in traditional religion and eager to talk about it. My research gave me the opportunity to participate in the ritual networks of four religious leaders representing a broad spectrum of contemporary religious practice, thought, and identity. I attended rituals; studied prayers, ceremonial songs, and beliefs; analyzed ritual behavior and social networks; and shared in the lives and practices of modern practitioners and their followers, trying to understand their role in the broader picture of contemporary reservation life and the dynamics of tradition. Broadly, my dissertation (Posthumus 2015) examines innovation and continuity in Lakota ceremonial life and how Oglala belief and ritual shape identity and ethnicity.

On a particularly sunny day at Pine Ridge my adoptive *lekší* (uncle), Richard Two Dogs, an influential practitioner, introduced me to his family, friends, and followers at his birthday party as an FBI secret agent because of the dark sunglasses I was wearing at the time. After everyone had a good laugh at my expense, he smiled and said, "No, just kidding. He's just our anthropologist." Lakota humor is really something special (see Bucko 2006). My experiences and participation at Pine Ridge as the "local anthropologist" allowed me to examine religious continuity and innovation, central topics of this study and my research in general.

When I first went to the field I had a strong scholarly foundation in historical Lakota culture, society, religion, ritual, and language. What I witnessed in terms of religious life seemed at first to deviate from the nineteenth-century models I was so familiar with. The practice of Lakota religion in the twenty-first century, at least on the surface, is quite distinct from what one reads in the classic ethnographies and collections of texts on the Lakotas. I was intrigued by the modern, practical adaptations and the transnational, global scope of contemporary Oglala religion. I searched the web for "Lakota medicine man" and found a number of fascinating sites, some more elaborate and convincing than others. I smiled when I received my first text message from a religious practitioner, informing me that the rocks for that evening's sweat lodge were almost ready to be loaded into the ceremonial lodge. Though I was a bit thrown at first, I persisted in my quest for understanding the deep continuities underpinning Oglala religious life, despite the clear presence of innovation and practicality, the darker, more sinister effects of settler colonialism, and the inescapable influences of modernity.

My major research questions came to revolve around these issues as I attempted to grapple with them. Is it possible to trace the historical development of contemporary Lakota belief and ritual? Is twenty-first-century religious practice based on continuities with the past, an entirely new phenomenon, or a hybrid of both? Is Lakota religion characterized by inventions of tradition or traditions of invention?[4] What does it mean to be traditional today from Lakota perspectives? And finally, why do Lakota people practice traditional religion in the modern world? These were the major questions I set out to explore, and I dove in headfirst, participating as much as possible in as many ritual networks as I could, interviewing people, listening, observing, and asking questions. Sometimes I felt like I *was* transforming into the FBI agent from my uncle's introduction with my endless interrogations.

Later, when I came across Descola's *Beyond Nature and Culture* (2013a), I felt that it provided some important keys to understanding many of the issues I was most concerned with. At the heart of both Lakota religious continuity and innovation is an underlying animist ontological orientation, a basic way of seeing, understanding, and being in the world that extends personhood—in the form of a soul or spirit—to nonhuman life-forms. This foundational understanding of the universe is poetically expressed in the common Lakota ceremonial axiom *mitákuye oyás'į*, meaning "all my relatives" or "we are all related," which refers not only to human kinship but also to the relationship shared by all life-forms, both human and nonhuman, and the reciprocal obligations, responsibilities, and mutual respect that naturally extend from it.

This ontological orientation is also apparent and persistent in the scholarly literature on the Sioux and in dialogue with contemporary Sioux people. For instance, at a council on Powder River in 1866 the great Hunkpapa leader Sitting Bull said, "Behold, my friends, the spring is come; the earth has gladly received the embraces of the sun, and we shall soon see the results of their love! Every seed is awakened, and all animal life. It is through this mysterious power that we too have our being, and we therefore yield to our neighbors, even to our animal neighbors, the same right as ourselves to inhabit this vast land" (Sitting Bull in Eastman 1991, 119). In 1933 the Oglala Lakota author Luther Standing Bear wrote,

> From Wakan Tanka [Great Mystery, Creator] there came a great unifying life force that flowed in and through all things—the flowers of the plains, blowing winds, rocks, trees, birds, animals—and was the same force that had been breathed into the first man. Thus all things were kindred and brought together by the same Great Mystery.
>
> Kinship with all creatures of the earth, sky, and water was a real and active principle. For the animal and bird world there existed a brotherly feeling that kept the Lakota safe among them. And so close did some of the Lakota come to their feathered and furred friends that in true brotherhood they spoke a common tongue. (Standing Bear 2006a, 193)

My task in this study is to outline the major elements of Lakota ontology, belief, and ritual and to explore the persistence and prevalence of these basic elements, embedded in an animist framework. The primary methods utilized herein have been participant observation, structured and unstructured interviews, intensive study of the Lakota language, and archival research.

This study is a reinterpretation of the ethnohistorical literature on the Sioux—supplemented by fieldwork among the Oglalas of Pine Ridge from 2008 to the present—from a Descolian animist perspective. Descola restores animism by stripping it of its social evolutionary aspects, rendering it anthropologically useful and productive. Briefly, he distinguishes between interiority—soul, spirit, or intentionality—and physicality or body, positing that this is a basic distinction made by all peoples throughout the world. Animism, according to Descola, is an ontological orientation that recognizes a common interiority and a dissimilarity of physicality. In other words, societies characterized by an animist ontology recognize that other species share an interiority or soul that is similar or identical to that of human beings. This commonality of interiority allows for the extension of sociality to nonhumans, thus abolishing the divide between nature and culture in societies characterized as animist from a Descolian perspective. It is the physicality—the body, manifest form, or habitus—that distinguishes human beings from nonhumans and specific human groups from others.

In animist regimes physicality distributes various species into collectives or social groups. Thus, there are as many tribes-species as there are different physical forms and the associated behavior patterns they permit. An indexical feature of animist ontologies is the capacity for transformation, that is, the notion that physicalities are akin to clothing, envelopes covering a common interiority, which are subject to change in certain domains of existence. I use Bruce Kapferer's notion of virtuality (2006b, 2010), developed largely from the work of Bergson, Langer, and Deleuze, to explore these domains in which transformation and interspecies communication and exchange are possible. In particular, I explore the realms of Sioux mythology, dreams and visions, and ceremony.

All the Sioux tribes shared homologous basic ontological assumptions and strategies for practice, what Descola calls modes of identification and relational schemas, respectively. This is because all Sioux groups originally shared common culture, language, and history. I attempt to demonstrate how a Descolian animist framework can bring these deep similarities to the surface and into focus, not only among the various Sioux tribal divisions but also among other (former) hunter-gatherer tribes characterized as animist.

This work also relies on A. Irving Hallowell's (1955, 1960, 1966, 1976) brilliant analyses of Berens River Ojibwe or Saulteaux belief and ontology for comparative purposes. Hallowell's pioneering work has had a great impact on the ontological turn in anthropology. The Sioux and Ojibwes share a long history of interaction and exchange, sometimes friendly and other times hostile or predatory. Both the Sioux and the Ojibwes may be considered animist in the Descolian sense, and hence the deep ontological similarities between these two groups are apparent in various domains. As Yankton Sioux ethnographer and linguist Ella Deloria writes, "In thought . . . and in ceremonies they [the Dakotas] resembled their Chippewa neighbors" (Deloria 1998, 17). Although many contemporary anthropologists might bristle at the notion of such broad comparisons I have found Hallowell's work on the Ojibwes both revealing and insightful in comparison to the Sioux ethnohistorical literature. While there are certainly many cultural differences, there are also many underlying similarities in terms of ontology and worldview. In identifying and exploring these similarities the differences come into sharper focus, allowing for studies that are both stimulating and consequential.

Finally, I explore how Sioux animist ontological orientations can teach us valuable lessons in the modern world. The work of Vine Deloria (1999, 2009) has also inspired much of this work, and in particular his ideas of mutual respect, responsibility, and the covenant guide my concluding remarks on our collective responsibility to ourselves, others, and the world in which we live. While traditional Sioux theosophy is certainly idiosyncratic and nondogmatic there is still much it can teach us today that can help us to live responsibly and respectfully in a multispecies world.

CHAPTER 1

Hallowell, Descola, Ontology, and Phenomenology

Alfred Irving "Pete" Hallowell's (1892–1974) impact on anthropology and ethnohistorical studies of American Indian cultures has been extensive and enduring. A student of Franz Boas via Frank Speck at the University of Pennsylvania and Alexander Goldenweiser at the Pennsylvania School of Social Work, Hallowell's professional output is staggering. His excellent analyses of American Indian culture, history, psychology, and experience, firmly grounded in an Americanist, Boasian historical particularist framework, were far ahead of their time and continue to be relevant and generative, inspiring new generations of anthropologists and fresh insights on perennial problems.[1] Hallowell's exemplary work with the Northern Ojibwes or Saulteaux of the Berens River and Lake Winnipeg regions of Manitoba continues to set the standard for engaged, reciprocal, theoretically based ethnography and ethnohistory (see Nash 1977). Particularly, his classic paper "Ojibwa Ontology, Behavior, and World View" (1960) has been influential, examining reality as a cultural construct and the nature and categories of being among the Berens River Ojibwes (see Darnell 2006, 13; Kohn 2015, 312).

Aside from his role as the father of modern scholarly interest in the history of anthropology and ethnoecology, Hallowell's contributions in psychological anthropology (he preferred "psychology and culture") and social organization are original and significant (Fogelson in Hallowell 1976, ix–xvii; Nash 1977; Spiro 1976). Franz Boas, writes Hallowell,

> commented that one of the central questions of anthropology "was the relation between the objective world and man's subjective world as it had taken form in different cultures." . . . The full significance of this knowledge cannot be brought to a logical focus without reference to an implicit psychological dimension. For a human level of existence not only necessitates a unique biological structure and a sociocultural mode of life, it necessitates a peculiar and distinctive kind of psychological structuralization, characterized by a level of personal adjustment and experience in which a unique and complex integration occurs between responses to an "outer" world of objects and events and responses to an "inner" world of impulse, fantasy, and creative imagination. Besides this, a human existence is one in which potentialities for readjustment, reorientation, change, are constantly present. (1955, viii)

Of particular relevance here are Hallowell's interrelated interests in worldview;[2] phenomenology; the ontological dimensions of self, other, and intersubjectivity; and interagency (Descola 2014b, 274; Ingold 1997) or interpersonal/interspecies relationships. As Hallowell's student Raymond Fogelson explains, Hallowell was "interested in how human beings perceived nature and acted within a culturally constituted behavioral environment" (Fogelson in Hallowell 1976, xiii).

In this study I discuss Hallowell's pioneering role in current anthropological studies of ontology, applying his insights to the ethnohistorical literature on the Lakota peoples of the Great Plains region, intermittent neighbors of the Ojibwes. The general aims of this study are threefold. First, to critically evaluate the veracity and utility of recent theories concerning ontological anthropology and "new animism." Second, to explore nineteenth-century Lakota ethnometaphysics, specifically ontology, notions of human and nonhuman personhood,[3] and worldview, through comparison with Hallowell's Ojibwe studies. And third, to suggest some new directions for ontological and new animist approaches by applying Bruce Kapferer's recent insights to extend their reach into various virtual domains, such as mythology, dreams and visions, and ritual.

This research also explores and celebrates my Americanist, Boasian intellectual genealogy, illustrating the continuing relevance of this tradition in contemporary theoretical and methodological debates in anthropology and beyond. The core tenets of Boasian anthropology continue to generate new ideas and insights in the field today (see Darnell 2001). My project is largely historical, and I realize that the nature of indigenous ontological alterity is articulated in various ways depending on context and a number of variables. The shifting realities and potentialities of indigeneity often lead to misrepresentations of contemporary indigenous life, denying indigenous individuals and communities the right to change and adapt and portraying these complex and diverse realities in binary opposition to modernity. Ontologically inflected anthropologies do not always adequately address change, diversity, and hybridity, as Bessire and Bond (2014, 443–44) point out (see also Lyons 2011; Greene 2009). This project explores traditional Lakota ontological conceptions as they operated within the magico-ritual realm, largely in the nineteenth century. I do not claim that these underlying beliefs apply equally to all Lakota people at all times or that multiple ontologies do not operate situationally and simultaneously in Lakota culture and thought.

Adopting an eclectic new animist or posthumanist position and one grounded in ethnohistorical methods,[4] I explore Lakota animist beliefs regarding the personhood of rocks, ghosts or spirits of deceased humans, animals, meteorological phenomena, familiar spirits or spirit helpers, medicine bundles, and so on. In this study I draw on insights from ontologically inflected anthropologies, particularly that of Phillippe Descola (2013a), in a (re)interpretation of nineteenth-century Lakota ethnography. Interestingly, Descola mentions the Sioux only twice in his voluminous magnum opus *Beyond Nature and Culture*, in both cases citing the comparative religionist Joseph Epes Brown (1997), a problematic source at best. Inspired by Hallowell (1955, 1960, 1976) and Descola, and frequently stimulated by the philosophical writings of Vine Deloria (1999), I demonstrate how a new animist framework and expanded notions of personhood connect otherwise disparate and inaccessible elements of

Lakota ethnography, offering new and exciting insights, along with the potential for a deeper understanding of traditional Lakota culture.

This work is anthropological in the broad, comparative sense of the term, rather than solely ethnographic. It is not focused on describing relative singularities alone. As Descola writes,

> Human beings . . . resort to a much more limited number of more general integrating schemas in order to structure their relations with the world. These schemas manifest themselves in what are, after all, a quite limited number of options available for distributing resemblances and differences between existing entities, and for establishing between the groups defined by that distribution and within them, distinctive relations of a remarkable stability. . . . Anthropology that seeks to be consequential has no choice but to gain an understanding of the logic of this work of composition, by lending an ear to the themes and harmonies that stand out from the great hum of the world and concentrating on emerging orders whose regularity is detectable behind the proliferation of different customs. (2013a, 110)

Following Descola, this study posits underlying, fundamental ontological similarities and commonalities among the various Sioux tribes, Lakota, Yankton, Yanktonai, and Dakota, as well as foundational affinities between the Sioux and the Ojibwes, demonstrated by Hallowell's work. Indeed, the general message of Descola's work is that there are schematic commonalities underlying *all* cultures characterized as animist, including many tribal societies of native North and South America that were historically hunter-gatherers. These common bedrock ontological orientations surface in noticeable correspondences crosscutting many Native American cultures and are particularly evident in the realms of religious belief and ritual.

This notion of shared ancient Native American origins and traditions is by no means novel or revolutionary. It is in fact a commonly held belief among many Native Americans, past and present. Likewise, the idea of mitákuye oyás'į (all my relatives, we are all related), the common Lakota ceremonial adage, is that all life-forms are related, children of the same earth and great mystery. As Minneconjou Lakota holy man John Fire

Lame Deer explains, "At the core of all Indian beliefs are visions gotten in various ways. . . . It is a good thing for Indians to look upon all Indian religions as a common treasure house, as something that binds us together in our outlook toward nature, toward ourselves, making us one, no longer just Sioux, Cheyennes, Navajos, Pueblos, Iroquois, Haidas—but something much bigger, grander—*Indians*" (Lame Deer and Erdoes 1972, 228–29; emphasis in original). More directly pertinent to this study is the fact that archaeologically it is nearly impossible to distinguish between Siouan and Algonquian sites, attesting to the underlying similarities of Sioux and Ojibwe lifeways through time (DeMallie 2001, 719).

I conclude this study with a discussion of the life-process *pimadaziwin*, the "central goal of life for the Ojibwe," which Hallowell describes as "life in the fullest sense, life in the sense of longevity, health and freedom from misfortune" (Hallowell 1960, 45; see also Pflüg 1996). In particular, I compare pimadaziwin with the Lakota concepts *wóniya* (life-transformation process) and *wicʻózani* (health) and with Jeffrey Anderson's term *life movement*, "the aim to generate long life, blessings, and abundance for self, others, family, and the tribe" (J. Anderson 2001, 5), which he developed through his work with the Algonquian Northern Arapahos. But before proceeding further I first explore the fundamental concepts, key theorists, and implications of the so-called ontological turn in anthropology.

The Ontological Turn in Anthropology and Reanimating Animism

On the heels of twentieth-century foci on language, interpretation, and epistemology, anthropology is now in the throes of an "ontological turn," a set of antianthropocentric and antisociocentric orientations, born largely from poststructuralist ideology, exploring the nature, properties attributed to, and categorization of being.[5] In practice, the turn toward ontology in sociocultural anthropology has veered in many directions over the last twenty years or so. Exploring the interface of nature and culture and notions of personhood and, in particular, expanding the person category beyond the human to encompass nonhuman life-forms, ontological anthropologies propose a reassessment and restoration of a modernized conception of animism, often referred to as new animism.

According to this view animism is no longer treated as the mistaken belief in an animated nature, as posited by E. B. Tylor (1871), but rather is viewed as an extension of social relationality to nonhumans (Kohn 2015, 317).

At the heart of this orientation is a theoretical assumption that humans are not exceptional or fundamentally separate from the rest of the world and a methodological thrust to develop a more robust analytic for understanding human-nonhuman interaction and relationship. The so-called ontological turn (see Kohn 2015 and Henare, Holbraad, and Wastell 2007 for summaries and Graeber 2015 for an indispensable critical overview and commentary) is most notably tied to the work of Philippe Descola, Eduardo Viveiros de Castro, Bruno Latour, Tim Ingold, Graham Harvey, Eduardo Kohn, and Rane Willerslev, among others.[6] Much ontological anthropology is also influenced by the poststructuralist philosophy of Gilles Deleuze, but I contend that it owes a great and somewhat underappreciated debt to Hallowell. Colin Scott (1989, 2006, 2013) and Robert Brightman (1993) also deserve special mention here. Their fine work exploring animist ontologies, human-nonhuman relations, reciprocity, and hunter-gatherer ethics among the James Bay and Rock Crees, respectively, exemplifies the tradition laid out by Hallowell.

In particular, Descola, Viveiros de Castro, and Latour have emerged as pathbreakers in this ontological turn but exemplify very different lineages and approaches (see Descola 2014a, 268–69; Kelly 2014). I focus on Descola's post- or neostructuralist posthumanist approach, the goal of which he generally describes as a "repopulating of the social sciences with nonhuman beings, and thus of shifting the focus away from the internal analysis of social conventions and institutions toward the interactions of humans with (and between) animals, plants, physical processes, artifacts, images, and other forms of beings" (Descola 2014a, 268).

As the ontological turn is closely linked to relational ontologies and a renewed interest in theories of animism ("new animism"), in this study I focus on animist ontologies as defined and discussed by Descola and others. Central to a new animist perspective (and prefigured by Hallowell) is a broader understanding of the concept of person that extends beyond the human and seeks to understand the interspecies relations between various persons—conceived of in terms of agency and as loci of causality and potentiality for social interaction and relationship—who people a specific behavioral environment. It is argued that human beings are capable of engaging in communicative relationships with nonhumans through various nonsymbolic semiotic means. In short, relationality, and its counterpart, representation, extends beyond the human and beyond symbolic language, as Kohn (2013), following Charles Peirce's triadic semiology, argues. This understanding also resonates with Harvey's (2005, 2013) practical definition of contemporary animism as the attempt to live respectfully within a multispecies community of persons, most of whom are not human but all of whom deserve respect. This is the "moral universe" characteristic of American Indian worldviews as described by Vine Deloria. In the moral universe mutual interspecies respect is required, and all actions, events, and beings are related, all participating in the ongoing (re)creation of the living cosmos. Mutual respect is in many ways a function of a strong sense of individual and collective identity (V. Deloria 1999, 46–51).

I have found Descola's work to be the most useful and applicable as a general theoretical orientation for exploring traditional Lakota ethnometaphysics. While decentering the position of human beings in social science theory, the foundations of Descola's framework are cognitive and logical (cf. Lévy-Bruhl 1926). Explaining that a universal feature of the cognitive process involves the awareness of a duality between material processes and mental states, he posits that individuals understand others, whether human or nonhuman, through self-comparison. Descola's poststructuralist brand of ontological anthropology employs a number of central concepts to postulate a fourfold schema of distinctive ontologies that he labels animism, totemism, analogism, and naturalism (Descola 2013a; 2014b, 274; Kohn 2015, 317). At the heart of his analysis is the universal distinction between the cross-cultural analytic concepts he labels interiority and physicality. According to Descola, "this distinction between a level of interiority and one of physicality is not simply an ethnocentric projection of the Western opposition drawn between the mind and the body. Rather, it is a distinction that all the civilizations about which we have learned something from ethnography and history have, in their own fashions, objectivized" (2013a, 116).

Descola (2013a; 2013b, 79–80) uses the term *interiority* to refer to the mind, will, soul, spirit, intentionality, or subjectivity and *physicality* to refer to the body, manifest form, materiality, or characteristic dispositions and behaviors, akin to Bourdieu's notion of habitus. He writes,

> The vague term "interiority" refers to a range of properties recognized by all human beings and partially covers what we generally call the mind, the soul, or consciousness: intentionality, subjectivity, reflexivity, feelings, and the ability to express oneself and to dream. It may also include immaterial principles that are assumed to cause things to be animate, such as breath and vital energy, and, at the same time, notions even more abstract, such as the idea that I share with others the same essence, the same principle of action, or the same origin: all these ideas may be objectivized in a name or an epithet common to us all. In short, interiority consists in the universal belief that a being possesses characteristics that are internal to it or that take it as their source. In normal circumstances, these are detectable only from their effects and are reputed to be responsible for that being's identity, perpetuation, and some of its typical ways of behaving. Physicality, in contrast, concerns external form, substance, the physiological, perceptive and sensorimotor processes, even a being's constitution and way of acting in the world, insofar as these reflect the influence brought to bear on behavior patterns and a habitus by corporeal humors, diets, anatomical characteristics, and particular modes of reproduction. So physicality is not simply the material aspect of organic and abiotic bodies; it is the whole set of visible and tangible expressions of the dispositions peculiar to a particular entity when those dispositions are reputed to result from morphological and physiological characteristics that are intrinsic to it. (2013a, 116)

Descola's fourfold schema of ontological orientations arranges interiority and physicality in different combinations. Descolian animism is an ontology characterized by a continuity or similarity of soul or interiority and a discontinuity or dissimilarity of body or physicality.[7] All beings are persons or subjectivities with selfhood that is comparable to that of humans. Persons and collectives are differentiated by their exteriorities.

In animist systems, humans endow plants, animals, spirits, and other elements of their environments with subjectivities and establish various personal relationships with these entities. Descola's central analytic concepts, interiority and physicality, hinge upon a basic mind/body dualism and are essentially reducible to the interplay of identity and relation (see Kapferer 2014a, 391): "My argument is that one of the universal features of the cognitive process . . . is the awareness of a duality of planes between material processes (which I call 'physicality') and mental states (which I call 'interiority')" (2014b, 274). Physicality refers to the manifest form of a species, the body, bodily equipment, exteriority, or materiality.[8] Interiority is a much more complicated term, referring to an array of concepts, such as eternal or spiritual essence, soul, spirit, vitality, potency, mind, will, agency, intentionality, subjectivity, and consciousness.

Both Hallowell and Descola, in startlingly similar terms, discuss the emphasis on the soul, spirit, or interiority in animist societies.[9] Hallowell basically equates interiority with the self, while emphasizing the independence of interiority from a particular physicality. The spirit or soul, Descola's interiority, transcends the body in space and time. According to Hallowell, "The soul is independent of a particular body; it transcends the body in time; an implicit concept of the self is intimately connected with the idea of the soul" (1955, 173). However, Hallowell notes that physicality is intimately connected to the self or interiority, so much so that physical possession of even a part of the body is considered to endanger the self. The ideal situation is a balance or harmony between soul and body. Death is a transformation that entails the permanent dissociation of interiority and physicality (Hallowell 1955, 173, 175–76; Descola 2013a).

Descola and Viveiros de Castro (1998, 470) posit that American Indian ontologies are essentially animistic, operating according to a belief in a spiritual unity or similarity of interiority and a corporeal diversity or dissimilarity of physicality. All persons have similar software, yet dissimilar hardware, so to speak. In animist societies, physicality is seen as fluid and unreliable, capable of transformation, while interiority is seen as the true, enduring, vital essence of a person. Interiority provides the common link that unifies all life-forms in the cosmos.[10] Due to this common subjectivity, animals, spirits, and other nonhuman persons are said to possess social characteristics: they live in villages, marry and have families, abide by kinship rules and moral and ethical codes, sing, dance, perform rituals, hunt, trade, go to war, and are capable of action, interaction, and relationship (Descola 2013b, 79–80). In this way, the distinction between nature and culture is blurred: nature is a reflection of culture and vice versa.

According to Descola and Viveiros de Castro, animist societies describe the variability of bodily appearance using the metaphor of clothing. While each tribe-species or collective has a characteristic outward form,[11] "a bundle of differentiated functions" or a "biological toolkit" (Descola 2013b, 80), physicality as clothing is changeable and removable. This is an expression of transformation or metamorphosis, a key feature of animist ontologies, in which animals, spirits, the dead, and other nonhuman persons have the potential to transform into human physicalities and vice versa. As Descola explains,

> Metamorphosis is what allows interactions on a common ground between entities with entirely different bodies, when animals and plants reveal their interiority under a human form in order to communicate with humans—in dreams and visions generally, or when humans—usually shamans and ritual specialists—don animal clothing in order to visit animal communities. Thus, metamorphosis is not an unveiling of the humanity of animal persons, or a way to disguise the humanity of human persons; it is the culminating stage of a relation where everyone, by modifying the position of observation to which he has been confined by his original physicality, strives to coincide with the point of view according to which he presumes that the other term of the relation apprehends himself: a human will not see an animal as he perceives it normally, but as the animal perceives itself, as a human; and a human is seen as he does not perceive himself ordinarily, but as he wishes to be perceived, as an animal. It is an anamorphosis, then, rather than a metamorphosis. (2013b, 80–81)

Metamorphosis often occurs in the virtual realms of mythology, dreams and visions, and ritual, allowing for interspecies interaction, relationship, and exchange. But more on this later.[12]

Before briefly discussing the complementary role of phenomenology in the ontological turn I will explicitly reiterate Hallowell's pioneering role in these developments. In particular, Descola's dual notions of interiority and physicality are practically identical to the concepts Hallowell articulated over fifty years ago. For Hallowell, all life-forms of the person class, whether human or nonhuman, share the same fundamental structure, consisting of an enduring, inner vital part and an unstable outer form that is subject to change. Describing the composition of *pawáganak*, the Ojibwe term for nonhuman spirit persons or "dream visitors" addressed by humans as "grandfathers," Hallowell writes,

> They have a "bodily" aspect, whether human-like, animal-like, or ambiguous. But this is not their most persistent, enduring and vital attribute any more than in the case of human beings. We must conclude that all animate beings of the person class are unified conceptually in Ojibwe thinking because they have a similar structure—an inner vital part that is enduring and an outward form which can change. Vital personal attributes such as sentience, volition, memory, speech are not dependent upon outward appearance but upon the inner vital essence of being. If this be true, human beings and other-than-human persons are alike in another way. The human self does not die; it continues its existence in another place, after the body is buried in the grave. (1960, 42–43)

Descola is not alone in his debt to Hallowell. Nurit Bird-David (1999), Ingold (2004), Viveiros de Castro (1998), Harvey (2005), and contemporary phenomenological approaches in anthropology all build on Hallowellian foundations. As this discussion illustrates, animism is not about belief per se. It ultimately hinges on processual social interaction, relationship, and experience. In other words, animism is grounded in phenomenology, one of the major poles, along with history and psychology, of Hallowell's theoretical contribution to Americanist anthropology and ethnohistorical studies of American Indian cultures.

Culture and Experience

Anthropology has long been interested in exploring how culture serves to shape worlds of experience (Throop and Murphy 2002, 186). Hence it should come as no surprise that anthropologists are keenly interested in phenomenology, the study of phenomena and structures of consciousness as they appear to and are experienced by a particular person or subjectivity. Understanding ontology is impossible without appreciating actual lived realities or experiences of being-in-the-world. In this way the project of ontological anthropology is intimately linked to phenomenological approaches in anthropology.

A pathbreaker of both orientations, Hallowell explored the interfaces of ontology, worldview, and phenomenology; of culture, psychology, and experience. As his student Anthony F. C. Wallace (in Hallowell 1976, 159) notes, Hallowell's ethnography is largely concerned with the perception of the individual actor. Another Hallowell student, Melford Spiro, describes this approach as the phenomenology of the self as understood by the actor. Discussing Hallowell's groundbreaking paper "The Self and Its Behavioral Environment" (Hallowell 1955, 75–110), Spiro (in Hallowell 1976, 353) writes, "It is probably not inaccurate to claim that this paper laid the foundation for the 'phenomenological' approach to the anthropological study of both culture and personality."[13]

Phenomenology plays a crucial role in the ontological turn and new animism. As Kapferer (2014a, 391–92) indicates, phenomenology is vital in Descola's *Beyond Nature and Culture*, particularly that of Husserl and Merleau-Ponty, which Descola (2013a) explicitly states. Descola basically adapts Husserl's body/intentionality distinction in his concept of physicality/interiority and follows his equation of consciousness with intentionality, the notion that all consciousness and thought has external reference beyond itself and is object-directed (Descola 2013b, 78–79; Thompson and Zahavi 2007). Descola writes of physicality "in the sense of dispositions enabling a physical action" and interiority "in the sense of self-reflexive inwardness" (Descola 2013b, 79).

Ingold and Willerslev exemplify a more phenomenologically oriented approach, emphasizing the practical, contextual modalities and situated nature of indigenous hunter-gatherer animism. Ingold's (2000, 2004, 2006, 2011) work examines the practical dimensions of lived experience in relation to ontology, seeing animism as being-(alive)-in-the-world. He is concerned not only with the nature of animism but also with how humans perceive the environment. As Willerslev points out, Ingold "adopts a phenomenological starting point, emphasizing that world and human reality are ontologically inseparable—an idea conveyed in the German philosopher Martin Heidegger's (1962, 107) phrase 'being-in-the-world.' The hyphenation of this expression signals that our everyday involvement with the various components that make up the world implies that we cannot regard them as a purely objective and value-free set of things waiting for our mental construction to render them meaningful. Rather, the things with which we deal have meaning for us in the immediacy of our dealings with them" (Willerslev 2013, 48).

Willerslev, drawing on Ingold's phenomenology, illustrates how giving primacy to "the personification of natural and other phenomena on the basis of one's practical engagement with the environment . . . reverses the ontological priorities of anthropological analysis by convincingly showing that everyday practical life is the crucial foundation upon which so-called higher mental activities of conceptualization are firmly premised. By taking seriously the actual experiences of the practitioners in this way, the theory allows anthropologists to analyze animistic beliefs in a way that is compatible with the indigenous peoples' own accounts, which tend to be based on hands-on experience with animals and things rather than on abstract theoretical contemplation" (2013, 48–49). Again, Hallowell anticipated these connections, masterfully elucidating the culturally constituted nature of both self and environment as phenomenologically conceived by social actors. Hence, in order to understand ontology, intersubjectivity/interagency, and behavior, one must first understand the interaction between culturally constituted selves and environments. Ultimately Hallowell was concerned with the meaning of experience and culture in relation to social behavior (Spiro in Hallowell 1976, 353–55).

Phenomenological approaches resonate deeply with Lakota, Ojibwe, and other tribal epistemologies, religious orientations, and worldviews (see, for example, V. Deloria 1999; Martínez 2004b). "Religion, as I have experienced it," writes Vine Deloria, "is not the recitation of beliefs but a way of helping to understand our lives. It must, I think, have an intimate connection with the world in which we live" (1999, xiii). Later he writes, "Indians consider their own individual experiences, the accumulated wisdom of the community that has been gathered by previous generations, their dreams, visions, and prophecies, and any information received from birds, animals, and plants as data that must be arranged, evaluated, and understood as a unified body of knowledge" (1999, 66). Both subjective and collective experience, along with practical adaptability, are at the very core of Lakota and other tribal worldviews.

In *The Metaphysics of Modern Existence* (2012) Deloria argues that perception is a fundamental epistemological principle that can produce knowledge capable of providing a context for human maturity and personality formation. Experience, observation, participation, and practical adaptation are fundamental elements of Lakota life, belief, and ritual, (re)generative of ontology, epistemology, and cosmology. For Deloria (1999, 14), Lakota perspectives focus on "the intensity of . . . experience and the perspective of the observer/participant." Rather than rejecting this world for some other transcendent realm, such as heaven, Lakota people embrace their lived realities as beings-(alive)-in-the-world, believing that everything humans experience has value and is instructive in some aspect of life. In the Lakota cosmos each entity, and by extension each place, is the center of the universe, and there is a distinct place, both literally and figuratively, for each tribe-species (Joseph Brown 1989; V. Deloria 1999, 5, 22–23, 45, 55–56).

Phenomenology, the subjective experience of beings-(alive)-in-the-world, is fundamental to the ontological and new animist frameworks. Phenomenology and ontology are mutually constituting and generative, operating in a dialectical fashion, so that neither can be understood without reference to the other. The intersubjectivity or relations between persons/subjects at the heart of ontological concerns cannot be grasped without understanding the culturally constituted and distinctive ways in which phenomena appear to and are interpreted by the self and collective in situated lifeworlds. Essentially both ontological and phenomenological projects destabilize and decenter natural/cultural attitudes. Ontological and posthuman anthropologies seek to decenter the privileging of human perspectives, opening the world to broader understandings and distinctly nonhuman moral vistas. Phenomenological description aims to destabilize or "bracket" the "natural attitude," those underlying, inherited, largely unexamined assumptions that organize our prereflective engagements with reality in which we assume that a world exists independently of our experience of it (Desjarlais and Throop 2011, 88–91). Ontological and posthuman anthropology effectively brackets our unexamined assumptions about animacy, personhood, causality, and the centrality of human beings in the universe. Next I build upon these insights from Descola, Hallowell, and Deloria, applying them in a reinterpretation of Lakota ethnographic material.

CHAPTER 2

Situated Animism and Lakota Relational Ontology

One of the fundamental (and in some ways unavoidable) shortcomings of much anthropological theorizing is its reliance on a distinctly Western philosophical tradition. In Western philosophy and thought there is a tendency, based on biblical and Cartesian notions, to separate humans from the rest of the world as superior, distanced, objective, third-party observers rather than acknowledging that humans are part of a system or web of relations and experience. Humans are encompassed and enmeshed within the universe rather than outside or above it. In this interconnected web of life humans are dependent upon everything else as interrelated parts of a system. In our contemporary lives we often forget that life is a dynamic process of transformation, interaction, and interrelation and that the line between self and other, subject and object, like the line between nature and culture, is blurred, if it is present or meaningful at all. The processual being of humanity, what Martin Heidegger (1962) refers to as "being-in-the-world" (and falling back into the Western philosophy trap), is often eclipsed in our day-to-day lived realities, in the chaotic and indeterminate actuality of our everyday existence. Nineteenth-century Lakota understandings of ontology, personhood, relationality, and the position of human beings in the universe were vastly different from both past and present Western understandings.

In the subsequent analysis I draw directly on Lakota thought, philosophy, and worldview as much as possible in order to gain a fuller and more nuanced understanding of "posthuman" ontology from indigenous perspectives. Utilizing historical texts written by Lakota people—many in their own language—and complemented by fieldwork and interviews with contemporary Lakotas, I explore Lakota perspectives on personhood, human-nonhuman social interaction, and relational ontology. Understanding this relational ontology is essential to understanding the world according to the Lakotas, their underlying assumptions, ideas, and life. The nature of this culturally constituted world defined their very possibilities of thinking and acting (cf. Hanegraaff 2015, 62). I stand firm in my belief, along with Hallowell and other Americanists or (neo-)Boasians, that native languages are the ideal entrée into native worldviews (see Darnell 2001). Along with native-language text analysis I also apply insights from the ontological turn and Hallowell's pioneering work on Ojibwe ontology and worldview. In a sense this work is equal parts critique, adoption, and adaptation of various themes encompassed within this anthropological shift of focus toward ontology, but it also explores the deeply rooted influence of Hallowell's particular and exemplary brand of ("pre-posthuman") Americanist anthropology.

For the Lakotas, all life-forms were related; the universe (*wamák'ognaka*, literally, 'all the things on earth') was experienced as being alive and characterized by its unity (V. Deloria 1999, 38, 46–53; 2009, 80; DeMallie 1987, 27–28; 2001, 806). Animals, spirits, ghosts, rocks, trees, meteorological phenomena, medicine bundles, and other objects were seen as persons or subjectivities, selves with souls, capable of agency and interpersonal relationship, and loci of causality. Indeed, the concept of person was directly related to notions of causality, so that impersonal forces were rarely the determinants of events (cf. Hallowell 1958, 80). Vine Deloria (2009, 184) writes that "the fundamental reality in our physical world is a strange kind of energy that is found within everything—from stars to humans to stones to quantum energy fields. This energy is personal—or can be experienced personally." Personhood was extended to most things in one's immediate environment with whom one communicated and interacted, and the potential for personhood was ever-present. In particular, ritual objects, such as swan or eagle down, red ochre or vermilion, stones, and so on, were linguistically classified as animate beings (Fletcher 1887b, 290n3).

The central religious concept of nineteenth-century Lakota life, the great animating force of the universe, and the common denominator of its oneness was *wakʻą́*, incomprehensible, mysterious, nonhuman instrumental power or energy, often glossed as 'medicine'.[1] Wakʻą́ is commonly translated 'sacred', 'mysterious', 'holy', or 'incomprehensible', but this polysemous concept is extremely complex, defying simplistic explanations. This force underlay all things in both the seen and the unseen realms and manifested itself in various ways in relation to humans as mysterious potency. The power concept wakʻą́ is the basic underlying principle of Lakota spirituality, integrating the Lakota cosmos. It is the animating force that flows through all things. Everything in the universe is imbued with and unified through wakʻą́ power or energy (DeMallie 1984, 80–81; Walker 1991, 68–80). In a pertinent passage Vine Deloria explains that "Sioux people understood that *Wakan Tanka* [Wakʻą́ Tʻą́ka, literally, 'Great Mystery']—a word that defies easy definition but reflects the 'great mysterious'—is in everything, so that there was no doubt that humans shared certain elements with all other creatures. As we probe more deeply into the mystery of life, we come to learn how closely related we are to other creatures" (2009, 14).

Around the turn of the twentieth century the Oglala Good Seat explained that, at base, wakʻą́ was "anything that was hard to understand" (in Walker 1991, 70). Around the same time the Oglala holy man George Sword said, "*Wakan* means very many things. The Lakota understands what it means from the things that are considered *wakan*; yet sometimes its meaning must be explained to him. It is something that is hard to understand. . . . Every object in the world has a spirit and that spirit is *wakan*. Thus the spirit of the tree or things of that kind, while not like the spirit of man, are also *wakan*" (in Walker 1917, 152). For Sword, Good Seat, Little Wound, and others of their generation the essence of wakʻą́ was its incomprehensibility, that "no man can understand it" (Walker 1991, 98). Significantly, wakʻą́ was often understood and classified in terms of its phenomenological manifestations or effects in context or in relation to human beings.

Stephen Return Riggs was a Presbyterian missionary to the Eastern Sioux or Dakotas at Lac Qui Parle, Minnesota Territory, throughout the mid-nineteenth century. Describing Sioux religious beliefs, he writes, "All life is Wakan. So also is everything which exhibits power, whether in action, as the winds and drifting clouds, or in passive endurance, as the bowlder [sic] by the wayside. . . . In the mind of a Dakota . . . this word Wah-kon . . . covers the whole field of their fear and worship. Many things also that are neither feared nor worshiped, but are simply wonderful, come under this designation" (Riggs in Dorsey 1894, 433). The power and utter incomprehensibility of wakʽą́ frequently evoked *wóyušʼiyaye* or *kʽokípʽa* 'fear' and *wóitʽųpe* or *iníhą* 'awe', which naturally led to the *wóohola* or *ohóla* 'respect, reverence' and *wóyuonihą* or *yuónihą* 'honor' paid to nonhuman spirit persons and other manifestations of wakʽą́ power (see Bushotter 1887–88, story 3). Consequently, wakʽą́ was considered extremely *wókʽokipʽe* 'dangerous'. The late Albert White Hat, a Rosebud Lakota educator and linguist, discusses the inherent dangerousness and ambivalence of wakʽą́ things, writing, "Every ritual we have is *Wókʽokipʽe*. You could translate that into English as 'dangerous.' It's not only our rituals; every creation, whether a blade of grass, a tree, a rabbit, a horse, or a human, is *Wókʽokipʽe*. And that's because every creation is *Wakʽą́*. . . . The reason they say every creation is *Wókʽokipʽe* is that everyone has a good side and an evil side. Every creation has good and bad in it, and in working with them, we might use the wrong energy" (White Hat 2012, 84). Wakʽą́, this powerful unifying and animating yet dangerous force, lies at the heart of Lakota metaphysical conceptions, but it was articulated in terms of kinship, the dominant interpretive principle of Lakota culture.

Wakʽą́ was the basis of kinship among humans and between humans and nonhumans (Joseph Brown 1997, xvi; DeMallie 2001, 806). Kinship, according to Ella Deloria (1998, 24), was the "all-important matter" in Lakota life and relationship the dominant interpretive principle. For nineteenth-century Lakotas kinship was the very center of existence, and all domains of human life operated according to its logic. As the dominant interpretive principle, kinship unified all lifeforms through the symbol of the *cʽąnúpa wakʽą́* 'sacred pipe', given to the people by Ptesą́wį 'White Buffalo Woman', a nonhuman spirit person and mediator figure. The pipe functioned as a means to unite disparate interiorities and establish relationship. As Sword explained in 1896, "The spirit in the smoke will soothe the spirits of all who thus smoke together and all will be as friends and all think alike" (in Walker 1991, 83). The gift of the pipe established a reciprocal relationship or covenant between humans and nonhumans; between the people and Wakʻą́ Tʻą́ka 'Great Mystery' (sometimes problematically glossed as 'Great Spirit'). Besides the pipe, the great symbol of interspecies unity and relationship was the circle, the *cʻągléška wakʻą́* 'sacred hoop' of existence (DeMallie 1984, 290–91; 1994, 1998; Densmore 2001, 63–68). Around the turn of the twentieth century, Thomas Tyon, an Oglala from the White Clay District of Pine Ridge Reservation, explained, "The Oglala believe the circle to be sacred because the Great Spirit caused everything in nature to be round except stone. . . . Everything that breathes is round like the body of a man. Everything that grows from the ground is round like the stem of a tree. Since the Great Spirit has caused everything to be round mankind should look upon the circle as sacred for it is the symbol of all things in nature except stone" (in Walker 1991, 160).

An essential feature of this relational ontology described by Tyon is the assumption that the universe and everything in it is alive and interrelated, and that all things in a specific environment potentially have a spirit, life, personality, subjectivity, intentionality, common energy, or, adopting Descola's concept, a similar interiority (V. Deloria 1999, 38, 48–50; Dorsey 1894, 433–34; Neill 1872, 266).[2] According to Charles Eastman, the Dakotas attributed "personality and will to the elements, the sun and stars, and all animate or inanimate nature" (1980, 122). He writes, "We believed that the spirit pervades all creation and that every creature possesses a soul in some degree, though not necessarily a soul conscious of itself. The tree, the waterfall, the grizzly bear, each is an embodied Force, and as such an object of reverence" (1980, 14–15). We might refer to this as a form of situated or site-specific animism, specific to particular spatiotemporal circumstances and experienced through relationship. As Riggs writes, "The Dakotas viewed every object *known to them* as having a spirit capable of helping or hurting them, and consequently a proper object of worship" (1883, 148; emphasis added). According to Vine Deloria, "it is not an article of faith in any Indian religion that everything has spirit.[3] What happens in the different Indian religions is that people live so intimately with environment that they are in relationship to the spirits that live in particular places. It is not an article of faith; it is part of human experience" (1999, 224).

Deloria (1999, 40–60, 224) asserts that this was not necessarily an all-encompassing belief that all things at all times had a spirit but rather an intimate experiential knowledge of and commitment to the spirits of particular places, situated in historical relationships. But on this point Deloria appears to contradict himself, making general claims such as, "the old Indians . . . saw and experienced personality in every aspect of the universe and called it 'Woniya' (Spirit)" (1999, 48); there was no "reason to suppose that other forms of life did not have the same basic intelligence as humans" (1999, 50); "American Indians . . . said that everything, including the rocks and grasses, was alive, and moreover had personality *and* intelligence" (2009, 80; emphasis in original); "we have no basis for believing that animals in a natural state do *not* demonstrate the aspects of personality and thought that we see in ourselves" (2009, 117; emphasis in original); and animals "had the same mental and emotional constitution as we do" (2009, 122). Perhaps the confusion arises from attempts to conceptualize and define complex Sioux notions of personality, will, soul, spirit, and so on and translate them for a largely nonnative, Western audience. Or perhaps Deloria is simply highlighting the situated, temporal, experiential, and relational nature of American Indian beliefs and lifeways.

In particular, Deloria opposes the notion that Native Americans were animists (see V. Deloria 2009, 80). Of course, his understanding of animism was based on the problematic theories of Tylor, Frazer, and other nineteenth-century thinkers, so that his resistance stems largely from the concept's embeddedness in social evolutionary theory, which held that animism was an erroneous belief in an animated nature, superstition, and evidence of racial inferiority, primitiveness, ignorance, and a lack of cultural, intellectual, and psychological accomplishment and development. In addition, Deloria seems to bristle at the notion of an overly dogmatic animism as a strict doctrinal creed that does not allow for the individualism, experiential idiosyncrasy, and innovation inherent in Sioux religious belief and ritual. In any case, Descolian animism involves extending social relationality to nonhumans and acknowledges subjective idiosyncrasy and hybridity within ontological orientations, thus cleansing animism of its intransigent, social evolutionary past. Further, all the notions discussed by Deloria above—soul, spirit, intelligence, subjectivity, personality, will, and so on—can be subsumed under Descola's general analytic concept of interiority, so that, from a Descolian animist position, we can agree that the *potential* for a generalized or similar interiority, extended across tribes-species to humans and nonhumans alike, was ever-present in nineteenth-century Sioux ethnometaphysics. This potential in no way detracts from the importance of experience or place in Lakota religious traditions and understandings (see V. Deloria 1973, 1999, 54–56, 323–38). The situated animism characteristic of the Lakotas is not a set of dogmatic concepts or creeds but a set of experiences based on both individual and collective (accumulated or intergenerational) knowledge.

This emphasis on the situated nature of Lakota animism, although somewhat oxymoronic, speaks to Kapferer's critique and re-expression of Descola's fourfold ontological schema. Instead of ontologies operating in an exclusionary manner, leading to a homogenization of a society as of one type or another, Kapferer argues that a number of different ontologies may operate under specific situated circumstances in a given society (Kapferer 2014a, 396; 2012). A notion of situated animism also speaks to the practical nature of hunter-gatherer animist cosmologies and ontologies in general, as articulated by Ingold and Willerslev. A practical, situated animism is inexorably bound to phenomenological experience and perception, particularly subsistence, trophic, and especially hunting activities. It is often restricted to particular historical and spatial contexts of relational activity, such as human-nonhuman encounters in actuality or in the realms of myth, dreams and visions, and ritual. This approach, argues Willerslev, subverts primitivism and romanticism by "taking seriously the actual experiences of the practitioners . . . [allowing] anthropologists to analyze animistic beliefs in a way that is compatible with the indigenous peoples' own accounts, which tend to be based on hands-on experience with animals and things rather than on abstract theoretical contemplation" (Willerslev 2013, 49; see also Willerslev 2007). Aside from ever so slightly amending Descola's notion of animism, recentering it in ethnography and the experiences of living indigenous peoples, a notion of practical, situated animism also explains why some things are bequeathed personhood at some times and others are not, an apparent contradiction observed by Tylor, Durkheim, Hallowell, and others.[4] But more on this later.

Many authors have overlooked the practical, situated nature of Sioux animist beliefs. Throughout much of the nineteenth century Thomas S. Williamson was a medical doctor and missionary to the Dakotas at the Lac Qui Parle mission and Kaposia, Minnesota Territory. The Dakotas, he writes, believed "every object, artificial as well as natural, to be the habitation of a spirit capable of hurting or helping them" (Williamson 1869, 435). James W. Lynd was a mid-nineteenth-century fur trader among the Dakotas turned Minnesota politician and amateur ethnographer. He was among the first casualties of the attack on the Lower Sioux (or Redwood) Agency by Little Crow and his warriors on August 18, 1862, the first major conflict of the Dakota War of 1862.[5] According to Lynd, the religious system of the Eastern Sioux "gives to everything a spirit or soul. Even the commonest stones, sticks, and clays have a spiritual essence attached to them which must needs be reverenced" (1889, 154). Despite the naïve overextension of animist principles and lack of focus on history and place, the ethnographic data recorded by these early observers is still useful.

A situated animist ontology, based on historical relationships, mutual respect, and the acknowledgement of a continuity of interiority, unifies an otherwise very individualistic Lakota belief system,[6] providing avenues for individualism and innovation (see V. Deloria 1999, 50–51). This relational ontology, centered on the notion of similar interiorities and symbolized by the sacred pipe and the circle, is the very basis of mitákuye oyás'į 'all my relatives, we are all related', a key cultural symbol and ceremonial benediction and blessing heard at all ceremonial and social gatherings.[7] The normative cultural values encompassed by mitákuye oyás'į are the very foundation of kinship, relational ontology, and the overarching interspecies collective, of which humans are only one hoop, one *oyáte* 'people, nation, tribe', in the company of many others. Articulating mitákuye oyás'į from a Descolian animist perspective reveals fresh insights and opens new horizons of meaning.

The key constituents of this animist ontology and worldview, of mitákuye oyás'į, are persons, a category that extends beyond human beings to nonhuman or other-than-human persons. Importantly, the Lakota worldview sees humans as the least knowledgeable and powerful beings, requiring the most aid and pity, upending the common Western biblical assumption that humans have dominion to rule over all other life-forms and subdue the earth (see V. Deloria 1999, 50; 2009, 99–100). For the Lakotas, the seed of all life is wak'ą 'sacrality, mystery, divinity'; hence all life-forms share a generalized interiority, whether human or nonhuman. Next we will examine Lakota perspectives on personhood and the nature, characteristics, and composition of human and nonhuman persons and collectives.

Oyáte 'People, Nation, Tribe' and the Nature of Collectives in Lakota Ethnometaphysics

There is no word in the Lakota language for nature as it is understood in the Euro-American, post-Enlightenment sense—as a passive, unchanging, impersonal, abstract domain of objects subject to autonomous laws that is antithetical to culture or society.[8] According to Standing Bear,

> We did not think of the great open plains, the beautiful rolling hills, and winding streams with tangled growth, as "wild." Only to the white man was nature a "wilderness" and only to him was the land "infested" with "wild" animals and "savage" people. To us it was tame. Earth was bountiful and we were surrounded with the blessings of the Great Mystery. Not until the hairy man from the east came and with brutal frenzy heaped injustices upon us and the families we loved was it "wild" for us. When the very animals of the forest began fleeing from his approach, then it was that for us the "Wild West" began. (Standing Bear 2006a, 38)

Writing years later, Vine Deloria observes, "Indians do not talk about nature as some kind of concept or something 'out there.' They talk about the immediate environment in which they live. They do not embrace all trees or love all rivers and mountains. What is important is the relationship you have with a particular tree or a particular mountain" (1999, 223). As Descola (2013a) argues, the strict division between culture or society and nature is a recent Western phenomenon that does not apply to animist societies.

In Lakota, there are terms—such as *manítu* 'wilderness, uninhabited regions', *ȟeyáta* 'back in the hills, out in the country, in remote areas', and *hókawiȟ* 'outside the camp circle'—that refer to the regions away from camp or human civilization and habitation, but not in the Western sense of abstract nature as strictly distinct and separate from culture or society (Powers 1986, 35, 204). The Lakotas did not objectivize nature as external to their subjective selves. Rather, they addressed the earth and other living beings inhabiting it as relatives, incorporating all life-forms into the sacred hoop of kinship, the dominant interpretive framework of Lakota culture (see Black Elk in DeMallie 1984). According to the Sioux animist ontology and worldview there was no sharp distinction between nature and society. Extending this insight, DeMallie writes, "In a very real sense, humankind and nature were one, just as the natural and supernatural were one. The distinction between natural and supernatural, so basic to European thought, was meaningless in Lakota culture" (DeMallie 1987, 28; see also DeMallie 1982, 390–91; Joseph Brown 1997, xiii).

Central to Lakota ethnometaphysics and worldview are the related notions that humans are not superior, or more intelligent, or separated from the other persons or life-forms in the living universe. Vine Deloria (1999, 28) writes, "There are few tribes . . . that would teach that humans are superior to animals, almost every tribe believing that each species forms a family or a people and has a specific relationship to humans, who merely constitute another species." There is continuity between nature and culture, and, in fact, humans are understood as the most dependent and helpless, the least knowledgeable and powerful, the pitiful and helpless "younger brothers" of the other life-forms.

Ethnographic accounts reveal a Sioux typology of "nature" as composed of a number of species or tribes of human and nonhuman life-forms. According to Vine Deloria (2009, 117), "First and foremost in the Sioux mind was the idea that other creatures were 'peoples' like us." Aaron McGaffey Beede, an Episcopal missionary to the Sioux in North Dakota in the early 1900s, elaborates, writing, "The Western Sioux believed that each being, a rock for instance, is an actual community of persons with ample locomotion among themselves, and such locomotion not regarded as circumscribed or restricted, save as the make (oicage) of the whole gives to each species his own sphere. And, as they reasoned, this limitation is merely in body (tancan), the mind, intelligence and spirit of each is privileged to range through and blend with totality by gaining a right attitude toward Woniya (Spirit)" (Beede 1912, Western Sioux Cosmology). Each species forms a family or a people, an oyáte 'people, nation, tribe', which I interchangeably refer to as *collective* or *tribe-species*. These collectives are both human and nonhuman, each having specific characteristics, dispositions, and historically situated spatiotemporal relationships with each other. Humans merely constitute another tribe-species in this schema, in which all forms of being are related in a cosmos characterized by its unity (V. Deloria 1999, 28, 48–55; 2009, 115–17; DeMallie 2001, 806; Powers 1982a, 46; 1986, 151–54).

The foundation of this view of collectives is the characteristic animist belief in a spiritual unity or similarity of interiority and a corporeal diversity or dissimilarity of physicality. Descolian animism is a mode of identification: a means of broadly schematizing our experience of things, specifying the properties of existing beings, and distributing those beings according to their attributes, which in turn forms the boundaries of identity and otherness (Descola 2013a, 309, 336). While animism provides the basic ontological orientation, it is relational schemas that specify the general form of the links between those beings and imprint a particular ethos upon a given society. Relational schemas, like modes of identification, are integrating schemas: "they stem from the kind of cognitive, emotional, and sensorimotor structures that channel the production of automatic inferences, orientate practical action, and organize the expression of thoughts and feelings according to relatively stereotyped patterns" (Descola 2013a, 310). Although a number of relational schemas may operate simultaneously and/or situationally in a particular culture, one is usually dominant or more prevalent, meaning that it is activated in a wide range of different circumstances in relations with humans or nonhumans, subjecting those relations to a particular logic (Descola 2013a, 310, 336–37).

Dominant relational schemas tend to distinguish collectives that coexist within a particular environment (Descola 2013a, 310). As we shall see, the major dominant relational schemas operating among traditional Sioux tribes were exchange and predation. In the Descolian framework, exchange refers to a symmetrical relationship between two entities in which any agreed transfer from one entity to the other requires something in return. Predation, on the other hand, is a negative asymmetrical relationship in which entity A takes something of value from entity B without offering anything in exchange (Descola 2013a, 311). According to Descola (2013a, 359), "The prevalence of a relational schema in a collective leads its members to adopt typical behavior patterns, the repetition and frequency of which are such that ethnographers who observe and interpret them feel justified in describing them overall as normative 'values' that orientate social life." Hence, dominant relational schemas systematize experience shared by a diverse collection of individuals, a group that is often characterized by internal variations—of territories, languages or "dialects," institutions, and practices. These schemas direct experience along well-entrenched pathways, bringing together the practices of complex collectives of variable sizes and natures. In many ways, a relational schema, the manner in which humans organize their experience in terms of their relations with other humans and nonhumans, defines the contours and limits of a collective (Descola 2013a, 361–64). Understanding Sioux lifeways in terms of relational schemas is particularly useful, considering the vast expanse of their territory in the nineteenth century, their cultural and linguistic variations, and the diversity and individuality characteristic of the various Sioux tribes from east to west.

Collective is here used in the Descolian sense, popularized by Bruno Latour (1993), meaning "a procedure of grouping, or 'collecting,' humans and nonhumans into a network of specific interrelations" (Descola 2013a,

422n1). *Collective*, which I use interchangeably with *tribe-species*, is distinguished from the classic term *society* in that it encompasses both human and nonhuman life-forms, corresponding in part to the notion of a social system. There are as many collectives as there are different forms and behavior patterns, but each is characterized by a social system. A common interiority dictates that human and nonhuman collectives share identical structures and properties. Animist collectives are characterized and qualified by human-type relations, and their members are aware that they form a particular collective and of their distinctiveness vis-à-vis other tribes-species. The composition of collectives in animist regimes is homogeneous or monospecific, each being a collection of human or nonhuman individuals who conform to a particular type and tend to be endogamous. In short, collectives are differentiated by form, morphological characteristics and dispositions, behavior patterns, breeding and feeding habits, habitat, or, in a word, physicality (Descola 2013a, 247–51, 254, 276, 279). Now let us see how all this works out among the nineteenth-century Sioux.

The Sioux, along with other animist hunter-gatherer societies, were endlessly fascinated by and naturally concerned with the vast array of physical forms manifested in the universe. "American Indians," explains Vine Deloria (1999, 52–53), "understanding that the universe consisted of living entities, were interested in learning how other forms of life behaved, for they saw that every entity had a personality and could exercise a measure of free will and choice. Consequently, Indian people carefully observed phenomena in order to determine what relationships existed between and among the various 'peoples' of the world." According to Šiyáka (Teal Duck), a Sioux man from Standing Rock Reservation who spoke with Frances Densmore in 1912, "Many animals have ways from which a man can learn a great deal" (Šiyáka in Densmore 2001, 184). Standing Bear, who refers to animals and other nonhumans as the "wise mentors and guides" (2006a, 75) of the Lakotas, writes, "The Lakota read and studied actions, movements, posture, intonation, expression, and gesture of both man and animal" (2006a, 18). Recall that physicality refers not only to the body or manifest form but also to habitus, behavior patterns, and dispositions and how these relate to the ways in which specific collectives interact with and occupy particular places or habitats. Physicality, then, using Vine Deloria's words, is tied to the prevalent idea among the Sioux that "particular places were designed for particular species, and, in human terms, for particular peoples. . . . Each place determined the various life-forms it would support and these creatures then worked cooperatively at their chosen location" (1999, 56).

Further, explains Deloria, "Careful observation of the behavior of other creatures by the Sioux revealed that each kind of animal—and here I am referring to birds, land animals and water animals—had its own unique way of adjusting to the world" (2009, 115). According to Eastman, a Santee Dakota writing in 1902, "The Indians divided all animals into four general classes: 1st, those that walk upon four legs; 2nd, those that fly; 3rd, those that swim with fins; 4th, those that creep" (C. Eastman 1971, 77). The familiar Lakota classification of living things was explained by the Oglala Thomas Tyon to James R. Walker, also around the turn of the twentieth century. According to Tyon's Lakota schema, breath or life was the common denominator of this classification, the stem being *ní* 'life', from which is formed *niyá, oníya,* and *wóniya,* variously translated as 'breath, life, life-breath', literally, 'that which causes life'. According to Tyon, the Lakotas recognized "four kinds of things that breathe: those that crawl, those that fly, those that walk on four legs, and those that walk on two legs" (in Walker 1917, 159–60). The differences between the Eastern and Western Sioux classifications of animals may be idiosyncratic and/or spatiotemporal/historical: the Dakotas mainly lived in a woodlands/riverine environment, while the Lakotas inhabited the vast prairies and plains where water, and the wildlife associated with it, was relatively scarce. Both schemas demonstrate the cultural significance of the number four among the Sioux. According to Vine Deloria, the Sioux metaphorically extended their classifications of nonhuman physicalities to humans as well: "The characterization of individuals in relation to the traits of an animal served as an Indian way of classifying and understanding strangers" (2009, 21). Clearly, the major Sioux criterion for classifying and differentiating life-forms was physicality in the

Descolian sense, that is, morphology, behavior, habitus, diet, particular modes of reproduction, and habitat.

The animist mode of identification distributes humans and nonhumans into as many collectives or social species as there are different physicalities. While physicality is the great ontological differentiator, a generalized interiority means all tribes-species are people, like humans, opening space for intertribal/interspecies commonalities, such as the extension of culture and sociality to nonhumans. In animist societies, explains Descola (2013a, 248), "species endowed with an interiority analogous to that of humans are reputed to live within collectives whose structures and properties are identical to those of human collectives." The Lakotas noticed correlations between humans and nonhumans, as well as specific relationships between various collectives (Powers 1986, 149–51). According to Deloria, despite differences in terms of forms and behavior patterns, nonhumans "also had many things in common with humans, and these things encouraged [human] people to seek to understand them. Like humans, the other creatures had limitations beyond which they could not go. Although these limits were largely dependent on the physical shape of the bird or animal, keen attention showed that they were quite like humans in having strong and weak individuals among their groups, in demonstrating joy and sadness, and in confronting unusual situations and finding ways to solve their problems" (V. Deloria 2009, 115–16).

Animist collectives are autonomous and isomorphic, conceived according to the model and logic of human society and comprehended and described using the language of human kinship (Descola 2013a, 247–51). In animism "nature" is thought of by analogy with "culture," so that animism is anthropogenic, rather than anthropocentric, in that "it derives from humans all that is necessary to make it possible for nonhumans to be treated as humans" (Descola 2013a, 258). As William Powers explains, "We might say that the Lakota employ metaphorical extensions between humans and animals: Nonhuman species are, in sacred language, treated as if they are human" (1986, 151). Extending this idea, Standing Bear writes, "The acceptance of a kinship with other orders of life was the first step toward humanization" (2006a, 202).

However, Powers contradicts himself and denies the notion that social organization and kinship among nonhuman spirit persons were modeled on that of human society. In a diatribe against his colleague Raymond DeMallie, Powers (1986, 120–25) claims that the relationships between the spirits were not modeled on or metaphorically related to the human kinship system, and that by and large the wak'ą beings were not addressed using kinship terms. As we shall see, Powers's denial is contradicted by virtually all the evidence: both the historical literature and contemporary ethnographic accounts, not to mention the opinions of many Lakota people, substantiate the similarities of the system of relatedness among and between humans and nonhumans in Sioux thought (see, for instance, Little Wound in Walker 1991, 67; Short Feather in Walker 1991, 115; Red Rabbit in Walker 1991, 127; Black Elk in DeMallie 1984; Standing Bear 2006a, 2006b; Posthumus 2008–17). In fact, earlier in the same work Powers blatantly contradicts his critical assessment, writing, "In sacred language . . . medicine men address all supernatural beings as Tunkašila 'Grandfather'" (Powers 1986, 36). In his attempt to discredit DeMallie Powers apparently lost sight of the very foundation of Lakota culture and society, namely, kinship, and its extension to nonhumans.

Powers (1986, 121–22) also denies that one sense of the term *wac'ékiya* or its stem *c'ékiya* refers to kinship: "The idea that it also means 'to address by kinship term' is erroneous. Since the authors do not cite a reference for this translation, presumably it is their own. . . . The term *cekiya* simply does not carry the connotation of kinship, and never has" (Powers 1986, 121). Apparently Powers was unfamiliar with the important work of the Yankton Sioux anthropologist and linguist Ella Deloria, who writes, "This need of first establishing proper relationship prevailed even when one came to pray. It gave a man status with the Supernatural as well as with man. The Dakota words 'to address a relative' and 'to pray' . . . are one. *Wacekiya* means both acts" (1998, 28–29). White Hat also gives a more recent account substantiating the cultural or idiomatic meaning of wac'ékiya, explaining that "today it is translated into English as 'prayer.' That's what people believe it means, and this takes the relative concept out of focus. Prayer is a way of addressing a higher power that is above you, above all of creation. Traditionally, *wac'ékiye* means to acknowledge or embrace a relative, to work together with each other with respect" (2012, 75n1). Again it appears that Powers lost sight of the literature—and the culture—in his attempt to refute DeMallie.

If there is no real distinction between nature and culture (or society) in the Western sense, then there is likewise no distinction between the laws, morals, sentiments, and values of human and nonhuman collectives.[9] Both conform to a system of shared attitudes and obligations, and, as Descola asserts, in a practical sense, the model extended to (or projected upon) nonhuman collectives is that of human society: human society is the paradigm of animist collectives (Descola 2013a, 247–51, 267). Animals, spirits, and other nonhuman persons are said to possess social characteristics, live in villages, marry and have families, abide by kinship rules and moral and ethical codes, sing, dance, perform rituals, hunt, trade, and go to war and are volitional agents, capable of action, interaction, and relationship (Descola 2013b, 79–80).

Although practically speaking, nonhuman collectives do conform to the structure of human society, traditional Lakota explanations invert this relationship in terms of primary origins or precedent. While kinship is the blueprint for all human and nonhuman interaction, according to most Lakota accounts nonhumans originally established kinship and the order and logic of the cosmos through their various doings and adventures in mythical times. It was Iktómi (Spider), the mythical trickster/transformer figure, who originally tricked the people who became the Lakotas into leaving their subterranean abode and emerging through a cave onto the earth's surface. But in those primordial times the earth as we know it was already occupied by nonhuman animal and spirit persons. In particular, the Old Man, Old Woman, and Double Woman had been exiled there, because they too had been tricked by Iktómi and had subsequently broken social rules and etiquette relating to kinship and marriage. These original nonhuman inhabitants of the earth apparently lived a hunter-gatherer lifestyle quite similar to that of the nineteenth-century Lakotas, based on the hunt or chase and living in tipis made of bison skins. Hence, the existence of sociocosmic order and law—in other words, culture, in this case tied to the capacity to feel and recognize shame or dishonor (*wówištece*)—prefigures human life on earth: the spirits already had an intricate kinship system that was later adopted as the model for human kinship (Walker 1917, 181–82).

Further, it was Iktómi, the trickster, who originally conceived language—naming all things and hence differentiating the various collectives by assigning them their distinctive physicalities—and taught the people culture (Bushotter 1887–88, story 105; Walker 1917, 166; Powers 1986, 152–54).[10] According to the Lakota ethnographer George Bushotter, whose Lakota texts were recorded in the late 1800s,

> [Iktómi] named everything that was to be found all over the world. . . . Whatever moved upon earth [i.e., animals] got its name from Ikto. We believe that he was the first to speak by using the words with which we express ourselves. Wherever there are here and there some animals that are peculiar, they were made so by Iktomi; and we believe too that he made all wild fruits. . . . He long ago named all the organs found within a man's body, and to this day we follow those names. . . . And in the olden times, Ikto was good friends with all sorts of animals, being related to them; and they took their orders from him. . . . He was able to converse with animals who cannot speak. (Bushotter 1887–88, story 105)

As the accounts above demonstrate, many Lakota perspectives hold that sacred nonhuman persons established the logic and order of the cosmos in mythical times (cf. Radcliffe-Brown 1952, 166).

In a similar vein, Deloria explains that "the oldest traditions say that humans learned politeness and courtesy from the animals. . . . Generations of elders had already observed the behavior of birds . . . and decided that emulating them was the proper way for humans to act" (V. Deloria 2009, 123). Standing Bear (2006a, 56) substantiates this, writing, "The Lakota enjoyed his association with the animal world. For centuries he derived nothing but good from animal creatures. From them were learned lessons in industry, fidelity, and many virtues and much knowledge." Culturally, human and nonhuman collectives were practically indistinguishable, equally united through kinship and a common interiority as they were differentiated by dominant relational schemas and physicality. For example, the Oglala Bad Wound (in Walker 1991,

124) discussed the spirit of the bison with Walker around the turn of the twentieth century, explaining that "the buffalo were given to the Lakota by *Inyan* [Rock]. They came from the earth. Their tipi is in the earth. They know all the ceremonies. They dance in their tipi." According to Black Elk (in DeMallie 1984, 127), "The birds and other animals are the only race that we really get along with. We, [the] Indian race, and the beings on this earth—the buffalo, elk, and birds in the air—they are just like relatives to us and we get along fine with them, for we get our power from them and from them we live."

But things get rather confusing when we consider that Lakota mythology holds that primordially humans and nonhumans lived in a state of indistinction, in which physicalities were not yet crystallized and differentiated.[11] Deloria references this notion in his discussion of the buffalo nickel: "Curiously, this coin suggests symbolically the Sioux Indians' belief that in a higher cosmic dimension they and the buffalo are one spirit, split into two separate entities upon taking physical form" (V. Deloria 2009, 25). The common belief in a shared interiority and distinctive physicality should be apparent.

Lakota traditions, as well as those of many other tribes, recall a time when all life-forms communicated with each other through speech and intermarried. In this original chthonic world, society was apparently structured much like nineteenth-century Lakota society, with chiefs, shamans, warriors, hunters, and the common people living communally in tipi villages. These "prehuman" people enjoyed meat, soup, and dancing and were envious of fine things, like bison robes and soft tanned animal hides, and hence were very much like humans in their social organization, subsistence strategies, material culture, tastes, dispositions, and emotions (Bushotter 1887–88, story 70; DeMallie 1984, 339; Standing Bear 2006b, 70; Walker 1917, 181–82). In other words, they epitomized the typical Sioux collective, whether human or nonhuman.

In addition, mutually beneficial and obligating covenants were forged between human and nonhuman persons and collectives, and interspecies/intertribal communication and exchange were important features of these close kin relationships (V. Deloria 1999, 51–52, 228–29). Descola writes,

Each collective is equivalent to a sort of tribe-species that establishes with other tribe-species relations of sociability of the same type as those that are held legitimate within the given human collective which ascribes its internal organization, its system of values and its mode of life to the collectives of non-humans with which it interacts. The so-called natural and supernatural domains are thus peopled by collectives with which human collectives maintain relations according to norms that are deemed common to all. For although humans and non-humans may exchange perspectives, they also and above all exchange signs, that is, indications that they understand each other in their practical interactions. (Descola 2013b, 85)

Movement is also crucial here as an indexical attribute of personhood, as discussed by Hallowell (1960) and Ingold (2004, 37–39). According to Sioux understandings, Táku Škąšką 'That Which Moves, Sky' presides over life, giving life to all living things at birth. Táku Škąšką is also the spirit associated with all movement (Walker 1991, 107–8). Things that move of their own accord are judged to be alive, as participating in a process of continuous birth, expressed in Lakota by the concept t'ų́ 'emitted potency', the sprout, emission, or emergence from a seed or germ, the seed or miracle of life resulting from the union of complementary male and female principles or energies. "Different beings," writes Ingold (2004, 38), "whether or not they qualify as persons, have characteristic patterns of movement—ways of being alive—that reveal them for what they are." The parallels between Ingold's notion of "ways of being alive" and Descola's physicality should be obvious. Speaking of the Lakotas, Clark Wissler writes, "That there was a time when the animals were as the people is the striking thought in many Indian myths, and this indicates a belief in the *fundamental life-identity of all moving creatures*" (Wissler 1907c, 52–53; emphasis added). Significantly, the generic Lakota word for animal is *wamákʿašką*, literally, 'things that move upon the earth'.[12]

The realms of Lakota mythology (*ohų́kaką*), dreams and visions (*ihą́blapi*), and ritual or ceremony (*wicʿóhʾą, wóecʿų*) were peopled by a diverse cast of characters, mainly various animal species and spirit persons commonly encountered in the plains environment in which the people lived. In these domains human-nonhuman communication and exchange is still possible, as it was in the primordial subterranean world. Aside from Iktómi and a few other key personalities, the literature suggests that the nonhuman persons of Sioux cosmologies should not be conceptualized as monolithic, timeless, immortal, singular entities but rather as a class (*oíc'aǧe*) of persons, a tribe-species or collective, an oyáte (see Riggs 1880, 266; G. Pond 1889, 219–20, 222; Walker 1917, 89). We must return to the root of Lakota life and culture, namely kinship, in order to more fully understand these nonhuman collectives in terms of human familial relationship, or t'iyóšpaye 'bands, lodge groups, tipi groups' (Walker 1982).

A t'iyóšpaye was composed of one or more extended families—often related through a set of brothers and other male relatives—usually averaging ten to twenty families or around one hundred people. The lodge group or band, as it is often designated in English, was the minimal social unit that stayed together throughout the year (DeMallie 2001, 734–35). Speaking of the t'iyóšpaye, Ella Deloria (1998, 40–41) writes, "This Dakota word is essential in describing tribal life. It denotes a group of families, bound together by blood and marriage ties, that lived side by side in the camp-circle. . . . All the families of a *tiyospaye* operated as a single unit in practically all activities." Substantiating Descola's insights on animist societies in general, Lakota traditions testify to the fact that nonhuman collectives were organized according to the model of human society: they too were composed of various nested social groupings (oyáte, t'iyóšpaye, *t'iwáhe* 'family, household');[13] males and females; husbands and wives; fathers, mothers, and offspring; brothers, sisters, cousins, and cross-cousins; grandparents, grandchildren, aunts, uncles, nieces, and nephews; affines and consanguines; friends and enemies; young and old; and so on (see G. Pond 1889, 218).

Crucial here is the concept *wac'ékiya*, inadequately and problematically translated as "to pray" but that more accurately means "to address a relative" (E. Deloria 1998, 28–29). Wac'ékiya is the critical link between humans and nonhumans, allowing for intertribal/interspecies communication and exchange. DeMallie writes, "When humans smoked the pipe together they bound themselves in recognized relationships that carried with them obligations for peace, friendship, and cooperation. In offering the smoke to *Wakan Tanka*, they likewise bound themselves to the *wakan* beings in recognized relationships, calling on the powers for pity and aid" (DeMallie 1984, 81–82). Significantly, wacʿékiya illustrates that the values of humans and nonhumans are essentially the same, based on the model of human kinship. As Deloria explains, through wacʿékiya nonhumans "could be counted on to answer with due respect, honor, and dignity as a man to his relative" (E. Deloria 1998, 55). According to Vine Deloria, Ella Deloria's nephew, "the Sioux saw everything as a matter of personal relationships even between and among sacred powers that stood as equals to each other" (2009, 16). Wacʿékiya is also the term for smoking the pipe ceremonially, functioning to unite the interiorities of humans and nonhumans through the smoke of the pipe, which carries the prayers of the people to Wakʿą́ Tʿą́ka 'Great Mystery' (Black Elk in Joseph Brown 1989, 6–7; E. Deloria 1998, 28–29; Densmore 2001, 66, 127, 389–90; Walker 1991, 76, 81–83, 87–90, 148–50). But more on this later.

Thinking of nonhuman collectives in terms of human kinship focuses otherwise vague aspects of the historical literature on the Sioux. From this perspective, for instance, the Wakį́ yąpi 'Thunder Birds' represented their own oyáte 'people, nation', composed of various tʿiyóšpaye 'bands, extended families' and associated with specific characteristics, dispositions, abilities, and symbols. The matʿópi 'bears' and heȟákapi 'elks' were autonomous but occasionally intersecting kinship units or collectives, and so forth. Each oyáte abided by kinship rules and had its leader or chief (itʿą́cʿq), warriors or messengers (akícʿita), hunters (wakʿúwa), medicine men or shamans, and so on. In the case of the Zįtkála Oyáte 'Bird Nation', for instance, the chief was Wąblí Gleška 'Spotted Eagle' (Powers 1986, 151–52).[14] Tʿatʿą́ka 'Buffalo Bull' was the spirit master and chief of the Pté Oyáte 'Buffalo People' (Walker 1917, 91). Further, each oyáte related to other oyáte according to dominant relational schemas— usually exchange or predation, often modeled on the food chain (see Descola 2013a, 361). Language plays a critical role here, as explained by White Hat (1999, 4): "Elders reminded us that language is wakʿą́, 'very powerful.' We use it to communicate with the other nations: the

Deer Nation, the Eagle Nation, the Buffalo Nation, and so forth. We talk to the *wamákʻašką*, 'living beings of the earth,' through spiritual communications."

The various collectives or oyáte composing the Lakota cosmos were conceived of largely in terms of human kinship, had specific attributes and dispositions, and were interacted with according to practical, situated animist and relational principles, often according to either predation or the formula mitákuye oyásʼį. As we have seen, categories of oyáte were distinguished according to physicality: winged (*waȟúpa*), two legged (*hunúpa*), four legged (*hutópa*), persons who swim or water species, persons who crawl or reptiles, persons who burrow in the earth or chthonic species, mediating persons who transition from beneath the earth to its surface or from the earth's surface to the skies, and so on. Within these overarching divisions were additional subcategories, such as Lakʻótapi 'the people' or *wicʻášapi/wįyąpi* 'humans', *matʻópi* 'bears', *pteȟcakapi* 'buffalo', *zuzécapi* 'snakes', *zįtkálapi* 'birds', *waȟįheyapi* 'moles', and so on, and within these subcategories there were further distinctions (see Powers 1986, 145–52).

Much like human tribes, such as the Dakotas and Ojibwes, these various oyáte did not always interact peacefully. Beede writes,

> To Western Sioux Indians each individual in a species (or kind or group), had its own unique Woniya-power [spirit power] (as well as its own "ton" [potency]), and the strifes within a group were explained as similar to family strifes, keen but not fundamental, for the group went on despite all such strifes, and the essential harmony overbalanced disharmony,—which was, as they thought, essential to progress. They trenchantly observed such strifes among communities of animals, beavers, for instance. They have showed me wars among ants and have told me of other such wars. They noticed how squirrels and gophers punish the lazy ones. And they also believed that the Woniya-power (and the "ton"), of all species and groups (though each had its particular endowment), was essentially harmonious with Woniya, the Fundamental of all things, despite all strifes of whatever nature. (1912, Western Sioux Cosmology)

Certain collectives, both human and nonhuman, were known for their historically situated mutual animosity. Gideon Pond was a Presbyterian missionary to the Dakotas in Minnesota Territory in the mid-1800s. Discussing the eternal enmity between the nonhuman collectives the Uktéȟipi 'Horned Water Spirits' and Wakíyapi 'Thunder Birds', Pond explains that "a mortal hatred exists between the different families of the gods, like that which exists between Indians of different tribes and languages. The two families already mentioned, like the Dakota and Chippewa, are always in mortal strife" (1889, 230). Lakota accounts from the late 1800s and early 1900s also testify to the animosity between the Uktéȟipi and Wakíyapi, who were said to always be at war (Walker 1991, 108, 118).[15] This predictable hostility between collectives was based on an empirical framework of practical, situated animism.

Like the chicken and the egg, these traditions make ascribing causality or provenience in terms of the original source of the model of Lakota society very difficult, whether it was based on human or nonhuman archetypes. But perhaps this is less important than demonstrating that, according to the traditional Lakota animist ethos, the distinction between nature and culture, the sociality and attributes ascribed to human and nonhuman collectives, was blurred or permeable, if it existed at all. This is why Standing Bear (2006a, 38) writes in exasperation, "We did not think of the great open plains, the beautiful rolling hills, and winding streams with tangled growth, as 'wild.' Only to the white man was nature a 'wilderness' and only to him was the land 'infested' with 'wild' animals and 'savage' people." Rather than sharp distinctions, relationship was stressed. There was continuity and a mutually constituting association between nature and culture. Further, if Powers is correct in stating that "the spirit world is simply an extension of the earthly world" (1986, 96), then all the semantic walls separating cultural, natural, and "supernatural" also come crashing down in a great domino effect. As Vine Deloria explains, in the Sioux mind "there is . . . no 'supernatural' as there is in the Western culture; the natural is simply larger and more comprehensive" (2009, 161). But more on this later.

Having established the nature of collectives in Lakota animist thought we shall now move on to the constituent elements of those collectives, namely, persons. As we shall see, the Lakotas and other American Indian tribes had an expanded understanding of personhood. For the Sioux, personhood included nonhuman entities who proved through experience to be alive, volitional, sentient beings capable of social interaction, speech, movement, and causal agency: subjective selves with souls. Next I explore nineteenth-century Sioux conceptions of persons and personhood.

Persons and Personhood in Lakota Ontology and Worldview

Animist subjects are everywhere: in a human, an animal, a bird, a spider, a spirit, the sun, the moon, the wind, a tree, a rock, a plant, a stream, a place, a weapon, a medicine bundle, and so on. But what constitutes a subject or person in animist ontologies? Following Descola, if all existing beings are endowed with an interiority analogous to that of humans, then all are potential subjects, animated by a distinctive will and holding a point of view of their own, albeit constrained by their physical apparatus or physicality. Personhood in effect comes down to the recognition of agency, autonomy, intentionality, rational discernment, moral judgment, and a point of view of the same basic nature as that of human beings (Descola 2013a, 282–83).

Epistemology in animist societies is based more or less entirely upon the act of perception and cumulative, practical, subjective experience in a particular environment, often interpreted according to a relational paradigm. This was certainly the case among the nineteenth-century Sioux. As Vine Deloria explains, "Knowledge was derived from individual and communal experiences in daily life, in keen observation of the environment, and in interpretive messages . . . received from spirits in ceremonies, visions, and dreams. . . . Indians believed that everything that humans experience has value and instructs us in some aspect of life" (1999, 44–45). In animist regimes the ability to perceive and experience in a subjective fashion is a critical indexical attribute of personhood, converting animist entities into subjects. Consequently, because an entity is recognized as a subject it is said to have a soul or spirit (Descola 2013a, 283–84). According to Descola, humans and their institutions provide the model for what an animist subject is, "namely a singularity occupying a position from which autonomous actions, perceptions, and statements are all possible. A soul is thus the concrete and quasi-universal hypostasis of subjectivities that, however, are definitely singular since they proceed from forms and behavior patterns that determine the situation and mode of being in the world that are peculiar solely to the members of the species collective that has been endowed with those particular attributes. This interiority is shared by almost all beings, but the mode of its subjectivity depends on the organic envelopes of beings that possess it" (2013a, 283). From these basic premises we shall now embark on the next phase of our exploration, incorporating some of A. Irving Hallowell's insights on Berens River Ojibwe ontology and worldview in an intertextual dialogue with Descola's *Beyond Nature and Culture* and the Sioux ethnographic literature.

Hallowell's insights on Ojibwe personhood, tied to notions of self, other, and their interrelations, parallel the major themes in Descola's *Beyond Nature and Culture* and the historical literature relating to Lakota ontology.[16] Following Hallowell, in Lakota ontology—the metaphysics of Being and beings—the action of persons is the focal point providing the key to worldview. Importantly, the person category is not synonymous with human being but transcends it.[17] Persons are inextricably linked to notions of agency as loci of causality. They are sentient, volitional beings who vary in power in relation to humans; they are social actors capable of communication, exchange, and relationship. Various types of nonhuman objects, or personified and subjectivized natural objects specific to a given place and time, are thought of as persons. They are addressed as such, and interaction with them is carried out in a personal idiom (Hallowell 1960, 20–22, 43–45; 1966, 274–75).

Personhood is not an inherent property of people and things. Rather, it is constituted in and through experience and the relationships into which people enter. It is a potentiality of being-(alive)-in-the-world (Ingold 2000, 97; Willerslev 2013, 49). Likewise, as Hallowell (1960) and others (Bird-David 1999, S71; Scott 1989) have argued, phenomenological experience is consistent with this expanded and inclusive notion of personhood in animist ontologies. As Kohn (2013, 132) suggests, "all beings, and not just humans, engage with the world and with each other as selves, that is, as beings that have a point of view." The Sioux understood that the cosmos was alive and consisted of living, perceptive entities, each having a distinctive personality and will. Vine Deloria (2009, 189) writes, "Recognition of the parity of other creatures in terms of psychological and spiritual capability was the hallmark of the Sioux understanding of other living beings." Further, he observes, "It would be difficult for people living with these animals and observing them daily, not to conclude that they had the same mental and emotional constitution as we do—animals were a 'people' in almost every sense" (2009, 122). This notion of extended personhood permeated the content of Lakota cognitive processes (perceiving, remembering, imagining, conceiving, judging, reasoning, etc.), guided strategies, and motivated behavior (V. Deloria 1999, 52–53; cf. Hallowell 1966, 273–74).

This broad notion of person is conceptually similar to notions of self: autonomous being that has a point of view, the culturally defined and constituted axis of worldview. Like Descola's subject, Hallowell defines self in terms of reflexive self-awareness and awareness of "the nature of the world perceived as other than self," self as "the individual as known to the individual" (Hallowell 1955, 75–80). As Spiro (in Hallowell 1976, 353) indicates, the Hallowellian self is "a mediating process between environmental stimuli and behavioral responses. . . . The self is the perceiving and experiencing ego as it is known to the actor himself."[18] For Hallowell, like Descola, notions of self are inextricably linked to notions of autonomy, perception, self-awareness, subjectivity, and volition.

The Lakota model of the person or self is processual and relational: it exists or becomes in the unfolding of spatiotemporal relationships with other persons or selves in the living cosmos. Hence, experience, perception, and subjectivity are central features of personhood (cf. Ingold 2004, 46–47; Descola 2013a, 282–84). According to Vine Deloria, "The world is constantly creating itself because everything is alive and making choices that determine the future" (1999, 46). The self is a locus of causality, constituted as a center of agency, perception, and awareness in the process of its active, practical engagement with and within a particular environment. This notion of self accentuates the situated, site-specific nature of Lakota animism. Life is a *growth process* or *process*

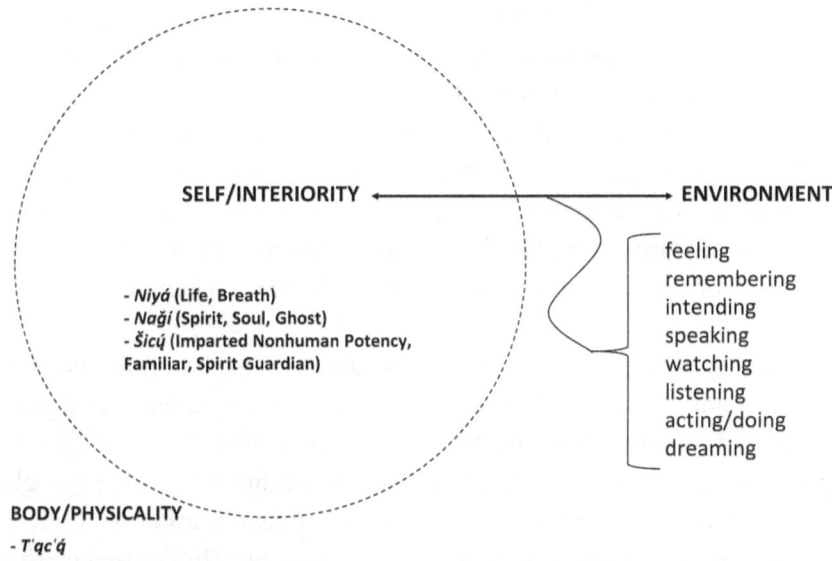

Fig. 1. The Lakota model of the person. Adapted from Ingold (2004, 46).

of transformation, a topic I address in detail in a later section. Feeling, remembering, intending, speaking, watching, listening, acting/doing, and dreaming are all aspects of a person's practical engagement with and within a specific environment. Through this process of engagement the self continually comes into being (being-[alive]-in-the-world), continuously creating and re-creating itself in an endless, emergent becoming, and life-transformation process is (re)generated and perpetuated.

I adopt a position that essentially unifies person and self, understanding both in terms of subjectivity, intentionality, and Descola's notion of interiority. This understanding of person/self is comparable to Heidegger's (1962, 27, 68) Dasein and the experience of being-(alive)-in-the-world, with a nod to Ingold (2011) and extended beyond the human.[19] Again, the common interiority at the base of animist ontologies focused the Sioux relational worldview, unifying the various human and nonhuman person-objects peopling the cosmos through shared substance, similar to what Richard Feinberg (1981; 2011, 84–89) calls the "extragenealogical" component in defining kin or Marshall Sahlins's (2013) notion of consubstantiality as the distinctive quality of kinship (see also Schneider 1969). A person, whether human or nonhuman, is a being who shares in this consubstantiality or common "extragenealogical" substance, spirit, or interiority, a relationship symbolized by the sacred pipe and the circle and expressed in speech by the phrase mitákuye oyás'į. A person is capable of social interaction and relationship and, as a volitional social actor, is a locus of causality and subject to moral dictums. Of course, persons in Lakota ontology also have more specific indexical characteristics.

The Lakota cosmos is alive, and everything in it has the potential for animacy and personhood. The attributes that index animacy and personhood are similar to those attributed to wakʻą́: life (ní), breath (niyá), spirit (nağí), growth (icʻáğa), the ability to communicate using speech or other semiotic means, the potentiality for transformation, sentience, volition, memory (wókiksuye), and movement or mobility (based on the stem šką́) all index animacy and the person category in Lakota culture. Recall that the word for animal is (táku) wamákʻašką, literally, 'things that move upon, across, or through the earth'. According to White Hat, "Many of our rituals come from what we know in English as animals, but in Lakota are called nations: Oyáte. . . . We don't have a word that means 'animal' in our language. As I understand it, in English an animal is a second-class citizen that doesn't have a discriminating mind. In our culture all living beings have such a mind, and in our relationship with them we have learned that they are more in tune with creation than we are. They provide us with medicine and advice and help us in our way of life" (2012, 78–79). Each phenomenal entity has an animating principle or soul (interiority) and a body (physicality) (cf. Hallowell 1934, 391).

Anticipating Descola's dual notions of physicality and interiority, Hallowell (1960, 42–43) reports that Ojibwe persons consist of a bodily aspect, a material form of some sort, and a persistent, enduring, inner, vital part. The outer form (physicality) is permeable, subject to change, and capable of transformation, while the inner essence (interiority) is the self and essential component that indexes personhood, marking a person as such. According to Hallowell (1960, 42), "Vital personal attributes such as sentience, volition, memory, speech are not dependent upon outward appearance but upon the inner vital essence of being." Thus Hallowell, like Descola, gives primacy to interiority in terms of identity, whereas physicality is central to relation.

The Sioux also privileged interiority in this manner, and this tendency is well documented, despite complicated notions of interiority among traditional Lakotas, according to whom there are up to four distinct types with various characteristics and functions.[20] Vine Deloria (1999, 58) writes, "The Sioux traditional people say that the important thing is the spirit of the creature; that it can and does change aspects of its physical shape in order to deal with changes but that basically it remains the same entity." This does not mean that physicality was not important as an indicator of difference and principle of classification vis-à-vis collectives. Rather, Deloria's words emphasize the fact that interiority was the defining feature of subjectivity and personhood. Deloria explains further, writing, "The world we live in, sustained by this power [wakʻą́], is ultimately spiritual and not physical" (2009, 184). In any case, this dual notion of physicality/body and interiority/spirit holds in nineteenth-century Sioux accounts, but their conception of interiority in particular was multifaceted and complex, calling for further explication.

Among the Lakotas, there was, and continues to be, a clear distinction between physicality (*tʻącʻą́* 'body') and interiority. But, as with everything else, relationship was essential, and these two aspects were considered to be interrelated; the physical and the spiritual were intertwined (see V. Deloria 2009, 84). Interestingly, the term *tʻącʻą́* is not used in reference to a corpse, emphasizing the relation between body and spirit. Tʻącʻą́ may be used in reference to the body or physicality, but *há* (the skin, hide, bark, outer casing or shell of anything) is also significant and may be translated as 'clothes' or 'clothing', indicating the unstable and unpredictable nature of outward appearances in Lakota culture. There was a widespread and well-documented belief in the potentiality for bodily transformation, which will be discussed in a later section, and different physicalities induced contrasting perspectives on the cosmos and different abilities and attributes, depending on a person's tribe-species (see Descola 2013b, 80; Viveiros de Castro 1998). The terms *oúcʻaǧe* 'form, likeness, shape, appearance, image, look, resemblance, growth' and *oúye* 'one's habits or way of life, lifestyle, one's situation or condition, one's nature' are also relevant here in terms of physicality and the habitus or distinctive behavior patterns and lifeways afforded or allowed by a particular physicality. But generally, physicality is less complex than the multifaceted and nuanced Sioux understanding of interiority. First I will discuss conceptions of human interiority before outlining nonhuman interiority and commonalities and differences between the two.

In the Lakota case human interiority was multifaceted, each aspect being interrelated with the others and integral to the proper functioning of the organic whole as long as a human lived embodied on earth. According to No Flesh,

> The *Wakan* [*šicų́*] is like a spirit. The spirit lives forever. When a man dies, his friends should give gifts to his spirit. The spirit was not his life. His life was his ghost [niyá]. His ghost is his breath. When a man dies, his spirit stays near for a time: the like-a-spirit [*nağíla*] of the gifts is pleasing to it. It takes them to the spirit land. . . . The spirit stays in the spirit world. It can come to the world. It can talk to mankind. A *wakan* man can talk with a spirit. A spirit can talk with its friends. If a spirit talks to one, that one is in danger. One who hears a spirit should ask his *Wakan* [šicų́] to help him. He should make gifts to the *Wakan*. He should ask a *wakan* man to help him. He should do as the *wakan* man bids him. (in Walker 1991, 116–17)

The constituent elements of Lakota interiority included the niyá 'life, breath', nağí 'spirit, soul, ghost', šicų́ 'familiar, "guardian spirit," imparted nonhuman potency', *wacʼį́* 'mind, will, intellect, consciousness', *cʼąté* 'heart, feelings, emotions', and *wówašʼake* 'strength, power'. Essentially, the combined niyá, nağí, and šicų́ constitute a triune conception of the soul or spirit, a common archetype cross-culturally, but the wacʼį́, cʼąté, and wówašʼake are no less significant in terms of the subjective self as a whole. However, I focus here on the triune niyá, nağí, and šicų́, which were conceptualized as the wakʼą́ aspects of human beings and hence immortal, having no birth or death.[21]

Niyá is a causative form of the verb *ní* 'to live' and can be conceptualized as the animating soul or spirit of the body. The niyá, closely associated with life and breath, is given to each human being at birth by Táku Škąšką 'Sky' (literally 'Something That Moves'), the spirit of the air who controls all movement (Densmore 2001, 67–68; Walker 1917, 156). In March 1914 Finger, an aged Oglala holy man, explained that stars are waníya—a nominalized form of niyá—and are the ghosts of human beings (in Walker 1917, 154–56). According to Finger (in Walker 1917, 154), "*Skan* [Táku Škąšką] takes from the stars a ghost [niyá] and gives it to each babe at the time of its birth and when the babe dies the ghost [niyá] returns to the stars. . . . A ghost [niyá] is *Wakan* (sacred, mysterious, holy), but it is not *Wakan Tanka* (Great Mystery)." If we take Finger at his word then we have isolated the origin of the niyá in the stars. Around the turn of the twentieth century the Oglala interpreter Thomas Tyon equated Wóniya T'ąka 'Great Life', based on another nominalized form of niyá, with Táku Škąšką: "*Woniya Tanka, Skanskan,* who is the *Wanagi Tanka* [Great Spirit] . . . gives the breath of life [niyá] and the spirit [nağí] to every child that is born alive" (in Walker 1917, 161).

In 1896 Sword explained that "a man's *ni* is his life. It is the same as his breath. It gives him his strength. All that is inside a man's body it keeps clean. If it is weak it cannot clean the inside of the body. If it goes away from a man he is dead" (in Walker 1991, 83). The niyá gives life to an organism and allows for its proper biological functioning (cf. Amiotte 1982, 27) and the continuation of life movement, "the aim to generate long life, blessings, and abundance for self, others, family, and the tribe" (J. Anderson 2001, 5). Although the final, permanent dissociation of the niyá from the physicality signals the death of the body, terminating one's bodily or earthly existence, the niyá lives on after the death of the body as an immaterial, dissociated spirit, likened to a shadow or smoke (Walker 1917, 86–87, 154–56; 1991, 70–72, 106).

Speaking of South American Indians, Viveiros de Castro (1998, 482) writes, "The fundamental distinction between the living and the dead is made by the body and precisely not by the spirit; death is a bodily catastrophe which prevails as differentiator over the common 'animation' of the living and the dead." Although it was revisited and expanded by Viveiros de Castro later, Hallowell initially blazed this path in the mid-twentieth century when he described death as the ultimate transformation entailing the dissociation of soul and body (Hallowell 1955, 173, 175–76). But more on this in the discussion of ghosts or spirits of deceased humans.

The naǧí is perhaps most fundamental in terms of Descola's notion of interiority, what Viveiros de Castro refers to as "'true soul', pure, formal subjective singularity, the abstract mark of a person" (1998, 481). The naǧí is the inner, characteristic, enduring essence of a person, usually translated as 'spirit', 'soul', or 'ghost', and also likened to a shadow. Oglala artist and author Arthur Amiotte provides a contemporary perspective on the naǧí, which he describes as much more personal and individualistic than the niyá, comparable to the ego, self-awareness, or self-consciousness. The naǧí is mobile and capricious. It retains the idiosyncrasies and personality of its worldly, human host, and, as Amiotte (1982, 29) notes, the naǧí "is much like a mirror image of the person's form, at once ephemeral when seen, transparent, and capable of easy transition to and from the spirit world."

The Lakota concept šicų́ is very complex. The Oglala holy man Finger describes it as the tʻų́ 'emitted potency' of a wakʻą́ or nonhuman spirit person, which fits the description of šicų́ as imparted, embodied nonhuman potency or influence, the familiar or spirit guardian. Like the niyá, the šicų́ is given at birth to each human by Táku Škąšká and hence has nonhuman origins. After the death of the physicality, when the niyá leaves and is dissociated from the tʻącʻą́, the šičų́ returns to the nonhuman person or star from whence it came (Walker 1917, 87, 156, 158–59; 1991, 72–73). When asked about the functions of the šicų́ Finger responded, "It remains with the body during life, to guard it from danger and help it in a *wakan* manner" (in Walker 1917, 156).

Sword provides a detailed description of šicų́, noting that every human has one šicų́ given at birth but may acquire others throughout life, mainly through experiences in the virtual realms of dreams and visions and ritual: "The word *Sicun* . . . signifies the spirit of a man. This spirit is given to him at birth to guard him against the evil spirits and at death it conducts him to the land of the spirits, but does not go there itself. In the course of his life a man may choose other *Sicun*. He may choose as many as he wishes but such *Sicun* do not accompany him after death; ... the *Sicun* that a man receives at birth is never found in anything but his body. This *Sicun* is like one's shadow" (in Walker 1917, 158).

Amiotte (1982, 30) describes the šicų́ as the "manifestation of spirit-like principle" and as an individual's personal power, reflected in one's distinctive abilities, gifts, and talents. In essence, by association and a sharing or union of interiorities a human takes on or embodies certain attributes and characteristics associated with a particular nonhuman spirit. According to Amiotte, the šicų́ is a special power that all things have that can be added to, expanded, and utilized to help others and oneself and to sustain and perpetuate life movement. When the naǧí of an individual leaves the body and travels to the other realm (ųmá wicʻóni 'other life'), for instance, in a vision or ceremony, it may be offered a portion of the partable šicų́ or potency of a nonhuman person, along with the prescribed prayers, songs, and rituals required for its activation and utilization in actuality (Amiotte 1982, 30–32).

White Hat provides some interesting additional insights into the nature of the šicų́ from a Rosebud Lakota perspective. He explains, "*Šicų́* means 'leaving your spirit or your influence someplace.' If you've ever read a book and got a sense of the author's feelings, then that's something like the meaning. The spirit of the author is in that book. Or it could be that somebody feels your presence when you're not there; that's your *Šicų́*" (White Hat 2012, 77). All the accounts above help to convey some sense of the complex, multifaceted šicų́ concept.

William Powers offers an alternative processual explanation of Lakota notions of interiority that is worth briefly exploring here. Some elements of his analysis correspond to my analysis above, relying largely on data from Walker's Oglala consultants, while others do not. Powers (1986, 134–36) likens his processual understanding of Lakota interiority to "four states of individuation." Through these states individuals come into being, are born and die, and then the process begins anew, over and over, in an endless cycle of reincarnation.[22] The first state is one of "having a potentiality for being," referred to in Lakota as šicų́. The second is "transforming this potentiality through birth into an essence that is independent of the body," referred to as tʼų́. The third state is "providing continuous evidence that this essence exists," referred to in Lakota as ní. And the fourth is "providing evidence that the essence independent of the corporeal existence continues after death," referred to as nağí.

Powers uses the analogy of the production of fire to illustrate his processual approach to Lakota interiority, in which (1) spark is equated with šicų́, (2) tinder with tʼų́, (3) flame with ní, and (4) smoke with nağí. While some aspects of Powers's analysis and analogy are slightly incomprehensible and seem exaggerated or forced, others are more plausible. Further, some contemporary Lakotas understand interiority in a similar, processual way, supporting Powers's claims, while others vehemently disagree with him. This discrepancy is a reflection of the individualistic nature of Sioux religious belief. It may also be due to the fact that many contemporary practitioners read the ethnohistorical literature on the Sioux, and some may subscribe to Walker's understanding while others subscribe to Powers's, the latter being largely inherited from the Red Cloud Community at Pine Ridge and in particular the practitioner George Plenty Wolf (Posthumus 2008–17; Powers 1986, xv–xvi; on practitioners and the ethnohistorical literature, see Bucko 1998).

Powers's explanation is intriguing, in part because one of the concepts used by Walker's Oglala consultants, nağíla, is problematic, having no real equivalent in any other source. According to Powers (1986, 228n9), nağíla was merely speculation by Walker, and tʼų́ is the appropriate "fourth" soul or aspect of interiority. There is some evidence in the literature to support this. For instance, Sword more or less equates nağíla and tʼų́, saying in a particularly ambiguous and cryptic passage, "*Nagilapi* are the *niyapi* of animals and the smoke of inanimate things. *Nagila* is the same as the *ton* of anything other than *Tobtob Kin*. Each thing, animate or inanimate, other than *Tobtob Kin* has a *nagi* or a *nagila*. The *nagi* of an animate thing is its spirit and of an inanimate thing that grows from the ground is its smoke. This is the potency of anything" (in Walker 1991, 98). But in this quote Sword also basically equates other aspects of Lakota interiority, namely, niyá, nağí, nağíla, and tʼų́. Is this evidence for a processual understanding of Lakota interiority or do we lack the vocabulary or data to differentiate these complex notions in English? Or was there little semantic difference between the various elements and terms used to conceptualize Lakota interiority? We may never know, as the literature is scanty on the topic, and much of this knowledge is lost or only vaguely comprehended and remembered by contemporary Sioux people.

Although Powers's explanation has some merit, certain aspects of it are problematic. For instance, it is generally accepted and supported by both the literature and Lakota people that humans *simultaneously* consist of a soul or spirit (nağí), a life or breath (niyá), and one or more nonhuman or "guardian" spirits (šicú) while they are alive and associated with a particular physicality. While this widespread belief could potentially encompass a processual understanding of soul in a broader, more abstract sense, the notion that there are distinctive stages in the development of the human soul—that one aspect or stage ends abruptly when another begins—is difficult to substantiate and support. Further, in dreams, visions, and ceremony the self, dissociated from the body, travels through time and space and is referred to in Lakota as nağí (see Beede 1912; Bushotter 1887–88). This usage of nağí while the organism is alive and functioning problematizes Powers's insistence that nağí only refers to the ghost: that aspect of interiority manifested only after the death of the physicality. In any case, the ethnohistorical literature has relatively little to say about these esoteric, theosophical aspects of Sioux belief, and so on one level analyses of Sioux understandings of interiority must always remain speculative.

Clearly, (life-transformation) process is central to Sioux ethnometaphysics, and all aspects of interiority must be understood as an integrated whole, each element of which is essential to the proper functioning of the organism. The collective interiority, composed of various interrelated yet distinct elements, is the potency of all things, central to both identity and relation. As Powers rightly notes, "One usually struggles to interpret the parts of the whole independently: *šicun* is 'potentiality'; *tun* is 'giving birth'; *ni* means 'life' or 'breath'; and *nagi* means 'ghost'. These interpretations are only partly convincing when we think of them as static concepts, but when we look at their interrelationships and dynamic quality, the parts blend neatly into an interpretation which emphasizes the whole life process as one in which immortality is achieved through reincarnation" (Powers 1986, 136).

Lakota notions of nonhuman interiority are slightly different from those of humans but built upon similar principles. In both cases the inherent individualism of Lakota belief renders neat categorizations and models difficult, if not impossible. Good Seat was an Oglala woman from the White Clay District of Pine Ridge Reservation born circa 1827. Around the turn of the twentieth century she explained, "*Anything that moves or does anything has a spirit.* Men give the spirits things to get their help or they give them things to keep them from doing them harm. If the spirits would stay away from men, then the men would care nothing for them, only for the spirits of their friends" (Good Seat in Walker 1991, 72; emphasis added). Good Seat clearly emphasizes the importance of movement as an indexical attribute of personhood.

All things in the cosmos had either a naǧí 'spirit, soul, interiority' or naǧíla 'spirit-like, soul-like, interiority-like'. Entities that had life or breath (ní) and could communicate in the language of the spirits— learned in the spirit or dream world (ųmá wic'óni 'other life')—were considered to have a naǧí. Humans belonged to this category but so did many other life-forms and objects, such as spirit beings, animal spirits (*wamák'anaǧi*), tree spirits (*c'ąnáǧi*), plant spirits, and the spirits of some inanimate things like smokes and foods (*wónaǧi*) (Amiotte 1982, 29–30; Beede 1912; Walker 1991, 71). According to Sword, "The *nagi* of an animate thing is its spirit and of an inanimate thing that grows from the ground is its smoke. This is the potency of anything. . . . There are many kinds of spirits (*nagipi*). All the spirits of one kind are the same as one spirit" (in Walker 1991, 98).

Naǧíla is a complicated concept, poorly documented in the literature, and apparently little is known about it today. Naǧíla may be defined as nonhuman spirit or interiority, the spirit-like or little spirit of nonhuman persons and things, or "the immaterial self of irrational [read nonhuman] things" (Walker 1991, 51, 73, 94).[23] James R. Walker (1991, 73), Pine Ridge Agency physician from 1896 to 1914, writes, "The old Lakota also believed that each thing except the *Wakan* and mankind had something like a spirit. This something they called a *nagila* (spiritish). These *nagipila* (spirits-ish) were *wakanpila* (*wakans*-ish)." Clearly some accounts differ and appear to contradict each other. Apparently there is very little semantic difference between nağí and nağíla, but the important distinction may be between human and nonhuman: nağí indexes human interiorities, while nağíla applies only to nonhuman interiorities. A key difference may also lie in the fact that nağíla appears to refer to *emitted* potencies, like t'ų́.

In any case, nağí and nağíla may be regarded as forms of the spirit, soul, or interiority, the potency or essence of humans and nonhumans. Along with life, breath, language, agency, movement, and so on, nağí and nağíla are important indicators or indexers of personhood in Lakota ethnometaphysical conceptions, marking something as a subject. Viveiros de Castro writes,

> To say . . . that animals and spirits are people is to say that they are persons, and to attribute to non-humans the capacities of conscious intentionality and agency which define the position of the subject. Such capacities are objectified as the soul or spirit with which these non-humans are endowed. Whatever possesses a soul is a subject, and whatever has a soul is capable of having a point of view. Amerindian souls, be they human or animal, are thus indexical categories, cosmological deictics whose analysis calls not so much for an animist psychology or substantialist ontology as for a theory of the sign or a perspectival pragmatics. (1998, 476)

Muddying the discourse is the great semantic overlap between the various concepts used to articulate Lakota understandings of interiority. Various terms for what might be called human souls or spirits are used, such as nağí, nağíla, and šicų́. In other contexts, the term *t'ų́* 'emitted potency' is used to describe the interiority or enduring spiritual essence of a person or object. Moreover, t'ų́ is likened to and even equated with wak'ą́ itself, as the wak'ą́ of anything. Speaking of offerings made to the spirit of a deceased human for its journey to the spirit world, Walker's consultants explain, "It should be provided with food for the journey. It should be given the things it enjoyed when the body was alive. The spirit cannot take these things with it, but the essence (*ton*) [interiority] of the things it takes with it and uses them. When things are given to the spirit, after it has taken the essence of them, then anyone may take the things and use them. But no one will do so unless he is in great want, for otherwise the things might be taken before the spirit has taken the mystery (*wakan*) from them" (Walker 1991, 106).

Human and nonhuman collectives are distinct and independent but closely interrelated in the Lakota cosmos, sharing common sentiments, structures, and properties. According to Brown, "Oglala people I knew on the Pine Ridge reservation invariably spoke of all animal categories as representing 'peoples as we are'" (Joseph Brown 1997, 13). Likewise, interrelations between human and nonhuman collectives were of the same basic character as intertribal relations, all structured according to the logic of human kinship. According to the Lakota animist ontology, all persons, whether human or nonhuman, share not only a similar interiority but also a common fundamental structure. I have articulated this structure by applying Descola's dual notions of interiority and physicality to the ethnographic literature on the Sioux, in conjunction with insights from Hallowell, Ingold, Willerslev, Viveiros de Castro, and others whose work with animist hunter-gatherer societies is relevant (see Descola 2013a; Hallowell 1960, 42; Ingold 2004, 31). To demonstrate the nature of nonhuman personhood among the Lakotas in context I shall now explore the personhood of rocks, inanimate objects from Western perspectives but characterized by nineteenth-century Lakotas as conscious, volitional persons capable of social interaction and relationship.

CHAPTER 3

The Living Rock, Grandfather of All Things

Hallowell (1960, 24) famously recounts an intriguing anecdote concerning the nature of rocks as volitional, sentient persons and social actors among the Berens River Ojibwes: "I once asked an old man: Are *all* stones we see about us here alive? He reflected a long while and then replied, 'No! But *some* are.' This qualified answer made a lasting impression on me." According to Ojibwe thought, all rocks have the *potential* for social interaction and relational personhood. How do we come to terms with this answer? It is puzzling both in terms of how something as apparently inert as a rock could be alive and also why some rocks are animate and others are not. In Western thought, the animate category comprises all things that are said to possess the property of life (see Ingold 2004, 35–36). From Lakota perspectives, life (ní 'life' or niyá 'life, breath') is certainly a qualifying attribute of the person category. But, as Hallowell (1960, 25) concludes, it is situated experience that ultimately determines whether a thing is animate, possessing the property of life: "The Ojibwe do not perceive stones, in general, as animate, any more than we do. The crucial test is experience. Is there any personal testimony available?" As Lynd (1889, 151) indicates, the Sioux appear to "deem the senses everything, the ideal nothing; and though there is no more imaginative being in existence than the Indian, yet it seems an essential idealism, having reference only to reality."

In a commentary on Hallowell's work, Ingold writes,

> The critical feature of . . . the liveliness of stones emerges in the context of their close involvement with certain persons, and relatively powerful ones at that. Animacy, in other words, is a property not of stones as such, but of their positioning within a relational field that includes persons as foci of power. Or to put it another way, the power concentrated in persons enlivens that which falls within its sphere of influence. . . . Whether a stone is alive or not will depend upon the context in which it is placed and experienced. . . . Animacy is attributed to artefacts that are closely bound up with the lives of persons.[1] . . . The animate stone is not so much a living thing as a "being alive." (Ingold 2004, 36–37)

Mary Black's studies among the Ojibwes in the 1960s lends weight to this conclusion. She notes that the Ojibwe term for living things, *bema.diziwa.d*, literally translates as 'those who continue in the state of being alive'.[2] However, Black suggests the term might be more accurately glossed as 'those who have power' (Black 1977, 143; see Ingold 2004, 37).

Alice Fletcher, based on her studies of Sioux belief and ritual in the early 1880s, reports a similar equation of life and power, describing "an offering to the earth" composed of a "chanted prayer [that] asks that the *life, or power in the earth*, will help the father in keeping successfully all the requirements of the ghost lodge" (Fletcher 1887d, 297; emphasis added). The connection between life/power, animacy, and personhood is evident in the following examination of rocks as persons/interiorities in Sioux ethnometaphysics, grounded in a condition of engagement, participation, and experience. These beliefs concerning rocks also emphasize the commonality of the Sioux animist understanding of the universe, spanning both time and space, from Sioux groups in the east to those of the west.

Rock as a nonhuman spirit person or interiority was considered wakʻą́, but, similar to Ojibwe belief, not all rocks were considered sacred or persons. Instead of the naïve animism of Tylor, Frazer, and others, in which the assumption is that belief in the animacy of *a particular* rock is necessarily extended to a belief in the animacy of *all* rocks, Lakota animism was site specific or situational. According to the Oglala Good Seat, "*Wakan* was anything that was hard to understand. A rock was *sometimes wakan*. Anything might be *wakan*" (in Walker 1991, 70; emphasis added). Stones symbolized and were associated with Táku Škąšką, the powerful and ubiquitous spirit of the air responsible for all movement and locomotion. This spirit was known to dwell in certain stones (G. Pond 1889, 230–31). According to Samuel W. Pond (1908, 403), a nineteenth-century missionary to the Dakotas in Minnesota Territory, "The Indians believed that some stones possessed the power of locomotion, or were moved by some invisible, supernatural power; and intelligent men affirmed that they had seen stones which had moved some distance on level ground, leaving a track or furrow behind them. . . . Some men of good common sense evidently believed that some stones could move or were moved by the god of which they were the symbol."

Íyą (Rock) existed first of all things. "He is most often addressed as the All-father," explains Walker (1917, 82), "for He is the ancestor of all things and all the Gods." Íyą is the father of Wakíyą 'Thunder Bird', the terrifying all-powerful spirit of the west, and Iktómi 'Spider', the ambiguous trickster of Lakota mythology.[3] Íyą, Wakíyą, and Iktómi are creator/destroyer figures, associated with the complementary powers of (re)creation/(re)generation/(re)construction, on the one hand, and destruction on the other, which are central to the sacrificial dynamic of ritual (see Kapferer 2006b). As such, Íyą is the patron spirit of revenge, destruction, violence, and (success in) warfare (Walker 1917, 132, 160; 1991, 275). According to Walker's Oglala consultants, "*Inyan* was the Spirit of the Rocks. He was a powerful spirit. The Indians invoked him more often than any other one. They made sacrifices to him frequently: when sick, when in want, when desiring anything, when going to a battle. The most acceptable sacrifice to *Inyan* was a piece of the skin of the person making the sacrifice. Anything could be given as a sacrifice to *Inyan*. The sacrifice was made on anything that represented *Inyan*. Usually this was a stone. A stone of a peculiar kind or shape was usually chosen" (Walker 1991, 102). It will become apparent that sacrifices or offerings, along with "praying to" (wac'ékiya) and ceremonially painting and adorning objects, functioned to subjectivize and personalize, facilitating ritual transformations that established relationship and enabled communication and exchange.

Stones were honored (*ohólapi* 'reverenced, honored') and considered holy and mysterious (*wakʿą́lapi*) because they were ancient, indestructible, hard, and durable. They figured prominently in Lakota mythology, especially the tales of the culture hero Stone Boy (see Walker 1917, 193–203). Stones were believed to have life-breath (niyá) and the potential for a common interiority with that of humans, animals, and other life-forms. Stones were known to move mysteriously of their own accord, to dance, produce visible sparks or blue lights, and communicate with humans through various means, such as speech and song. One tradition describes a holy man who stabbed a sacred stone from which blood flowed out (Bushotter 1887–88, story 28; E. Deloria n.d.h, 193; Dorsey 1889a, 153–55).

Certain stones were held to be particularly sacred or potent, and if an individual was lucky enough to find one of these rare stones or be given one by a medicine man or a spirit, it would often become (part of) that individual's personal medicine or power.[4] These sacred stones tended to be perfectly round, translucent stones that were pushed up from beneath the earth's surface by powerful nonhuman life-forms able to traverse and mediate between various domains, in this case between the earth's surface and the subterranean world. The ant, mole, coyote, and wolf are representative of such mediating life-forms. Sacred stones of this kind were also found on top of buttes, often after thunderstorms, and some believed they were products of lightning strikes (V. Deloria 2009, 93; Powers 1986, 113). According to William Powers, in order for such stones to be effective, that is, wakʿą́, they had to be given a name through the performance of a naming ceremony (*cʿaštʿų́*) (1986, 113–14). This ritual naming invested the stone with a nonhuman spirit and personality, a šicų́, believed to be immortal and capable of being reinvested in other objects, human or nonhuman, animate or inanimate (Powers 1982b, 11).

According to Walker's Oglala consultants, "A shaman must impart a *ton* [tʿų́ 'emitted nonhuman potency'] with the right ceremony done in the right manner. . . . When a shaman imparts a *ton* to anything the thing is made a *sicun* [šicų́]. A *sicun* is like the God.⁵ . . . A shaman must put the container on a *sicun* and this makes it a *wasicun* [*wašícų*]" (Walker 1991, 95–96). Through the proper ritual, stones are invested with a nonhuman interiority generally referred to as šicų́ but specifically named after one of the spirits or grandfathers who attends the ceremony. Once a ritual practitioner encases the stone in a container of some kind, a skin bag or casing, it is referred to as a wašícų and invested with and an embodiment of *wówakʻą* (sacredness). In the case of stones these sacred bundles are called *wašícų tʻųką́*, a šicų́-ized stone (Powers 1986, 114–15). Powers writes, "Every Oglala who believes in the omnipotence of Wakantanka wears or carries a small spherical stone carefully rolled up in a wad of sage and deposited neatly in a miniature buckskin pouch no more than an inch in diameter" (1982b, 11). These sacred stones imbued with a nonhuman interiority and power are addressed and prayed to in times of sickness, distress, or danger (Powers 1986, 226n7).

Through visionary and dream experiences humans could establish relationships with Íyą, become adoptive members of the Rock collective, so to speak, and have it for their familiar or spirit helper (*tʻawášicų*). Rock dreamers typically practiced the yuwípi ceremony, tied to divination and prophecy, in which their Rock spirit helpers assisted them in locating lost objects, animals, or people. Sacred stones were associated with Táku Škąšką́ (Sky) as the best physical representation of the great mysterious energy. In ceremony, Rock spirits helped the Sioux by healing, locating lost people, animals, and objects, bringing objects or animals to the medicine man, and divining the future. In pre-reservation times the major use of stones in this ceremonial way was to locate game or enemies and detect the approach of enemy war parties (V. Deloria 2009, 94, 96). A Rock dreamer would boil food for a mystery feast (*wakʻą́ wóhąpi*), and the people would ceremonially appeal to Rock. Remembering served to activate power through (re)invoking relationship, while imitation brought nonhuman spirit persons to life (Deloria n.d.h, 193, 1998, 61; Dorsey 1889a, 153–55; G. Pond 1889, 248–50; Walker 1991, 69, 107, 153–55). For these reasons, explains Dorsey (1889a, 154), "the Lakota learned to prize the stones, and they decorated them with paint, wrapped them up, and hung a bunch of medicine with each one."

Rocks were considered to be persons or subjectivities if they interacted and communicated with humans, engaging in relationships of exchange and dependence. Ritual was a key avenue through which rocks and other "inanimate" objects were phenomenally experienced. Ella Deloria (n.de., 24) vividly describes a yuwípi ceremony in which stone spirits manifested themselves to the human senses by producing whistling sounds and mysterious blue sparks or lights. At one point in the ceremony a stone fell on the ritual altar with a thud, and a member of the ritual gathering was struck in the chest with a ball of rope used to tie the practitioner, flung by the spirits. Disappointed at the behavior of his spirit helpers, the practitioner scolded, "Please don't do that!" The sparks (táku škąšką 'pebbles') continued to land on the altar and began speaking to the people. They remained there for the people to examine. When the light was lit at the conclusion of the ceremony one small translucent stone lay upon the altar. Upon closer inspection the people discerned a tiny face on the side of the pebble with "a decidedly hooked nose." The lights were put out again and the pebble placed back upon the altar. Suddenly it whispered, "Sing for me; I shall dance then." When the people sang the pebble bounced rhythmically around the room and returned to the altar like a spark in the dark.

The potency of Rock is represented, and hence manifested, in "natural" stones, key elements in ritual and ceremonial altars, bundles, and paraphernalia (Walker 1917, 128–31). According to Tyon, "there is a different kind of *wakanla* rock; they are the sweat lodge stones (*tonkan yatapika*), as they say. These act differently" (in Walker 1991, 154). Samuel Pond notes that among the Dakotas "the same kind of stones were used [in the sweat lodge] as they were accustomed to worship" (1908, 420). These stones were heated and prayed to in the sweat lodge, in which their niyá 'life, breath' rose as steam when the hot rocks were sprinkled with water, providing physical and spiritual purification and healing for the ritual gathering, the audience or spectators not directly engaged with the production of the rite but nonetheless participant and vital in it and its dynamics (cf. Rappaport 2000; Kapferer 2010, 239).

Sweat lodge rocks are referred to as *t'ųką* (*yatápika*) and addressed ceremonially as grandfather (*t'ųkášila*).[6] In general, the kinship terms tʿųkášila 'grandfather' and ųcí 'grandmother' are most commonly used in ritual invocations addressing nonhuman spirit persons, implying protection, dependence, respect, and the recognition of authority. The claim of relationship is imperative and central to the Sioux worldview, not to be ignored or disregarded (Joseph Brown 1989, 5–6; E. Deloria 1998; DeMallie 1994, 1998; Fletcher 1887a, 276n1; G. Pond 1889, 219; Powers 1982a, 46). *Grandfather*, explains Vine Deloria (2009, 14), is the term used by the Sioux, and many other tribes, "when they describe experiences in which *Wakan Tanka*, the Great Mystery, has become personified."[7]

In the sweat lodge ceremony the rocks, carefully placed in the center of the sacred lodge, are addressed as tʿųkášila, or grandfather. They are nonhuman spirit persons who are reenergized by heating them in a ceremonial fire until they are red hot, like glowing embers. This process causes the stones to "come to life," as one contemporary Lakota man put it (Posthumus 2008–17). They are prayed over and sprinkled with culturally significant plants and herbs, such as tobacco, cedar, sweetgrass, and sage. When the ritual leader of the sweat lodge orders the door closed and pours water on the rocks from a dipper steam is produced, which is the visible breath of the living rocks. According to Tyon, "The breath of the rocks [*įyą tʿaníya*] is very *wakan*" (in Walker 1991, 155).

According to some contemporary Lakotas, when one prays and sings to the grandfather spirits in this way, that is, in the sweat lodge, they come and hear you. They are pleased by the people praying in this way. Not only do the grandfathers come and hear the people's desires and concerns in the context of the sweat lodge, but they are also present in numerous other ceremonies—in particular the yuwípi and vision quest—when addressed, invoked, and honored in the appropriate manner. This Lakota belief in the very real presence of the spirits during ceremonies is comparable to what Hallowell says about Berens River Ojibwe beliefs concerning the narration of myth. The Ojibwes also address the spirits as grandfather. According to Hallowell, "The *ätíso'kanak*, or 'our grandfathers,' are never 'talked about' casually by the Ojibwe. But when the myths are narrated on long winter nights, the occasion is a kind of invocation: 'Our grandfathers' like it and often come to listen to what is being said" (Hallowell 1960, 27).

Whenever the people pray with the pipe and address the spirits as relatives, sing, dance, honor, make offerings, dedicate feasts, humble themselves, and so on the spirits come and listen and help. They are persons sharing a common interiority and motivated by the same kinship structure and mutual obligations. They love the Lakʿól wicʿóȟʾą 'Lakota way of life, Lakota traditions' and are pleased to see its preservation through practice. Sioux ritual, then, plays a dual role: it ensures, maintains, and perpetuates the continuity of the relationship between humans and nonhumans, and at the same time ritual also ensures, maintains, and perpetuates the continuation of life movement in general. As Powers notes, the basic intention of all Sioux healing or doctoring ceremonies is the desire to (continue to) "live with all my relatives" (Powers 1986, 85, 97). White Hat puts it slightly differently: "Our rituals are designed to help us stay focused on Mitákuye Oyásʾį. They also give strength, endurance, courage, or encouragement" (White Hat 2012, 74).

The Oglala chief Little Wound explains that Íyą dwells in the rock, and Tʿųká is the Wakʿą́ 'spirit master' of the natural or common rock (in Walker 1917, 179; 1991, 197).[8] The Oglala Ringing Shield elaborates, "*Tunkan* is the spirit which fell from the sky. It is a stone. It knows all things which are secret. It can tell where things are when they are lost or stolen. It is the friend (*kola*) of *Taku Skanskan* (the spirit or power which causes things to vanish like smoke or clouds that fade away)" (in Walker 1991, 112).

According to Mary Henderson Eastman, the wife of the army officer and illustrator Captain Seth Eastman, who lived among the Dakotas at Fort Snelling, Minnesota Territory, in the 1840s, "The Dahcotahs say that *meteors* are men or women flying through the air; that they fall to pieces as they go along, finally falling to the earth" (1995, 22; emphasis in original). This substantiates earlier claims concerning nonhuman spirits as stars. In particular, Finger (in Walker 1917, 154–55) explained to Walker in 1914 that a meteor is called *wóȟpa* or *wóȟpe* and is wakʿą́ 'sacred, mysterious, holy'. When pressed, Finger explained that Táku Škąšką́ causes stars to fall, just as he chooses which nonhuman spirits, taken from the stars, will be given to each human at birth. Táku Škąšką́ is also known as Sky, and his people are the stars (Walker 1917, 81–82,

178–79). Significantly, Wóȟpe 'the Beautiful Woman' is the name in the esoteric symbolic language of the shamans for the sacred mediator, also known as White Buffalo Woman (Ptesą́wį), who is the daughter of Táku Škąšką́ and the adopted daughter of the Wind (T'até). Wóȟpe brought the sacred pipe to the people, hence establishing relationship between humans and nonhumans. She originally descended to earth from the stars like a falling star, and her spirit (t'ų́) is in the smoke of the pipe, carrying the people's prayers to the spirits.

As a means of consecration, invocation, and subjectivization, "common" stones were often painted with sacred red earth paint or vermilion (*wasé*), decorated with swan or eagle down, given offerings, and then addressed and prayed and sung to. As Walker (1917, 135) explains, "Red paint on a stone consecrates it and makes of it an altar on which may be placed offerings to the God, the Rock, which one should make when about to undertake some dangerous deed." According to Mary Eastman, the Dakotas "sacrifice to all the spirits; but they have a stone painted red, which they call the Grandfather, and on or near this, they place their most valuable articles, their buffalo robes, dogs, and even horses" (1995, 56). Pond writes, "Stones were much worshipped by them, both with prayers and offerings. They chose granite boulders and painted them red. . . . [They] were covered with votive offerings, such as tobacco, pieces of cloth, hatchets, knives, arrows, and other articles" (S. Pond 1908, 405).

In essence, these personified or subjectivized rocks were transformed into portable altars, *ųmáni* or *ową́ka*, doorways to the other world, technologies for the descent into ritual virtuality, and interfaces between common, quotidian realities and the spirit world, actuality and virtuality. Bison skulls serve a similar ritual function as portable altars consecrated, addressed, and prayed to as media of communication with the wak'ą́. Properly consecrated, these objects are essentially indistinguishable from the spirit persons they represent or symbolize, as the spirit and natural object share a common interiority, a point I will develop further below.

However, as Fletcher (1887a, 276n1) notes, these objects are understood as "exponents of a mysterious life and power encompassing the Indian and filling him with vague apprehension and desire to propitiate and induce to friendly relations." These consecrated (personified, subjectivized) objects were ceremonially addressed, prayed to, and propitiated and offerings and sacrifices were made to them as "media of communication with the permeating occult force [wakʿą̇] which is vaguely and fearfully apprehended." Ella Deloria (1998, 52) confirms Fletcher's statement: "My informants all felt that it was an error to say the Dakota actually worshipped rocks, trees, the four winds, and other manifestations of nature. 'They are not themselves Wakan, but the Wakan is in all things. When our people wished to pray, they selected some common tree or rock, untouched by man, and set it apart for its sacred use by painting it red. And then they addressed it, for now it was Wakan.' One man so explained it." Finally, the famous Yanktonai artist Oscar Howe (2004) substantiates many of the claims outlined above in a description of his piece *Calling on Wakan Tanka*: "The buffalo skull . . . represents life, a Sioux symbol for life. . . . Sioux Indians believe that unusual formations in nature are closer to the Wakan Tanka (Great Spirit). These physical attractions have spiritual meaning (a small spirit resides in an unusual thing), and are used as altars, generally trinkets, charms, etc. are left there to mark it as an altar—or paint (ceremonial) is sometimes dabbed on them. Many non-Indians believe that Indians pray to objects in nature. But the Sioux only prays through these unusual nature things to reach the Great Spirit."

Sioux belief and ceremony pertaining to Rock is ancient and pervasive, transcending modern tribal divisions. Riggs equates Íyą with Tʿųká, referring to it as the greatest terrestrial power or force (he lists Wakíyą as the greatest aerial power or force). Rock was the oldest spirit, hard and indestructible, naturally coming to symbolize the cultural values of endurance and strength (Riggs 1880, 267–68). Lynd (1889, 168–69) refers to Dakota "adoration" of Íyą as "an every-day affair." According to Riggs, rocks "came to be the most common object of worship.[9] Large boulders were selected and adorned with red and green paint, whither the devout Dakota might go to pray and offer his sacrifice. And smaller stones were often found, set up on end, and properly painted, around which lay eagle's feathers, tobacco and red cloth. Once I saw a small dog that had been recently sacrificed. In all their incantations and dances, notably in the circle dance, the painted stone is the god supplicated, and worshipped with fear and trembling" (1880, 268).

In a similar vein, Lynd (1889, 169) writes, "The most usual form of stone employed in worship is round, and about the size of the human head. The devout Dakota paints this *Tunkan* red, putting colored swan's down upon it, and then falls down and worships the god [interiority] which is supposed to dwell in it or to hover near it." George Bushotter (1887–88, story 28), a Lakota man born in Dakota Territory in 1864, provides a parallel Lakota account of stone rituals, illustrating a number of key cosmological and ontological commonalities in both stone symbolism and ritual practice in general.[10] According to Bushotter, a stone is placed in a tipi and ceremonially painted red (*šayápi*) to honor and consecrate it. Human hair, tobacco, and other fine articles are given or left to it as offerings (*iȟpéyapi*), and whenever someone is sick the consecrated (subjectivized, personalized) stone is addressed in prayer (*c'ékiyapi*). But only through the dynamic of subjectivization and consecration could the stone hear the wishes of the people. "The stones are hard," explains Bushotter (1887–88, story 28), "and when the people made a fire over one, and some steam [*p'ó*] came forth, they took it to show that the stone was a man (i.e., alive) and that it was his breath [*íyq-t'aniya*] they saw; by which many a man was saved from death [*nípi*], they believed."

Lynd provides an excellent explanation of these beliefs and the imaginal dynamics of Dakota ceremony:

> Frequently the devout Dakota will make images of bark or stone, and, after painting them in various ways and putting sacred down upon them, will fall down in worship before them, praying that all danger may be averted from him and his. It must not be understood, however, that the Dakota is an idolater. It is not the *image* [physicality] which he worships, . . . but the *spiritual essence* [interiority] which is represented by that image, and which is supposed to be ever near it. . . . The God must be present, by image or in person, ere he can offer up his devotions. (1889, 154; emphasis in original)

The forming of an image, so common in Sioux ceremony (see Walker 1917, 108–10; M. Eastman 1995, 12, 19–20; Riggs 1893, 225–26) is an example of symbolic identification or representation and the magical performative character of ritual, whereby the act *does* what it says or represents, and the ritual force or magicality is performatively present in the ritual gestures themselves. The virtual dynamics of rite operate as a means for engaging immediately with the ontological ground of being (Kapferer 2006b, 510, 516; 2010, 245).

These effigies (*wakáǧapi, wasábglepi*), ritually forged of stone, wood, bark, hide, and so on, function to focus the psychic energies of ritual participants and the ritual gathering, providing a visualization for the mind or will (wacʻį́) to focus upon. This multipurpose process of creation, consecration, and invocation calls or invites the interiority of a particular nonhuman person to be present or embody a sacred space for a particular purpose. As these examples indicate, certain elements are common or essential in Sioux ceremonial dynamics, such as ritual painting, adorning with down, music and song, dance, offerings and sacrifice (of food, water, tobacco, red cloth, flesh, etc.), and ritual address or prayer (wacʻékiya). In fact, all might be considered forms of "prayer," a multifaceted ritual symbol.

Lakota Ritual Dynamics and Establishing Interspecies Relationship

As we have seen, translating the Lakota verb *wacʻékiya* and its nominalized form *wócʻekiye* as "prayer" is inadequate and misleading, as Ella Deloria pointed out in the 1940s. Most Western Christian religious notions, such as God, prayer, and worship, distort traditional Sioux understandings of belief and ritual. Human-nonhuman relationships tended to be very practical. According to Tyon (in Walker 1991, 124), "The Indians did not worship the spirits. They only feared them and endeavored to propitiate them or obtain their help in what they desired to do." Speaking of Wakʻą́ Tʻą́ka, the impersonal totality of all that is mysterious in the universe, Vine Deloria writes, "Only later, when Christian missionaries attempted to link Sioux traditions to their own religious systems, did this mysterious presence begin to take on human forms and demand a groveling, flattering kind of worship" (1999, 48).

Coming largely from Western Christian backgrounds, early nonnative ethnographers were puzzled by Sioux understandings of the nature of the spirits. According to Paul Beckwith (1889, 253), the Indian agent for the Sisseton-Wahpetons at Devil's Lake Agency in present-day North Dakota from 1875 to 1876, the Sioux made sacrifices "as often to the bad as to the great or good spirit." Apparently Beckwith was unfamiliar with the widespread Sioux belief that nonhuman spirit persons are ambiguous in their interactions with humans (neither good nor bad; simultaneously creative, generative, and destructive; amoral in terms of human understandings), which complicates the application of core Western religious notions to Sioux ethnography. Speaking of the Dakotas, Gideon Pond reports, "Evidence is wanting to show that these people divide their *Taku-Wakan* ['Holy Things', i.e., nonhuman spirit persons] into classes of good or evil. They are all simply wakan [incomprehensible, strange, mysterious]" (1889, 217).

Rather than prayer, address as a relative, placation, lamenting, or propitiation is more accurate (literally, 'crying to someone' or 'crying for something'). Through ceremony, the Sioux sought to (re)establish relationship and to placate, and appease ambiguous, powerful, and often frightening and dangerous spirits. Generally, they wanted to be left alone, free of anxiety, misfortune, sickness, and death. Honoring, respect, and reverence (ohóla, yuónihą) are more appropriate from Sioux perspectives than worship. As Vine Deloria explains, "This attitude was not a 'worshipping' of the animals, as uniformed theologians might say, but rather the adoption of a posture of humility before an aspect of nature that they did not fully understand" (2009, 189).

The Sioux deemed sacred (*wakʻą́la*) mysterious entities and processes that induced fear (kʻokípʻa, wókʻokipʻe, kağí) and awe (*wóitʻupʻe*, iníhą, kağí). The natural response to fear and awe is respect and honor, which led to adoration and placation, but in a very practical sense aimed at maintaining and perpetuating life movement. As Good Seat (in Walker 1991, 72) explains, "Men give the spirits things to get their help or they give them things to keep them from doing them harm." Fletcher (1887a, 276n1) writes, "The Indian stands abreast with nature. . . . He appeals to it, but does not worship it." A major dynamic of placation was invoking aid or pity (*ų́šila*) in an attempt to induce the spirits to intervene in actuality and perpetuate life movement. In this way, honor, respect, and reverence are functions of fear and awe, and the notion of wacʻékiya as lamenting, crying, or weeping is intimately linked to the desire to induce or invoke aid or pity (ų́šila). From Sioux perspectives, respect does not mean worship but involves two attitudes: (1) the acceptance of self-discipline by humans and their collectives to act responsibly toward other life-forms; and (2) to seek to establish communications and covenants with other life-forms on a mutually agreeable basis. Respect and self-discipline were essential in human interaction with wakʿą́ things and processes of power and significance (V. Deloria 1999, 51, 56).

A deeper understanding of the cultural significance of wacʿékiya, tied to kinship, is central to understanding Sioux animist ontology and worldview. Ella Deloria's role in developing this understanding is one of her greatest contributions to Sioux ethnography. She writes that the "need of first establishing proper relationship prevailed even when one came to pray. It gave a man status with the Supernatural as well as with man. . . . *Wacekiya* implies that in every meeting of two minds [interiorities] the kinship approach is imperative; it is the open-sesame to any sincere exchange of sentiment between man and his neighbor or man and his God. Once the channel is clear between the two, a reciprocal trust and confidence are guaranteed" (E. Deloria 1998, 28–29). Wacʿékiya is the polysemous Lakota term for 'to address a relative', 'to pray', and 'to smoke the pipe ceremonially'. Its stem is *cʿéya* 'to cry, weep, wail', the dative form of which is *cʿékiya* 'to pray to someone, pray for something, beg, beseech, entreat, to address someone by the proper kinship term'. Thus Black Elk (in Joseph Brown 1989) preferred the English 'to lament' over 'to pray' in translating wacʿékiya.

Dorsey lists a number of essential elements, features, or accessories of wacʿékiya among the Sioux, important and common ritual dynamics that transcend Sioux tribal divisions. First is ceremonial crying or wailing, from the stem *cʿéya* 'to cry, weep, wail', sometimes, but not always, accompanied by articulate speech. Second is the practice of *yuwį́tapi* 'to stroke or rub something with the hands', as in *ité yuwį́tapi* 'to stroke the face', a gesture of gratitude, respect, and honor. In relation to wacʿékiya, yuwį́tapi refers to the supplicant elevating his arms with the palms outstretched toward the object or face of the person or power being invoked or addressed, followed by the passage of the hands down toward the ground without touching the object or person.

Third is the offering of the pipe to the object or person being invoked or addressed by pointing or holding it with the mouthpiece toward the power invoked (see figure 2). Fourth is the practice of *wazílya* 'smudging, incensing', in which smoke from the pipe or other culturally significant things (tobacco, sweetgrass, sage, cedar, willow bark, bison chips, etc.) functions to banish unwanted malevolent influences, invite and please benevolent influences, demarcate and frame ritual space, and unite the interiorities of the various persons present at a given ceremony.[11] The belief underlying the practice of wazílya is that the spirit or interiority (nağíla or t'ų́) of anything is released in its smoke, highlighting the sacrificial dynamics of (re)creation/(re)generation/(re)construction/(re)composition via destruction/decomposition. In many Sioux rituals the drama of life and death is thus played out. Fifth is the application of kinship terms of address to the objects, persons, or powers invoked, usually t'ųkášila 'grandfather' and ųcí 'grandmother', depending on the context.[12] And sixth is the offering of sacrifices (*waúyąpi, wóšnapi*), usually goods, food, animals, or pieces of the supplicant's flesh (*waíc'išpapi*) (Dorsey 1894, 373, 435; cf. Bad Heart Bull and Blish 1967, 86; Walker 1991, 76–77, 81–83, 86–89, 94–95, 98, 113, 119, 194).

Samuel Pond provides a fine example of the semantic depth of the term *wac'ékiya* and the inadequacies of translating it with the Western, Christian notion of prayer. Pond (1908, 412–13) describes a scene in which a group of Dakotas were preparing the food for a sacred feast (wak'ą́ wóhąpi), writing, "While the food was being cooked two or more were engaged in praying, or rather wailing in loud recitative tones. They called it praying, but the word to pray is derived from the word weep, and in these feasts they wept rather than prayed. The devotional exercises were continued most of the time while the food was being prepared."[13] In any case, a broader, more culturally nuanced understanding of wac'ékiya aids our understanding of ethnographic accounts of stone rituals described above in that the nonhuman interiority of the stone had to be properly treated (sacrifices, offerings, ceremonial painting and adornment) and approached in order to address, lament, and "pray" (cry to or for) to it.

Ceremonial painting and adornment are central to Sioux ritual dynamics of framing, originally taught to the people by nonhuman persons in

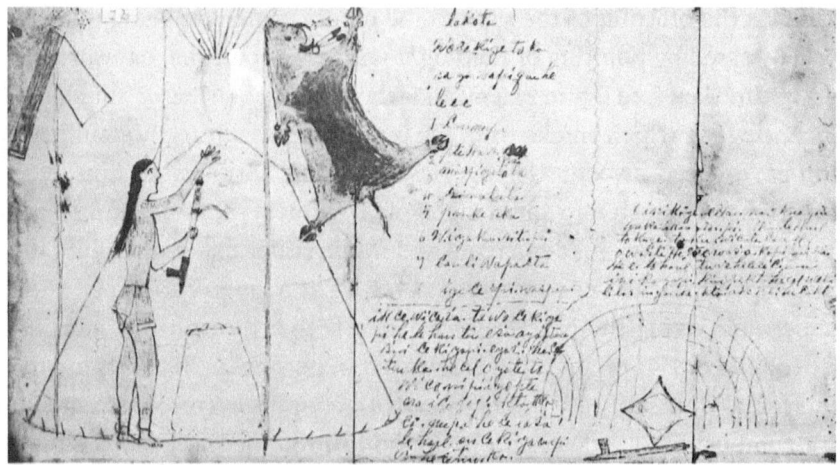

Fig. 2. *Yuwı̨́tapi* 'ritual supplication' and *c'aṇúpa iyáȟpeyapi* 'ceremonial pipe offering'. Reproduced from Bad Heart Bull and Blish (1967, 86), by permission of the University of Nebraska Press.

mythical time/space, each spirit teaching which colors and designs it preferred and required. "There is said to be wakan virtue in this paint, and the manner of its application," writes Gideon Pond (1889, 225). Scarlet or red is a sign of active "worship" or propitiation and the most common color for sacrifices (Lynd 1889, 169–70; G. Pond 1889, 222). According to Fletcher (1887a, 285n9), "The putting on of paint is always a part of Indian ceremonial, religious or social. It forms a part of the formal approach in religious ritual so essential to the Indian mode of thought. The dead are painted that the person may meet the spirits in proper guise. It is also regarded as an offering of prayer."

In ceremonial contexts painting was an act of invocation, intensification, and manifestation. Designs received from nonhumans in virtual space/time actualized and activated power. Paints prepared and applied ceremonially were considered wak'ą́, infused with potency that was transferred to the person or object painted. Rocks were often painted, adorned, propitiated, and offered sacrifices by men setting out on hunting or war expeditions in order to secure either power to destroy and good fortune or power to avert destruction and misfortune from themselves.

Red stripes, similar to those made during the *huŋká* 'making of relatives' ceremony, were painted on rocks where such interactions and offerings were deemed appropriate (Walker 1917, 137; 1991, 232–33). "The symbolic color of God the Rock is yellow," explains Walker (1991, 235), "but red is put on a stone in veneration of the Rock, for red is sacred and the Rock is pleased with this mark of reverence and may bestow perseverance and endurance on one showing it." According to Little Wound, "It pleases *Inyan* to have red placed on a stone. When you would please the spirits put red paint on a stone" (in Walker 1991, 197). As Riggs explains, "Paint occupies an important place in all their worship. Scarlet or red is the religious color for sacrifices, while blue is used in many ceremonies. The use of paints, the Dakotas aver, was taught them by the gods. . . . No ceremony of worship is complete without the *wakan'*, or sacred application of paint. The down of the female swan, colored scarlet, also forms a necessary part of sacrifices" (1869, 77).

More than just a symbolic representation, down embodies and *is* the spiritual essence or interiority of the nonhuman person or collective from whom it is derived.[14] "Swan's-down, dyed red," reports Riggs (1869, 472), "is a sacred article, and used continually in their worship as an offering to the gods, and as an ornament of consecrated articles, such as the weapons and feathers of the warrior. It is much delighted in by the gods, who are said to wear it largely." Down painted red is referred to as *wadúta* and *walúta* among the Dakotas and Lakotas, respectively, literally 'red thing', and may be applied to any red offering or sacrifice, including down, cloth, or human scalps.

Further, down and cloth offerings or prayer flags (*šiná wóuye*) serve parallel functions. Nonhuman spirit persons are known to be very sensitive to wind, atmospheric changes, abrupt or violent movements, and loud noises.[15] Hence, down and prayer cloths are essential in all formal ceremonials, the fluttering of which is believed to attract the attention of the spirits so that the ceremonial appeals (wac'ékiya) will be heard (Fletcher 1887a, 283n5; G. Pond 1889, 227). Fletcher (1887a, 284n5) writes, "Among the tents of the Dakotas one may see poles with bits of cloth hanging from their tops, leaning up against the logs cabins, thrust between the smoke flaps of the tent, or stuck in the ground beside the lodge, showing that someone is sick or in trouble and is thus seeking help and a blessing. In great distress several poles may be raised." As the Sioux peoples moved westward in pursuit of the bison, eagle down gradually replaced swan down. In some ceremonies, like the Dakota raw fish feast, the dancers/ritual participants "are painted all over in various colors, and ornamented with white and red swan's down" (Riggs 1869, 85). In this way, and in others, such as the foods and offerings made to spirit persons, "the Dakota honors his god as he would be honored himself" (Riggs 1869, 78), speaking to an inherent anthropogenic quality in the dynamics of ritual subjectivization.

Painting and adorning a rock or other nonhuman person or object is key to the dynamics of Sioux ceremonial practice, providing the frame within which the ritual habitus operates through wac'ékiya or formal address or appeal (see Kapferer 2006b, 2010, 238, 245–46).[16] Kapferer writes, "The ritual frame effectively establishes the events of action occurring within it as a self-referencing system that has its own relatively independent legitimacy and meaning. Thus the framing of acts and events as ritual constitutes rite as its own domain of belief and veracity. . . . The framing of . . . ritual action is created by the action itself and can operate as an invisible membrane surrounding the action, momentarily setting it off from the ongoing flow of life yet simultaneously pragmatically engaged with it" (2006b, 515–16). Demarcating an altar or sacred space, as in the painting and adornment of a stone or buffalo skull, is one obvious form of framing in Sioux ritual practice. Standard verbal ritual appeals, such as aid/pity me (ų́šimala yo/ye), hear me (onámaȟʔų wo/we), behold me (wamáyąka yo/ye), and help me (ómakiya yo/ye), along with ritual music and other aesthetic dynamics, also function in terms of framing, initializing and sustaining a human-nonhuman joint-attention situation that allows the ritual habitus to operate (on joint attention, see Tomasello 1999, 2000, 2014). Only after spirits were honored and properly consecrated and invoked through painting and adornment could they be addressed and offered sacrifices. An offering of this kind was usually "something fine," writes Ella Deloria (n.d.h, 195), "and inside it they tied whatever was symbolic to them."

Ritual framing, explains Kapferer (2006a, 517), "opens participants to the particular logics of transformation and transition that are integral to the teleological process that the frame defines." It also constitutes a particular lived-in space whose dynamics are comparable to Bourdieu's notion of habitus, a structuring structure of dispositions that mediates between agency and structure and is of ontological import, impacting how an individual agent perceives, thinks, and behaves (Bourdieu 1977; Kapferer 2006a, 517–18). Kapferer (2006a, 518) writes, "Rituals can be conceived as complex dispositional structures through which participants are made to move. These structures are not static but are brought into different relations of meaning and signification through ritual events in which the bodies of participants are centers of meaning production and themselves laden with import." There is also a clear sacrificial dynamic—consisting of the ritual demarcation of sacred or virtual space/time and processes of (re)creation and (re)generation via destruction—involved in the offering of sacrifices to nonhuman persons in an attempt to interact and establish intersubjective relationship and exchange (see Kapferer 2006b).

Having examined in detail the personhood of rocks as an ethnographic vignette and various key ritual dynamics at work in traditional Sioux ritual practice, I now turn to an exploration of transformation or metamorphosis as a key indexical attribute of personhood.[17] As Ingold (2004, 31) writes, "The inner essence, or soul, [interiority] holds the attributes of sentience, volition, memory, and speech. Any being that possesses these attributes is a person, irrespective of the intrinsically unstable form in which it appears." Although humans and nonhumans are alike in terms of a common interiority and structure, they differ in degree or qualitatively in terms of the amount of power they possess, which is directly correlated to their capacity or potential for transformation.

CHAPTER 4

Persons and Transformation

A classic feature of many animist ontologies and a fundamental attribute of persons basic to the cognitive and ethnometaphysical (ontological and epistemological) orientation of nineteenth-century Lakotas was the capacity for metamorphosis or transformation. According to Vine Deloria, "The Sioux traditional people say that the important thing is the spirit of the creature; that it can and does change aspects of its physical shape in order to deal with changes but that basically it remains the same entity. As the Indian interest is in the spirit or soul of the other creature and not in its morphology, some substitutions can be made in ceremonial objects, provided that the substituted materials have the same spiritual relationship to people that the former objects had" (1999, 58).

Persons, as conscious, subjective beings-(alive)-in-the-world and loci of causality in a position to know and reflect upon the nature of existence, could appear in both human and nonhuman forms while maintaining an enduring fundamental interiority and/or identity. As Joseph Epes Brown (1997, xiv) observes, "Underlying the fluidity of appearances there is the binding thread of the *wakan* concept, the ultimate coalescence of the multiple into the unifying principle of Wakan-Tanka. Wakan-Tanka is the Great Mysterious whose multiplicity of aspects does not compromise an essential unity. Given this emphasis on underlying unity, the Oglala categorize beings not on the basis of physical similarity, but on the basis of shared, qualitative power." Vine Deloria (1999, 47) elaborates on this theme, writing, "There are many accounts of people traveling to other worlds, of people becoming birds and animals, living with them, and experiencing the great variety of possible modes of existence."

Metamorphosis entails a revealing of common interiority through the shedding of one corporeal envelope and the adoption of another, allowing for interspecies/intertribal interaction, relationship, and exchange. Thus a human could be embodied in an animal or a plant, an animal could adopt the physicality of another animal, and an animal or a plant could shed its customary clothing and adopt the form of a human being. While this change in physicality—and consequent shifting of perspective—may not have occurred often in actuality, it certainly occurred in other existential realms of experience (Descola 2013a, 135–38). The instability of outward form in both human and nonhuman persons was experienced and dramatized in mythology, dreams and visions, and ritual. For the Sioux, the Ojibwes, and other indigenous peoples of North America the realms of myth, dreams and visions, and ritual were continuous with waking life or actuality rather than separate from it. Myth was understood as the past experiences of nonhuman persons, and dreams and visions were considered the past or future experiences of human selves. Along with ritual, these experiences were continuous with other cumulative self-related experience. In these virtual realities, often referred to by Lakota people today simply as "the spirit world," a person's vital essence, the self or interiority, was afforded a degree of mobility in time and space normally impossible in actuality or everyday experience (cf. Hallowell 1960, 34–35; 1966, 284; Ingold 2004, 34–35, 41–43).

The Wakíyą (Thunder Birds) provide a classic example. Wakíyą were conceptualized as animate beings who had the ability or power to change their physicality at will, usually exhibiting either an avian or human form, while maintaining an enduring and recognizable interiority and/or identity. The Wakíyą were also manifested, of course, as thunder (*wakíyą hot'ųpi*) and lightning (*wakíyą tųwápi*), the former known as the Wakíyą's characteristic call or cry and the latter as its stare or glare. This ability or potential for transformation was common among the mythical personages and nonhuman spirit beings peopling the Lakota cosmos and was indexical to the person category. Clearly, physicality, while essential in terms of differentiating collectives, was a more or less incidental attribute of being, arbitrary, transmutable, and potentially deceiving, while interiority was a much more reliable indicator of identity, enduring and transcendent of outward appearances.

Sioux ontology reflected a highly transformational cosmos and lifeworld. Metamorphosis indexed great wakʻą́ power, involving an alteration of manifest appearance, while the vital essence or interiority of the person continued in existence in some other form (cf. Ingold 2004, 31). Transformation was a common motif in Sioux mythology and oral tradition. For instance, recall that White Buffalo Woman was originally one of the Star People, daughter of Táku Škąšką́, who fell from the sky as a meteor and was able to take the form of both a beautiful woman and a white buffalo cow. The Ųktéȟi, or water monster spirits, were known to capture humans and transform them into water animals (Walker 1917, 89). Tʻatʻą́ka, the spirit master of the buffalo and chief of the Buffalo People, could appear as an animal or as a human, as could the Buffalo People themselves. The latter, in human guise, were known to intermarry with humans and had the ability to transform their spouses into animal form (Walker 1917, 91). In one of the Stone Boy mythical narratives, humans are transformed into cherry stones when Íya, the evil mythical giant, sucks them in with his breath. Luckily, Stone Boy is able to change them back into their original human form (Walker 1917, 202).

Transformation also figured prominently in dream and vision experiences. Joseph White Bull (1849–1947), renowned warrior, nephew of Sitting Bull, and a chief of the Minneconjou Lakotas, had a vision in which he saw a man coming from the west painted with red lightning streaks and riding a black horse. When the rider attacked a human enemy, piercing him with a lance, symbolic of lightning striking, the victim transformed into a plant. Later in the vision, White Bull led a group of men in a charge toward the west, before they all transformed into swallows (Vestal 1984, 12–15; see DeMallie 1984, 84–86). Lone Man, an elder from Standing Rock who spoke with Densmore in the early 1900s, had a vision of the Thunder Birds from the west that parallels White Bull's. In his vision, Lone Man attacks an enemy, thrusting him through with his lance, causing his enemy to transform into a reed standing in water (Lone Man in Densmore 2001, 160). Frequently in visions animal and other nonhuman spirits appeared to the visionary in human form, only to transform into various significant plants and animals (see, for example, Densmore 2001, 66, 173–74, 176–77, 184–85, 187–88, 251–52). Black Elk's great vision is full of instances of metamorphosis. For instance, he strikes a human enemy who then turns into a turtle, a group of horses transform into buffalo, and a red man transforms first into a buffalo and then into an herb (DeMallie 1984, 86–87, 118). As DeMallie (1984, 87) explains, "For the Lakota, the powers granted in visions can be thought of as the ability to recognize and utilize transformations of the natural world. Implicit to this belief system is a conception of interdependence that is more fundamental than mere interrelationship: the universe is one, and its varying life forms are different configurations of the universal animating power."

Both living and deceased humans were known to be able to assume the form of animals, but usually this ability was rare and an indicator of great power. At Pine Ridge Reservation in 1898, Short Feather explained to Walker that evil shamans could kill people using incantations, make bad medicine, and transform humans into animals. For all these reasons they were feared by the people (in Walker 1991, 115). According to Vine Deloria, "For the Sioux it is possible in ordinary life for a man to have the power to assume or adopt other forms in which to express himself" (2009, 177). In animist societies, subjects are potentially everywhere. Speaking of the Berens River Ojibwes, Hallowell explains, "So far as appearance is concerned, there is no hard and fast line that can be drawn between an animal form and a human form because metamorphosis is possible. In perceptual experience what looks like a bear may sometimes *be* an animal and, on other occasions, a human being. What persists and gives continuity to being is the vital part, or soul" (1960, 38; emphasis in original). The concepts of transformation and "medicine," the latter conceived of in terms of power (wówašʾake 'strength, power, energy') and knowledge (wóslolye), were intrinsic to the "natural attitude" of the Lakotas, deeply ingrained since earliest childhood through processes of socialization and enculturation.

In animist regimes metamorphosis is often not a covering up but an opening up of the person to the world, a revealing of a common interiority (cf. Descola 2013a, 31, 135–38; Ingold 2004, 33). This is not always the case, however, as in sorcery/witchcraft or the Ojibwe bear/man or bear walker, in which transforming one's bodily clothing serves to disguise one's true identity and nefarious intent. Transformation as a revealing of a common spirit is more relevant in the contexts of dreams and visions and ritual, in particular the vision quest. The physicality does not conceal or enclose the interiority of the person like a container, insulating it from immediate contact with the environment. Rather, it is a transitory bodily envelope or clothing that can be donned or discarded as circumstances dictate. Beede (1912) explains that among the Northern Lakotas there was a traditional belief that

> the "soul" or "mind" is not *in* the body, as many or all white people believe, but is *around* the body as the heavens and the "all-animated space" is around the earth—though connected with the earth as the "soul" is with the body. That with some Indians more than with others this "soul" which is around the body, at times, may expand so as to reach regions far away and sense the things there, both the physical things on the earth and also things in the "world invisible" which is around the tera firma. That in this "world invisible" around the physical earth there are almost countless spheres of movement of living persons of some sort (not at all emphasizing departed spirits, if including them); these spheres generally harmonizing in their movements, though sometimes in conflict; and that all human persons here in this earthly living are connected with some one of these invisible spheres.

The human mind (wacʻį) and soul (naǧí) were all around human beings and could journey far away from the body (tʻącʻą́). During sleep, ritual, paralysis, or sickness the mind and soul might wander to other planes of existence or to the spirit world. This explains many beliefs concerning the Lakota dream experience and disease theory. Yet in many ways the mind and soul were codependent on the body: they were interconnected (Beede 1912, Western Sioux Cosmology). The physicality enables rather than constrains, providing the distinctive equipment, skills, dispositions, anatomical devices, or habitus, the hardware, which is the basis of Viveiros de Castro's (1998) notion of perspectivism, through which various life-forms experience and interact with the world in their own distinctive ways.

For nineteenth-century Lakotas wakʻą́ indicated the potential ability and power to transform, a notion tied to growth and development (icʻáǧa), which marked a phenomenon, person, or thing as *tʻókeca* 'different, strange, weird', an anomaly. Wakʻą́ was a semantic category with ontological import that distinguished ordinary, everyday realities from the extraordinary or incomprehensible aspects of life and the universe. Wakʻą́ as incomprehensible and beyond the scope of human understanding stems from an important categorical attribute of nonhuman power and potency in relation to humans and manifested in concrete acts: transformation. Transmutation, the act or state of changing or altering form, and the potential capacity to transform were significant Lakota religious concepts and defining features of wakʻą́.

Beede discusses the significance of transformation among the Northern Lakotas: "With the Western Sioux Indians 'miracle' is life-transformation-process (not life-process)" (Beede 1912, Western Sioux Cosmology). An important indicator of transformation among nineteenth-century Lakotas was the category tʻókeca 'difference'. "'Taku tokeca' [something different or strange] and 'taku winihan' [something causing fear or excitement], and many other expressions are applied to something that is wonderful, and to some extent arousing fear also, perhaps," writes Beede (1912, Western Sioux Cosmology), "but the word 'wakan' connoted a life-transformation-process always, as Indians understand. And Great Spirit (Wakan-tanka), whatever the origin of the term, is, to them, the Being Who is the Master of, or Lord of, or Source of, or Totality of the total life-transformation-process in the entire world or species or groups." In doctoring songs, for instance, the term *tʻókeca* is frequently used to index the power of the practitioner and the patient's transformation from sickness to health (Densmore 2001, 275–77).

Transformation is also related to the concept *tʻų́* 'emitted spiritual essence or potency; power and ability to do wakʻą́ things'. As Walker's Oglala interlocutors explain, "All the God persons have *ton*. The *ton* is the power to do supernatural things" (Walker 1991, 95). William Powers also weighs in on the religious significance of transformation, writing, "To the Oglalas, the totality of natural and cultural phenomena are capable of undergoing transformations which require that behavior toward these phenomena be altered, or somewhat modified. The causes of these transformations and the Oglala explanation for concomitant changes in behavior are subsumed under the concept of *taku wakan* 'sacred thing(s)'. The phenomena which are regarded as *taku wakan* may be temporarily or permanently transformed. Those which are permanently transformed are regarded collectively as *Wakantanka*" (Powers 1982b, 45). Summarizing Walker, Powers (1982a, 52) states, "Energy has two aspects: visible and invisible. The potential to transform visible energy into invisible energy, and the reverse, is called *tun*. The tun of every invisible aspect is its visible aspect. The transformation from visible to invisible, and the reverse is called *wakan*, as is the resultant state. Invisible aspects are to be feared." T'ų́ indexes wakʻą́, both of which are related to the potential capacity for metamorphosis, which indexes power, which is another way of understanding Lakota conceptions of wakʻą́.

Hallowell (1960, 39; 1966, 284) concludes that the capacity for transformation is one of the generic properties of the person category and a feature that links humans with nonhumans in their behavioral environment or lifeworld. However, t'ų́ and the potential for metamorphosis index power, understood in the sense of strength, energy, exceptional abilities, and knowledge or wisdom, the differential reserve of t'ų́ and wakʻą́ potency. Within the person category there is a quantitative and qualitative gradation of power: humans in their natural state are the least powerful and knowledgeable, while specific nonhumans occupy the top rank in this power hierarchy. According to Kenneth Morrison,

> If person is a principle of ontological similarity, power is the principle of differentiation. Persons are powerful in various degrees, but significantly some human beings, particularly those who have ritual knowledge, exercise power equal to, if not superior than, other-than-human persons. For all persons, power is at once knowledge and the ability to apply knowledge to novel situations. Since power itself is

ethically neutral, it must always be grounded in intentional activity. Power is therefore dangerous because it can be used to achieve either good or ill. In effect, power is the existential postulate which accounts for those personal decisions which make for both human and cosmic order and disorder. (1992, 203)

A foundational assumption among nineteenth-century Sioux was that nonhumans could assume a variety of bodily forms, whereas this ability among humans was rare and a marker of unusual power. Power of this degree could be acquired by human beings only from and through the help of nonhuman persons.

In relatively rare cases nonhumans purposely sought out intersubjective interaction with humans, as in the case of Ptesą́wį and what Ella Deloria (n.d.e, 4–5, 26) refers to as a vision of obtainment, an honorary intersubjective or interpersonal transfer of power and knowledge in which a human is called by a nonhuman person without conscious striving.[1] But more commonly human beings bore the brunt of establishing relationships with nonhuman persons, desperately trying to invoke and induce them to see and hear them and have mercy and intervene in earthly human affairs. This was accomplished through various means and ritual dynamics, many involving forms of self-mortification, including song, dance, wacʽékiya 'crying to/for, addressing as a relative, "prayer"', evoking pity,[2] ritual, fasting, sensory deprivation and overload, sacrifice, suffering, and self-torture. In some cases a trance or altered state of consciousness was attained in order to commune with the nonhuman persons of the Lakota cosmos. Ella Deloria (n.d.h, 194) gives the impression that there was a positive correlation between the extremity or degree of the "great hardships in crying for a revelation out in the wilderness when they are questing" and the amount and quality of the power and knowledge (Hallowell's [1955] "blessings") attained, manifested in concrete "magical" acts (*wakʽą́ wicʽóȟʔq*).

In their spiritual practices the Lakotas purposefully sought out nonhuman things, persons, and spaces far from human habitation and activity. In the late 1800s missionary-turned-ethnologist James Owen Dorsey recognized the importance of the human/nonhuman distinction in Siouan cultures. He perceptively deduced that the most significant distinction was not between natural and supernatural but rather between human and nonhuman.[3] "In considering the subject from an Indian's point of view," he writes, "one must avoid speaking of the supernatural as distinguished from the natural. It is safer to divide phenomena as they appear to the Indian mind into the human and the superhuman, as many, if not most natural phenomena are mysterious to the Indian. Nay, even man himself may become mysterious by fasting, prayer, and vision" (Dorsey 1894, 365). In Dorsey's astute estimation Siouan ontologies and worldviews index and process phenomenological experience according to a human/nonhuman binary.[4] Dorsey's insight represents an important first step toward the realization of the central role of personhood in the ethnographic and anthropological literature on the Sioux.

Nonhuman things and persons were conceptualized as mediums or intermediaries through which the wakʻą́ 'sacred, mysterious' could be reached. As Little Moon, one of Ella Deloria's Hunkpapa consultants, illustrates,

> In old times the Dakotas also had God, though they did not know just what it was. But the only thing they were sure of was that somewhere there was something incomprehensible who had power surpassing the power of men, and that if he wanted to aid men he did; and if he wanted to withhold his aid, the people suffered.
>
> That was why, when they needed help, they wished to pray. But of course, not knowing just where to reach God, and not being able to say just where God was, they sought out something that was not man-made, like a rock or tree. They thought that whoever made rocks and trees was more powerful than man, so that through them as mediums, he might be reached. That was why, when they wanted to pray they sought out a rock or tree far from human habitation and reverently they painted it with sacred wasé (red paint) and thus they consecrated it; and then they were ready to address it. Then if they so wished and had it, they left a sacred object there, an offering. It was something fine, and inside it they tied whatever was symbolical to them. And then he who was to pray stood by the offering on the rock

or tree and said, "Grandfather, take pity on me and tell this for me: I would live long. I would have horses," or else whatever they wanted they asked for. (Little Moon in E. Deloria n.d.h, 194–95)

In a similar vein Fletcher explains,

> Careful inquiry and observation fail to show that the Indian actually worships the objects which are set up or mentioned by him in his ceremonies. The earth, the four winds, the sun, moon, and stars, the stones, the water, the various animals, are all exponents of a mysterious life and power encompassing the Indian and filling him with a vague apprehension and desire to propitiate and induce friendly relations. The latter is attempted not so much through the ideas of sacrifice as through more or less ceremonial appeals. More faith is put in ritual and a careful observance of forms than in any act of self-denial in its moral sense, as we understand it. The claim of relationship is used to strengthen the appeal, since the tie of kindred among the Indians is one which cannot be ignored or disregarded, the terms grandfather and grandmother being the most general and implying dependence, respect and the recognition of authority. (1887a, 276n1)

Usually each nonhuman or spirit person had a characteristic and recognizable messenger who carried out his wishes and spoke for him, acting as intermediary between humankind and the nonhuman person in question. Akíc'ita, sometimes translated as 'scout' or 'lieutenant', is the Lakota term for these sacred mediators who represented the plans and wishes of the spirits to the people and executed them, acting in all things on behalf of her or his spirit master (E. Deloria n.d.c, 41).

Powerful individuals were known to have the ability to transform from humans into various animals, such as elk and buffalo, and back again. When a person was in a wak'ą́ state or doing something in a wak'ą́ manner (*wak'ą́yą*) he or she was transformed in some way, whether the interiority was momentarily out of its usual time/space or embodied in some unfamiliar physicality or the physicality was altered or transformed in some way. These altered states are flip sides of the same coin. In any case, transformed humans were said to be wak'ą́ or t'ókeca, sacred, holy, powerful, incomprehensible, different, anomalous, as were children, the elderly, sick people, and the insane (see Little Wound in Walker 1991, 69).

In the domains of mythology, dreams and visions, and ceremony transformation was a regular occurrence, whereas it was less frequent in actuality, yet still possible for those possessing great power. Humans had the potential to transform into animal or plant physicalities, and animals and spirits were known to take human form in order to communicate and interact with humans. Hence, transformation provided a common ground between life-forms with different physicalities and a space for interspecies interaction, relationship, and exchange (cf. Descola 2013b, 80–81). Next I examine these major themes in light of specific ethnographic examples, exploring the role of nonhuman persons (the spirits and ghosts of deceased human beings), transformation, and relational ethnometaphysics in three interrelated virtual domains: mythology, dreams and visions, and ritual or ceremony.

CHAPTER 5

Spirits and Ghosts

Whereas social relations with human beings belonged to the chaotic sphere of waking life, everyday reality, or actuality, the most intimate social interaction with nonhuman persons was experienced chiefly, but not exclusively, by the self in mythology (ohúkaką), dreams and visions (iháblapi), and ceremony or ritual ([wakʻą́] wicʻóȟʼą, wóecʻų). Virtuality is a concept developed by Henri Bergson (see Ansell-Pearson 2005), Susanne Langer (1953, 1957), Gilles Deleuze (1988) and Deleuze and Félix Guattari (1987, 1994), and Bruce Kapferer (2004, 2006b, 2010, 2013b). My use of the term comes largely from Kapferer, who was also heavily influenced by Victor Turner. For Kapferer, virtuality is no less a real, fully lived existential reality than is actuality, yet it is substantially different in two key ways. First, virtuality is a kind of phantasmagoric, self-contained, imaginal space, a dynamic or plane of immanence that allows for all kinds of potentialities of human experience to emerge and actualize. Second, virtuality is a technology for the slowing down of the tempo of actuality and holding in abeyance or suspension some of the vital qualities of lived reality. The latter aspect is referred to as the descent into the virtual and explains the (re)generative, (re)constitutive force of ritual, vision experiences, and other virtual dynamics in the context of everyday realities. Virtuality has ontological import as a technology for bringing forth and changing the very ground of being, concentrating the dynamics of cosmological, social, and personal (re)construction.

In the following section I explore the nature of nonhuman spirit persons and the dynamics of human-nonhuman interaction in the interfaces of mythology, dreams and visions, and ritual. Virtuality, like transformation in the Descolian animist sense, provides a common ground for interspecies communication, relationship, and exchange (see V. Deloria 2009, 179–81). Importantly, as Hallowell noted many years ago in reference to the Ojibwes, social interaction for nineteenth-century Lakotas involved no vital distinction or polarity between self-related experience in virtual space as opposed to self-related experience in actuality. Hallowell writes, "Social relations with other-than-human persons are not metaphorical but intimately meshed in their thought and experience with interrelationships between human beings" (1966, 279). All self-related experience was considered together as a cumulative whole, not divided, demarcated, and compartmentalized. Yet at the same time virtual experiences were not confused with events that occurred in actuality. The Sioux recognized significant qualitative differences between the two domains while maintaining a unity of thought in terms of the cognitive orientation of self to others and environment (cf. Hallowell 1966, 274–76).

At the heart of human-nonhuman relationships and covenants were dynamics or relational schemas of exchange. Medicine or power, often in the form of knowledge or specific abilities, symbolically equated with life (ní) or life-giving potency, was transferred from nonhuman to human in these spaces, effecting symbolic identification, a convergence of interiorities and identities, and ritual transformation. For their part in this exchange humans humbled themselves and evoked pity and kinship obligations. They offered patronage and respected, honored, and propitiated the nonhuman persons peopling the living cosmos, making offerings and sacrifices to them. Speaking of the Berens River Ojibwes, Hallowell writes, "The other-than-human grandfathers are sources of power to human beings through the 'blessings' they bestow, i.e., a sharing of their power which enhances the 'power' of human beings" (1960, 22).

Among the Sioux, human-nonhuman relationships were defined in terms of human kinship, namely friendship (k'olátakuya and huƙátakuya):

a human being "made friends" with a bird, animal, stone, spirit, or other nonhuman person. The kʻolá 'friend' and hųká 'adoptive relative' relationships were extremely serious matters traditionally, not to be entered into or taken lightly. The kinship obligations and responsibilities of these relationships were equivalent to those of blood or consanguineal relatives, in many cases even more binding (Walker 1982, 40–41; V. Deloria 2009, 116, 145; Powers 1986, 81–82, 206). According to Lame Deer, "The young men who vowed to be a *kola* to each other would almost become one single person. They shared everything—life and death, pain and joy, the last mouthful of food, even their women. They had to be ready at all times to give their lives for each other. In the same way an older man could adopt a younger one by becoming his *hunka*. By this ceremony, the younger man became the son of the older, even if only a few years separated them in age. Men sealed these special friendships with a ceremony" (Lame Deer and Erdoes 1972, 203). Likewise, nonhuman spirit persons related to one another according to these same forms of human kinship, namely kʻolá and hųká (see Black Elk in DeMallie 1984; Densmore 2001; Standing Bear 2006a; Walker 1917, 1991). For instance, Tʻatʻą́ka, spirit master of the bison, was considered the kʻolá of Wí 'Sun', Táku Šką́šką́ 'Sky' was the kʻolá of Tʻaté 'Wind', and the West Wind was the kʻolá of Wakį́yą 'the Thunder Birds' (Walker 1917, 64, 81, 84, 130–31, 167).

The nonhumans peopling the Sioux cosmos were vested with collective-specific powers and knowledge, often glossed as "medicine," which they shared with humans by agreeing to be friends with them—and hence establishing exchange relationships (V. Deloria 2009, 116). In the early 1900s Brave Buffalo of Standing Rock Reservation described his Elk dream to Densmore. In the dream Brave Buffalo was escorted to a beautiful spirit lodge occupied by elk persons. Once he was seated in the lodge, explains Brave Buffalo (in Densmore 2001, 177), "the elks rose and said they had heard that I was a great friend of the buffalo, and that they wanted me to be their friend also." After establishing a friendship and alliance with Brave Buffalo the elks taught him a sacred song and gave him instructions and powers, such as wakʻą́ swiftness, protection, and specific designs for painting his tipi and adorning himself. Illustrating the connection between the actual and the virtual, Densmore concludes,

"The elks told him further that before he would be fully entitled to make a request for help from them he must go through a performance which he himself should devise, by which he would show the people that he was acting under their patronage" (2001, 178).

Speaking of Sioux interspecies relations, Vine Deloria explains:

> Among the tasks and favors that the animals performed are included the knowledge of healing herbs that humans could use to cure illnesses, locating sources of food, warning humans of future events, and giving them powers to deflect or avoid dangers. It was essential, therefore, that individuals have as many animal friends as possible, since each animal had its own unique powers to share with them. Great honors had to be shown to these animals, and songs were composed to express human thanks for favors bestowed. The birds and animals also gave the people songs that could be used to call the animal for assistance. Some restrictions were placed on humans when entering into a relationship with another creature. Animals and birds were always to be treated with respect and often could not be hunted without first gaining their permission. (2009, 116–17)

Importantly, it was the nonhuman, as an active subject, who most often initiated interspecies friendship. These relationships were reciprocal and symmetrical, which is why I categorize them as exchange, rather than gift giving, according to Descola's framework of relational schemas (V. Deloria 2009, 127–28; Descola 2013a, 311). These nonhuman-initiated exchange relationships also had practical effects and applications in the physical world, illustrating the real impact of virtuality in actuality: nonhumans gave humans instructions and powers, healed sickness, shared significant knowledge, and identified medicinal plants that had immediate practical value in human life and aided in the maintenance and perpetuation of life movement (V. Deloria 2009, 128, 175).

Recall that the person category extended beyond the human to include animals, plant life, meteorological phenomena, celestial bodies, and what Western philosophy and science consider inanimate objects or things. There were many types of nonhuman persons encountered in the Lakota lifeworld. There were the familiar characters or personages from mythology and religious belief, collectively labeled Wakʿą́ Tʿą́ka or Táku Wakʿą́, such as Tʿaté 'Wind', the Tʿatúye Tópa 'Four Brothers or Four Winds' (whose dwelling places in the four directions spatially defined the Lakota cosmos), Ptesą́wį (White Buffalo Woman), Táku Škąšką́, Wakíyą, Ųktéȟi, Iktómi, Stone Boy, Blood Clot Boy, Anų́gite 'Double Women', and so on. There were the animal spirits and the platonic spirit masters of what we term natural species of plants and animals, such as Tʿatʿą́ka 'Buffalo Bull', Matʿó 'Bear', Heȟáka 'Elk', Sįtésapela 'Black Tail Deer', Wąblí 'Eagle', Šų́kawakʿą 'Horse', Šų̄gmánitutʿąka 'Wolf', and so on. These nonhumans were commonly referred to collectively in English as "the spirits." To illustrate some of the general characteristics of nonhuman persons I now briefly explore Lakota perspectives on the nature of nonhuman spirits.

The Spirits

In often-bungling nineteenth-century accounts early missionaries and others described the spirits peopling the Sioux cosmos in Western moralistic terms. Unfortunately, this model has tended to hold in much scholarship on the Sioux since then. In 1869 Riggs (1869, 92–93) explained, "The sum and substance . . . [of Dakota religion] is *demon-worship*. The gods they worship are destitute of all the attributes of the true God. Even the best of them, or the Great Spirit, has but a negative character." According to Lynd, the "Great Spirit," a problematic notion at best, was conceived of as a negative good, neither positive nor active. In 1889 he wrote that the Dakotas "never pray to Him, for they deem Him too far away to hear them, or as not being concerned with their affairs. No sacrifices are made to Him, nor dances in His honor. Of all the spirits, He is the Great Spirit: but His power is only latent or negative" (1889, 151–52). Riggs explains, "The Dakota, having his eyes shut to the presence and character of the true God, misinterprets the kindly discipline of life, and credits the chastisements of a loving father to the spite of these vengeful demons, whose special delight it is to make man more miserable, or to destroy him. Demons wander through the earth, causing sickness and death. Spirits of evil are ever ready to pounce upon the unwary" (1869, 93–94). Although the accounts of Riggs, Lynd, and their contemporaries tend to be melodramatic and ethnocentric, reflecting their own cultural and religious biases and traditions rather than Sioux understandings, some useful data can be gleaned from them nevertheless.

By framing the matter in terms of Christian morality early missionaries completely missed the point, and some contemporary scholars, such as Julian Rice (1998, 14–15), continue to perpetuate the misconception that all spirits in the Lakota cosmos were evil or malevolent in their interactions with humans. On the other end of the spectrum, the notion that all spirits were good or benevolent is not supported by the literature either, as demonstrated by the destructive, death-dealing ways of the Wakíyą, the dreaded Thunder Birds who struck fear into the hearts of the Sioux. Clearly, certain spirit persons were more inclined toward negative interrelations with humans than were others. Interactions with certain spirits, such as Wakíyą, Iktómi, Íya, Wíyą Nupápika, Anúgite, and Gnaškíyą, for instance, tended to be more negative and detrimental to humans, while interactions with other spirits, such as Tʻatʻą́ka, Matʻó, Ptesą́wį, and Makʻá, tended to be more positive and beneficial (see Walker 1917, 1991).

But we are framing this in the wrong way. First of all, good and bad, benevolence and malevolence, are relative terms dependent on the position or perspective of a subject in relation to an object or other, who is himself a subject, self, or I. In reality, many binaries are two extremes of the very same thing, not absolutes. In the case of good and evil we are talking about relative ends of a spectrum that indexes how one subject interacts with and relates to another. From a Lakota perspective we might consider whether one treats another as a relative (*takúye*)—a Lakota (*lakʻóta*)—or as an enemy (*tʻóka*). Perhaps these poles best correspond to positive and negative, where indifference lies in the center, a complete lack of feeling or relatedness between two terms or subjects. Understood in terms of Descola's relational schemas, positive interaction is characterized by exchange or gift giving, while negative interaction is characterized by predation.

A Descolian animist framework provides a lens that illuminates an untrodden middle ground and satisfactorily resolves this old debate in the literature concerning the nature and morality of spirits in Sioux belief. Nonhuman spirit beings, much like humans, and particularly shamans, were neither inherently good nor evil, benevolent nor malevolent (cf. Basso 1970, 38). The behavior of spirits in relation to humans was relative, dependent on context and history. Particular spirits did not possess moral sanctity and were neither unequivocally benevolent nor malevolent. They were reactionary, emotional, capricious, whimsical, and volatile, and, much like humans, they could be proud, jealous, and easily offended by disrespectful behavior, rituals performed improperly, breaches of taboo, and other varieties of what Hallowell refers to as "bad conduct" (1955, 268; 1966, 280). Just as human society is the model for nonhuman society in animist collectives, so too humans provide the model for nonhumans in terms of personalities, dispositions, emotions, characteristics, behaviors, and so on.

In particular, the idea that spirits could be offended is an ancient, pervasive, and fundamental Sioux belief. Spirits were offended by all varieties of bad conduct and, once offended, could wreak havoc on people and cause extreme misfortune and hardship (Curtis 1908, 70; E. Deloria n.d.e., 20–21, 33–34; DeMallie 1984, 393; Dorsey 1894, 469; G. Pond 1889, 231–33, 247; Walker 1991, 25, 75, 82, 85, 87, 170). As the Oglala Ringing Shield (in Walker 1991, 114) warns, "Men should be careful and not offend the spirits." Animal ceremonialism and hunting ritual functioned to circumvent offending animal spirits and was closely linked to sacred interdictions, taboos, or ritual prescriptions and proscriptions. According to Walker (1917, 92), "A man may so offend game animals that they will escape from hunters, and if so a Shaman should penalize the offending one by making taboo to him some portion of the offended animals."

The spirits could be offended by bad conduct (*wówahtani, wic'óȟ'ą šíca*) or propitiated by honor (*yuónihą*) and respect (*wóohola*). The former led to hardship, misfortune (*wówahtani, wóak'ip'a, wót'eȟi*), sickness (*wówayazą, wók'uže*), and even death. The latter led to spirits pitying humans and establishing friendships or medicine-exchange relationships essential to the maintenance and perpetuation of life movement. But once such a relationship was established it entailed binding obligations. One had to live in accordance with certain rules and in a way that was pleasing to his particular spirit helper.

This is why spirits, like wakʻą́ energy in its latent state, are best conceptualized as amoral and ambiguous, contextually benevolent or malevolent in their interrelations with humans. This, along with the inherent individuality characteristic of Sioux religious belief, also explains why spirits were cursed by humans when they were ineffective, vengeful, merciless, aggressive, or believed to be the cause of misfortune, sickness, and so on and why one revered his personal spirit helper(s) and derided the spirits and beliefs of another. As Samuel Pond (1908, 405) explains, the Dakotas "did not always speak of their gods with the greatest respect, and it was uncertain how much or how little confidence some of them had in them. The writer happened to be standing with Shakopee near some painted stone gods, when he spoke of them with the utmost contempt, and of their worshippers as silly fools; but he acknowledged that he would not venture to speak so before the Dakotas, and he appeared to be a zealous worshipper of such things as long as he lived." According to Walker's (1991, 105) Lakota consultants, "Each one believes in the spirits his sect believes in, and laughs at the spirits that another sect believes in. One seeks a vision to learn what sect he must belong to."

Pond goes on to describe a trip he took with a Dakota chief. When they encamped for the night the chief "made the figure of a turtle in the earth, and prayed to it for good weather. He seemed somewhat offended when I told him that his prayers would avail nothing, and stoutly maintained that it was not a vain thing to pray to turtles for good weather" (S. Pond 1908, 405). As it turned out the weather was fair the next day, and consequently the chief was pleased by the efficacy of his prayers, which Pond begrudgingly acknowledged. At their next encampment the chief "renewed his devotions to the turtle . . . but this time the turtle failed to respond." Pond recalls, "In the night we were drenched by a cold rain. I suggested to the old man that it would be well for him to get up and call upon his god; but he was in a bad humor, and spoke very disrespectfully of turtles and declared he would be revenged on the next one he met" (S. Pond 1908, 405). Pond's narrative accentuates the fickle and contradictory nature of humankind and the emotional aspects of religious belief in general.

He concludes that "many of the Dakotas were unsettled in their minds, not being firm in their belief of all that was taught by their prophets" (S. Pond 1908, 406).

In any case, the motives of nonhuman spirit persons were not easily interpreted by humans, especially without reference to human dispositions and understandings. The doings of spirits as wakʻą́ beings were by definition often incomprehensible, mysterious, and beyond the narrow scope of human understanding and comprehension. The nineteenth-century Sioux clearly defined wakʻą́ nonhuman spirit persons by their incomprehensible, mysterious, and powerful nature, yet because of a common interiority and structure, nonhuman behavior and effects could be interpreted by medicine men or shamans who specialized in interpreting the wakʻą́ and conducted diagnostic ceremonies. According to Samuel Pond's younger brother Gideon, diagnosis was an important part of the doctoring process among the Dakotas in the mid-1800s. He writes, "The doctor ascertains the sin which has been committed, and the particular god which has been offended and inflicted the disease" (G. Pond 1889, 247). Many Sioux ceremonies involve an initial diagnostic phase, most notably yuwípi and other doctoring rituals.

Understanding the nature and morality of spirit persons as ambivalent and incomprehensible—in a word, humanlike—provides a way out of Willerslev's (2013) dilemma, namely, that animism is not taken seriously by native peoples and is basically ideology. The spirits, like wakʻą́ energy in general, are neither inherently good nor bad. They can be helpful or harmful in contexts, and this belief plays out and is manifested through concrete social interaction and experience. Familiar spirits with whom one has an established relationship are usually beneficial and more predictable. Other unknown spirits, impersonal in the sense that one has no direct phenomenological or personal experience with them, are more unpredictable and may interact with people in a more negative way, from human perspectives. This, along with inherent individualism and innovation, explains why Lakotas may joke about or with spirits and may curse one and praise another, propitiate or honor one and laugh at another. Lynd describes an inextricable maze of gods, demons, spirits, beliefs and counter-beliefs, earnest devotion and reckless skepticism, prayers, sacrifices, and sneers, winding and intermingling with one another, until a labyrinth of pantheism and skepticism results, and the Dakota, with all his infinity of deities appears a creature of irreligion. One speaks of the medicine dance with respect, while another smiles at the name—one makes a religion of the raw fish feast, while another stands by and laughs at his performance—and others, listening to the supposed revelations of the circle dance, with reverent attention, are sneered at by a class who deny *in toto* the *wakan* nature of that ceremony. (1889, 63)

While the Sioux certainly attempted to placate and influence the spirits and alter their actions through suffering (*wókakiže*), sacrifice (*waúyąpi, wóšnapi*), evoking aid or pity (*ųśika, ųśila*), and other ritual dynamics, they did not *worship* the spirits, aside from thank offerings and rites of thanksgiving (*wópʻila*) in recognition of a sickness cured, a death averted, a horse stolen, an honor or battle won, and so on. According to Walker (1917, 56), "The Oglala did not worship their deities and their ceremonials were not devotional. They considered their Gods as merely superhuman, whose aid could be invoked, or who could be pleased so that they would grant favors, or who could be displeased so that they would punish." Elaborating on this theme, Walker (1991, 45) writes, "The Oglalas were very religious, but not at all pious. They did not worship anything. By sacrifices and ceremonies they propitiated their Gods to secure their aid, or placated them to appease their anger." The nineteenth-century Sioux feared and respected the spirits and called on them for aid and protection as relatives (*wacʻékiya*), but they did not worship them in the Christian sense. Accordingly, Sioux rituals (*wakʻą wicʻóȟ'ą* or *wóecʻų*) were generally conceived of as "doings": practical, goal-oriented, teleological actions performed to get results and inextricably linked to power (DeMallie and Parks 1987, 211). Sioux ceremony was not meant to praise or worship spirit beings in the Western sense.

Ella Deloria also problematizes the notion of nature worship among the Sioux, while substantiating many of the claims made herein vis-à-vis animism and ritual dynamics: "My informants all felt that it was an error to say that the Dakotas actually worshipped rocks, trees, the four winds, and other manifestations of nature. 'They are not themselves Wakan, but the Wakan is in all things. When our people wished to pray, they selected some common tree or rock, untouched by man, and set it apart for its sacred use by painting it red. And then they addressed it, for now it was Wakan.' One man so explained it" (1998, 52).

In this way the Lakotas effectively flipped the Christian religious system, epistemology, and philosophy, an insight that sheds light on their ethos, worldview, religious belief, and ritual practice. Spirits by nature were inexplicable, mysterious, amoral, and ambiguous. Like humans, they could relate to other persons either positively (exchange, gift giving) or negatively (predation). Malevolent nonhuman interventions in the human sphere, such as bad luck, sickness, and so on, tended to provide the major impetus for ritual action. Instead of explaining the universal human problem of suffering in terms of the "chastisements of a loving father" (Riggs 1869, 93), nineteenth-century Lakotas understood suffering in terms of the active agency and intervention of ambiguous, powerful, and dangerous spirit beings. To this day many Lakota people consider spirits to be dangerous, frightening, and awesome, in the sense of horrific, incomprehensible power (Posthumus 2008–17; White Hat 2012, 84–85). When offended or angered these spirits could be spiteful, vengeful, destructive, and deadly, but ultimately their motives and actions could not be easily interpreted or understood by humans: they were wakʻą́. Highlighting the differences between humans and nonhuman spirits, Ringing Shield explains, "What a man knows is what has been done. What the spirits know is what has been done and what will be done in the future. The spirits can tell what is to be in the future. They can tell this to anyone" (in Walker 1991, 113).

This reversal of the role of nonhuman forces in human life mitigates some of the contradictions inherent in Christianity, such as the concept of original sin, atonement, the guilt associated with sin, and the perennial unanswerable question, Why do bad things happen to good people? Understanding this significant epistemological difference also explains why sacrifice was so central to ritual practice and why supplication and propitiation characterized Lakota belief and ritual much more accurately than worship. Understanding the ambivalent, contextual, relational, and sometimes antagonistic relationship between nonhuman spirits and human beings allows us to better comprehend core nineteenth-century Sioux cultural values and norms, which are essential to and embedded in religious ideology and ritual practice.

To demonstrate various ontological themes discussed herein I now turn to an examination of Lakota beliefs concerning the disembodied spirits of deceased human beings, commonly referred to as ghosts (*wanáǧi*), a common type of nonhuman spirit person encountered in the Sioux cosmos and lifeworld.

Wanáǧi 'Ghosts'

Just as stones and other nonhuman entities were known to move, speak, and interact with humans—experienced phenomenologically—so too were ghosts or the spirits of deceased humans. According to Tyon, "Dead people [*wicʻáša tʼápi*] exist among the tipis, the people believe; and on that account everyone is always afraid of the night" (in Walker 1991, 164). I have already outlined the complexity of Lakota notions of human interiority. The ghost or spirit of a deceased human is called wanáǧi or naǧí.[1] It is a disembodied, unbounded, pure interiority that maintains some semblance of the character, attributes, dispositions, intentionality, or habitus of the person, yet is no longer localized, embodied, or associated with a particular physicality (tʻącʻą́ 'body'). More specifically, the ní 'life' or niyá 'life-breath' has left the physicality, signifying the organic death of the organism, after which the spirit or spirits travel and do various things. Therefore, it is the tʻącʻą́ and the ní or niyá, the body and the soul of the body, that distinguish the living from the dead.

Some believe a living human has multiple wanáǧi: one that remains near its relatives and its grave after bodily death and another that travels the *wanáǧi tʻacʻą́ku* 'Milky Way' (literally, 'ghosts' road') toward the south on its way to the *wanáǧi tʻamákʻocʻe* 'spirit world'. Interestingly, the spirit world of the dead is apparently much like the human world of the living. The journey to the spirit world southward along the Milky Way is perilous. According to some Sioux this road splits or is bisected by a raging river bridged by a slippery log that must be crossed. An old woman sits there and judges the souls: those who are worthy proceed to the spirit world, while those who are not are pushed or fall back to the earth. The spirit world is said to be at the other end of the spirits' road, beyond the pines and the path of the winds, at the edge of the world, but no human knows exactly where it is. Some say it is in the west, some say the south. The utopian spirit world includes both human and nonhuman souls and is full of bison and other game and free of cold, hunger, work, pain, sickness, and death. It is composed of a series of ghost villages or camps (*wanáǧi wic'ót'i*), each composed of various bands (t'iyóšpaye) and families (t'iwáhe) living in spirit tipis, where the people feast and dance, producing the northern lights (*wanáǧi t'awác'ipi* 'spirits' dance') (Bushotter 1887–88, story 12; Standing Bear 2006a, 197–98; Walker 1917, 86, 132, 156, 1991, 71, 102, 116–17, 126, 141–42; Joseph Brown 1989, 29n13).[2]

According to Sword (in Walker 1991, 99), "A Lakota has a spirit that goes to the spirit world and never dies. He has other spirit-like selves. His breath of life is like a spirit. His strength is like a spirit. His influence is like a spirit. These are all spirits but when his body dies, they go to where they came from and are no more." Other Sioux see this process as a spatiotemporal transition, each person having only one wanáǧi that remains near its body, relatives, home, clothing, and other personal belongings after death for a period of time, usually four days, before transitioning to its journey south toward the spirit world (Bushotter 1887–88, story 12; Dorsey 1889a, 143). This belief explains why the Lakotas often bury the dead in their clothing or burn the clothing, belongings, and even the homes of the dead. It also substantiates the taboo against making loud noises and violent, sudden movements that disturb the atmosphere, as spirits are very sensitive to such things, and the prescription for behaving in a good and proper manner in the presence of the dead (Dorsey 1889a, 144; Fletcher 1887c). For instance, it is believed that if one acts inappropriately or engages in bad conduct in the presence of the dead within four days of the death he will be mysteriously compelled to repeat those actions throughout the rest of his life. This belief is well-documented. According to Ella Deloria, "The Dakotas firmly believed that what a person felt, thought, and did during some emotional crisis in life, became a habit supernaturally operating, almost like a spell, from which he could hardly change. Times of grief were such times. The period of a girl's passing into womanhood was for her definitely such a time" (1998, 66). Birth is another example (see V. Deloria 2009). Hence, many ceremonies involve lengthy harangues emphasizing core Lakota values. These beliefs are tied to what might be termed "supernatural retribution," the recognition of the inherent danger of the wakʻą́ and a common belief in immanent justice tied to notions of bad conduct and cause and effect: that things come back to you, and bad behavior results in bad effects later. This is an important part of the native system of logic: if you make mistakes, you pay for them (Grobsmith 1981).

Specifically, it is believed that if a person does something bad around the time of a relative's death he will be doomed to repeat it forever. Robert E. Daniels reports that a man who stole something during his mother's wake was compelled to steal for the rest of his life: "The explanation followed that anyone committing a transgression during the period between the death and the interment of a close relative would be destined to repeat the act uncontrollably for the rest of his life" (1970, 228). Elizabeth Grobsmith (1981, 66) corroborates Daniels's findings, writing that beliefs concerning the dead stem "from the Keeping of the Soul ritual. Lakota who no longer formally observe this ceremony are still cautious about the four-day period immediately following a death. One informant stated: 'You really have to be careful about what you do then. You can't do anything bad—like drink or steal—or that's what you'll be for the rest of your life.'" Many of these beliefs, embedded in an animist ontological orientation, persist today among contemporary Sioux people.

However, not every wanáǧi successfully makes it to the spirit world. For various reasons some are cast back to earth and must thereafter wander aimlessly among the living, whistling, moaning, and striking fear into the hearts and minds of the people, especially in cases of unnatural death. Sioux mythology and oral tradition are full of examples of humans interacting with ghosts. Ghosts are not always visible to the living, but sometimes they materialize in human form. When visible, they are known to dress in a particular way—usually wearing a gray blanket or a winter buffalo robe with the hair outside or dressing in the "old way"—and to hover above the ground with no feet visible to the human eye. They have been known to take human spouses and appreciate eating, drinking, smoking, and music, just as living humans do. More often, however, ghosts are audibly experienced. Whistling, moaning, and other macabre sounds are characteristic of ghosts as they interact with and are experienced by humans. Ghosts have been known to sing and speak with humans, and sometimes they whisper in people's ears, a decidedly ominous omen (Bushotter 1887–88; E. Deloria n.d.c, 50; n.d.e, 25; Dorsey 1889a, 143–50). According to Tyon, the people believe that "Ghosts bring messages" (in Walker 1991, 165).

Ghosts were feared and respected because they were known to cause trouble for the living: anxiety, fear, misfortune, sickness (physiological, psychological, psychosomatic, and spiritual), and even death. Seeing or hearing a ghost was a bad omen that could result in sickness, insanity, changes in personality, and eventually death. Ghosts were believed to visit the sick at night, prompting people to incense or smudge (wazílya) their lodges with protective cedar or some other medicine. If someone heard a ghost whistling he would leave the lodge and fire a gun to frighten it and drive it away. Seeing a ghost was also believed to cause a paralysis of the face called *wanáǧi ktépi* (literally, 'ghost killed'), known today as Bell's palsy (E. Deloria n.d.e, 25; Dorsey 1889a, 144–45; S. Pond 1908, 404; Walker 1991, 164–65). According to Dorsey (1889a, 144), "Before death the lodge is surrounded by ghosts of deceased kindred that are visible to the dying person." For all these reasons the spirits of the dead were and continue to be feared, respected, and avoided.

Yet to preemptively avert such inauspicious outcomes, and to sustain and perpetuate life movement, people propitiate, honor, and make offerings to ghosts in various ways. As Good Seat explains, "When a man dies, his *wanagi* leaves his body. It stays near it for a short time. It is well to please it while it lingers near the body. If it is not pleased, it may do some harm to someone" (in Walker 1991, 71). Speaking of the Dakotas, Samuel Pond (1908, 404–5) writes, "Many prayers were addressed to ghosts, who were never very far away, and, if the Indians did not see them, they often heard them whistle, especially in the night. . . . [The Dakotas] called frequently upon ghosts without much formality. The hunter or traveler, stopping to smoke, would fill his pipe and holding it up would say, 'Here, ghosts, take a smoke and give us a good day.'"

Clearly, the disembodied interiorities of deceased humans maintained a liking for the things enjoyed by the living.

Offerings are commonly made to ghosts, including tobacco, flesh, cloth, and various small valuables, but most frequently food is offered. The ritual known as the ghost plate is an extension or truncation of the compound ghost-keeping ceremony. To this day it is normatively performed at the outset of feasts, which are foundational elements of all Sioux ritual. Small amounts of each type of food are carefully and reverently placed on a dish, smudged (wazílya) with medicines, and then publicly prayed over by a holy man, the master of ceremonies, a veteran, or some distinguished elder. These foods, especially the choicest bits, are ceremonially fed to the ghost to honor and please it. Afterward the dish is taken outside and left in a secluded place, buried, or burned, before the feast commences. The food offerings may also be buried or burned without being placed on a plate. In this food offering to ghosts, as in many other rituals, technically nonhuman (disembodied) interiorities are addressed and cried to (wac'ékiya), ultimately as a means of placation (evoking aid or pity [ų́šila]) and honoring (ohóla, yuónihą), inducing the ghosts to intervene positively in human affairs (ókiya 'to help'), avert misfortune (wót'eȟi[ka], wakíȟtani, wóak'ip'a), and allow life movement to flow on unabated. In the offering of the ghost plate the interiority of the deceased human is addressed, as well as the interiority or life of the (animal) food represented on the plate (wamák'anaǧi 'animal spirit'; wónaǧi 'spirit of food') (Bushotter 1887–88, story 230; Fletcher 1887c, 300; Walker 1991, 71).

Fletcher describes the food offering at the outset of an Oglala ghost-keeping ceremony she witnessed at Pine Ridge in 1882. The father of the deceased "takes a bit of food from the dish with his fingers and, lifting it, says: 'We offer this food that you may help us, that we may escape ill fortune. We ask you to help us to avoid any sickness or misfortune that may lie in our path.' The offering is then dropped upon the mellowed earth [owáka, ųmáni 'altar'] and buried in it" (Fletcher 1887c, 300). Tyon gives a complementary account from the early twentieth century. When the people eat, he explains, "they always give food to the ghosts. They do it in this way. They take a little bit of food and spill it out near the fire. They say this as they do it. 'Ghosts, say for me "I will live long,"' they say. The ghosts accept it, they think. If they don't do this, the ghosts take offense, they say" (in Walker 1991, 164).[3] Eating before the ghosts are fed is a gross violation of proper conduct and a breach of taboo, causing the ghosts to become angry and punish the offender. They might cause him (or his relatives) misfortune, illness, or bad luck in love, hunting, or warfare.[4] They might cause him to drop his food before it reaches his mouth, spill water as he attempts to drink it, gash himself with a knife, or cause other injuries (Dorsey 1889a, 148).

The most lavish and complex of all ghost-related ceremonies is the *wanáǧi yuhápi* 'ghost-keeping'. Accentuating elements of what has been called contagious magic in Sioux belief,[5] Fletcher (1887c, 296) writes, "These Indians entertain the belief that after death the soul will linger near the body so long as it is preserved or any part of it kept intact, particularly if not exposed to the air. The clothing too, which was needful to the comfort of the body, partakes of the individuality of the person and the spirit will linger about these articles . . . the soul being like a shadow continually with the body and at death gradually fading away." In the ghost-keeping ceremony the physicality is dead, the ní or niyá having left or broken its life-sustaining association with the body, and so it is buried or placed on a scaffold according to custom. The interiority, however, the person, subjectivity, or intentionality, is kept and maintained, symbolized by a lock of hair cut from the deceased's head and ceremonially wrapped in a bundle.

The lock of hair and bundle, the interiority transferred into a new physicality, is referred to in Lakota as wanáǧi 'ghost, soul, spirit' as long as it contains the essence of the person. The ghost is released in the final rite of this compound ritual, a lavish feast and giveaway called the *wakíc'aǧapi*. During the wakíc'aǧapi the ghost or spirit bundle (*wanáǧi wap'áȟta*) is ceremonially opened, the interiority is ritually released, and the now-empty physicality or shell, the hair encased in the bundle, is taken out, away from human habitation, and burned or buried. Sometimes the mother of the deceased keeps the lock of hair. The deceased is supposed to retain his usual place in the household circle, his interiority continuing to be present, until this final releasing of the spirit, which is now free to depart and make its journey to the spirit world. Throughout the ritual there is much weeping and feasting, and the relatives of the deceased honor the ghost by giving away to the point of impoverishing themselves (Bushotter 1887–88, story 230; Dorsey 1889a, 143–47; Fletcher 1887c).

Riggs's (1869, 466–67) discussion of the Dakota Sounding Cloud's sun dance song supports this equation of hair with the interiority or soul. In the song, which embodies the human-nonhuman communication sought in the sun dance, "four souls" are equated with four scalps and/or four enemies.[6] The significance of hair in Sioux magico-ritual belief and practice is pervasive, as Ella Deloria's work suggests. The Lakotas normatively believed that hair was sacred, intimately connected to the life and identity of a person. The Lakotas believed that the little white ball or bulb at the root of the hair follicle was "part of the actually living individual from whom the hair was extracted." A similar dynamic operates in the Dakota medicine dance (wakʻą́ wacʻípi), in which new members are ritually gifted a lock of hair of their deceased predecessor. They reverently keep this hair in their sacred bundle and in many ways take on the identity of the individual they replace (E. Deloria n.d.c, 33).

For these reasons, explains Ella Deloria (n.d.e, 11–12), "The Dakotas were religiously careful not to leave a single strand of hair lying about." Beliefs concerning hair and dynamics of what has been referred to as contagious magic underpin Sioux notions of sorcery/witchcraft. Apparently mice were the model of and for this type of nefarious hair magic. If a mouse were to obtain a specimen of someone's hair it might use it in a nest and otherwise abuse or defile it, sending poison or bad medicine through the vacant root from whence the hair came, causing the victim to experience mysterious headaches and nosebleeds. For this reason, "women always carefully wrapped their combings into a ring on their finger and saved it till one day they burned the entire collection and then started in again" (E. Deloria n.d.e, 12). A similar dynamic operates in what Deloria (n.d.e, 12–14) calls wicʻápʻehį yužų́pi 'they pull out the human hair', a Lakota sorcery/witchcraft practice involving the ritual extraction of hair from a victim at a distance via the assistance of the practitioner's helper spirit, leading to the same symptoms, namely, headaches and nosebleeds.[7] If left unresolved this practice resulted in the death of the victim, although usually the inflicting party had a change of heart and intervened to preserve the victim's life.

Similar beliefs vis-à-vis interiorities also hold in reference to images and the plastic arts. Many Sioux refused to allow their portrait to be painted or picture taken because of a widespread and persistent belief that their spirit (wanáǧi) would remain in the image instead of traveling to the spirit world after the death of the body (Dorsey 1894, 484; M. Eastman 1995, 12). Camped at the mouth of the Teton River in the 1830s, artist George Catlin painted the portrait of Lone Horn, a chief of the Minneconjou Lakotas. Catlin's narrative demonstrates Sioux beliefs concerning images and contagious magic, important themes in ritual as well. He writes, "After the exhibition of this chief's picture, there was much excitement in the village about it; the doctors generally took a decided and noisy stand against the operations of my brush; haranguing the populace, and predicting bad luck, and premature death, to all who submitted to so strange and unaccountable an operation!" (Catlin 1973, 1:248). Noticing how the Sioux carefully guarded their portraits, Catlin was puzzled until he "learned that it was owing to their superstitious notion, that there may be life to a certain extent in the picture; and that if harm or violence be done to it, it may in some mysterious way, affect their health or do them other injury" (1973, 1:255).

Speaking of the ghost-keeping ceremony, Deloria writes,

> My informant said, "like a picture" the hair of the dead was kept. That means something very special in Dakota. The likeness of the dead is or was believed to have something of the essence of the person about it. To look at a dead person's picture was a very solemn act.
>
> In my Teton material I have "pictures", representations, made of the personalities of the dead for whom a ghost keeping ceremony was held. The women were represented with a certain diagrammatic drawing on an oblong piece of skin tacked to a stick, and the stick was nailed into the ground in the ghost-lodge. The men by another. But they did not look like the faces of the dead; they were in no sense an attempt to represent the faces. It was enough that they represented the dead and to that extent, those representations were treated with awe and reverence, quite as much as if the dead were lying in the tipi.

This idea is prevalent. When I was a small child, I was visiting my grandmother and grandfather on the Yankton [Reservation] when there was a "ghost feast" being held at the home immediately south of us.

My grandma took me with her. The women sat in a half circle, the men completed it on the other side. I sat by my grandma a while, but then I went off to play with the other children. I suppose speeches and give-aways went on, but it was only when we heard one person cry; and then another and another in pretty regular succession, until the volume of wailing increased enough to bring us in, that I tried to find the reason.

The girl had been dead over a year. I don't think they really kept her hair; it was not being done among the Christian Dakotas which these were.

Nevertheless, I saw that the wailing was evoked by the crayon image of the dead girl, which someone was showing to each seated woman. And immediately she looked at it a moment, she murmured perhaps something like, "Ah, my grandchild!—or Ah! My niece!" and then she would pull her shawl up over her head and begin to wail aloud. . . . To me it was only a picture; but to the people it was of the essence of the girl herself. And several women got up and gave away certain fine belongings, "because they could not allow the day to go unmarked on which they had 'seen' her again." (E. Deloria n.d.c, 31–33)

Clearly, there was a strong belief in the connection or continuity between the hair, clothes, weapons, other significant or distinctive objects, images or representations of a deceased human (or of a nonhuman spirit person), and so on and that person's personality, subjectivity, or interiority. This insight sheds light on other dynamics of Sioux belief and ritual explored in the following chapters, particularly in reference to ceremonial bundles, offerings and sacrifices, and *káǧapi*, ceremonial (re)enactments of vision experiences and sacred imitations of nonhuman spirit persons publicly performed before the people. These connections are apparent and reoccur with great frequency in the domains of Sioux mythology, dreams and visions, and ritual.

CHAPTER 6

Nonhuman Persons in Lakota Mythology

The nineteenth-century Sioux lived in a universe (wamákʿognaka) that was alive, peopled by various human and nonhuman persons and collectives (oyáte), and they operated according to an interpretive method based on the principle of relatedness. Experience, coupled with this interpretive schema, fueled the practical belief that other virtual dimensions of life—mythology, dreams and visions, and ceremony—were part of an organic whole, the cumulative experiences of the self and collective, and not distinct from other experiences, times, and places (see V. Deloria 1999, 38–39). In a very real sense the people, the "natural world," and the "supernatural world" were one: there was no demarcation of culture, nature, and supernature in terms of practical individual and collective experience. A virtual domain of key importance was mythology. Speaking of the Berens River Ojibwes, Hallowell explains, "The world of myth is not categorically distinct from the world as experienced by human beings in everyday life. In the latter, as well as the former, no sharp lines can be drawn dividing living beings of the animate class because metamorphosis is possible. In outward manifestation neither animal nor human characteristics define categorical differences in the core of being. And, even aside from metamorphosis, we find that in everyday life interaction with nonhuman entities of the animate class are only intelligible on the assumption that they possess some of the attributes of 'persons'" (1960, 35).

Mythical virtuality is a dimension of the real or actuality. For nineteenth-century Lakotas the space/time of myth was not separate or demarcated from actuality or lived, existential, everyday realities, it was simply different. Myth was a phantasmagoric, imaginal space, a plane of immanence, potentiality, and emergence.[1] It was a technology for the slowing down and retooling of chaotic actuality, for the direct and immediate entrance into the compositional dynamics or processes of reality and its formation, referred to by Kapferer as the descent into the virtual (Kapferer 2006b, 673–74). Mythical virtuality was akin to a beneficial cognitive simulation and had a very real (re)generative, (re)creative, and (re)constitutive effect on the dynamics of cosmological, social, and personal construction in actuality. It was not, however, a model, ideality, or representation of ordinary or quotidian realities.

Elaine Jahner describes the powerful, transformative, phantasmagoric space of the Lakota mythical realm and its potential to alter actuality. Speaking of the Oglala storytellers with whom Walker collaborated around the turn of the twentieth century, Jahner (in Walker 2006, xxiii) writes, "Their presentations of traditional tales have genuine psychological power attained through effective and subtle realizations of traditional motifs, and their creative dramatizations of the meanings of beliefs are important examples of imaginative oral literature." The "genuine psychological power" noted by Jahner is related to virtual dynamics and the potential to alter the ontological ground of being underpinning actuality. Sebastian Braun (2013, 17) also emphasizes the transformational aspects of American Indian storytelling.

In most cases Hallowell's insights into Ojibwe ontology obtain well for the nineteenth-century Sioux. One of the major sources of information about nonhuman persons in the Lakota cosmos is mythology. Myths, explains Hallowell, "are not fiction. On the contrary, they narrate the past activities of well-known other-than-human persons who are their chief characters" (Hallowell 1966, 278). This distinction between mythology or folklore and fiction is equally significant among the Lakotas, as Ella Deloria discusses in a letter to Franz Boas (Deloria to Boas, February 24, 1938, in Deloria 1927, B.B. 61; see also Jahner in Walker 2006, 22–23).

In traditional Lakota society myths were told in the winter camps during long winter evenings by a narrator who utilized various dramatic performance techniques, such as gesture, voice, mimicry, flow, and so on (for more on Plains sign and body language, see Clark 1982; Farnell 1995). The telling of a myth as part of oral tradition was in fact a kind of invocation of the nonhuman characters involved. These culturally central personages are conventionally referred to as "the spirits" or, using kinship terms, as grandfather (t'ųkášila) or grandmother (ųcí), attesting both to their psychological and ontological status as persons and to their incorporation within the boundaries of the Lakota kinship system. Myths and the nonhuman persons they evoke are beings-alive, and in motivation and behavior these nonhumans are similar to human beings. Through the performance of oral narrative children growing up in traditional Sioux society became extremely familiar with their nonhuman grandfathers and grandmothers. Sioux children were reared hearing about, hearing, interacting with, and otherwise existentially *experiencing* various nonhuman personages through the oral tradition, the narration of myth, dreams, and so on. As interaction between humans and nonhumans continued throughout the life cycle, the latter became deeper entrenched as familiar subjective agents in everyday life. In this way epistemic trust developed between Sioux individuals and nonhuman persons, the trust required for social learning to take place between two entities, allowing for relationship and the exchange of knowledge and medicine. The individuality and personality of nonhuman persons was reinforced through performance. Hence, the reality of these personages did not depend on conceptualization alone but was strongly reinforced by actual perceptual and phenomenological experience (see Hallowell 1960, 30; 1966, 278–79; compare to Lévi-Strauss 1963, 206–31).[2] In this way the performance of mythological narratives was a descent into the virtual, plugging individuals and communities into the ontological ground of being, providing them with direct access to the compositional dynamics of actuality, and allowing for its adjustment.

Here I am referring to ohúkaką, which may be conceptualized as folktales, myths, or the histories of nonhuman persons, the oldest and most complex genre of traditional Lakota tales.[3] Jahner describes Ella Deloria's (1932, ix–x) classification system of Lakota narrative genres.

Ohúkaką were subdivided into two groups, writes Jahner: "The first group of *ohunkakan* are situated in a mythic past when the world as we know it was still in process of formation; the second group involve more recent but still amazing events" (in Walker 2006, 25). According to Ella Deloria, the ohúkaką are

> the best known, oftenest repeated, and farthest removed from the events of everyday life of the Dakota people. They are the real *ohunkakan*. To our minds, they are a sort of hang-over, so to speak, from a very, very remote past, from a different age, even from an order of beings different from ourselves. These tales, in which generally some mythological character like Iktomi, Iya, the Crazy Bull, the Witch, or Waziya (the Cold), takes part together with human beings, are part of the common literary stock of the people. Constant allusion is made to them; similes are drawn from them which every intelligent adult is sure to understand. (1932, x)

Deloria (1932, x) emphasizes that the purpose of the ohúkaką was "to amuse and entertain, but not to be believed," but as Jahner notes, "belief did affect these tales. People made constant allusions to them and drew similes from them because they told of an order of existence that provided a basis for interpreting the present one" (in Walker 2006, 26). As one of Deloria's Lakota consultants in the late 1930s noted, "Doubtless those stories were our people's folktales before the white man appeared; and our people believed in them in those early days" (Deloria to Boas, May 12, 1939, in E. Deloria 1927, B.B. 61). But Deloria's statement as to the truth value of Lakota mythology seems like a rationalization for the benefit of a largely non-Lakota audience. Myth in general tends to express eternal truths in the form of symbolic themes and metaphors rather than "historical truth" in the Western sense. Myth and other virtual realities have real ontological import in actuality.

Hallowell describes a similar rationalization process among Ojibwes attempting to explain to outsiders the "bearwalk," in which a human temporarily transforms into a bear: "All such statements, of course, imply a skeptical attitude towards metamorphosis. They are rationalizations advanced by individuals who are attempting to reconcile Ojibwe beliefs and observation with the disbelief encountered in their relations with the whites" (1960, 37).[4] As DeMallie notes, "Insiders' perspectives tell the story of the past according to perceived cultural dynamics that invariably differ from those of western historians; they are filled with concrete exhibitions of supernatural power that shape and motivate the course of events" (1993, 524).

Sioux ohúkaką dramatically and vividly depict the exploits of a common stock of nonhuman personages. For the most part the characters in Lakota myth are regarded as living entities who have existed since time immemorial. These are the *wak'ápi* (spirits): wak'ą́ persons who have no birth or death and yet tend to behave like humans (cf. Hallowell 1960, 27). As Finger (in Walker 1917, 156) explains, "Anything that has a birth will have a death. The *Wakan* were not born and they will not die." Included in this group are the mythical figures Iktómi 'Spider, Trickster', Wí 'Sun', Táku Škąšką́ 'Sky, Moving Spirit', Íyą 'Rock', Mak'á 'Earth', T'áté 'Wind', the T'atúye Tópa 'Four Winds', Yumní 'Whirlwind', Wakį́yą 'Thunderbird', Hąwí 'Moon', Wazíya 'Old Man, the Wizard', Wakąka 'Old Woman, the Witch', Anúgite, Wíyą Nųpápika 'Double Woman', Íyą Hokšíla 'Stone Boy', Wé Hokšíla 'Blood-Clot Boy', Íya 'Giant Eater, Cannibal', Gnaškį́yą 'Crazy Buffalo', Ųktéȟi 'Water Monster', and so on. Also various animal spirits figure prominently in Lakota mythology, such as Hunúp or Mat'ó 'Bear', T'at'ą́ka 'Buffalo Bull', Heȟáka 'Elk', Šųgmánitut'ąka 'Wolf', and so on. These animal spirits are herein designated with initial capital letters to indicate that they were considered the platonic, representative master spirits or "chiefs" of important game animals (oyáte, or collectives) and other flora and fauna in the Plains environment, usually tied to subsistence patterns (Densmore 2001, 174; Jahner in Walker 2006, 30–33; Walker 1917, 91, 179). Finally, the spirits of deceased human beings (wanáǧi 'ghosts') also appear frequently in Lakota mythology.

There is some debate as to whether or not natural phenomena were commonly personified or anthropomorphized in Lakota mythology, which speaks to current discussions in ontological approaches in anthropology.[5] According to Walker, the Oglalas "attributed to natural phenomena personalities and God-like qualities" (2006, 4). However, throughout her investigation of the Walker material in the 1930s Ella Deloria found this alleged anthropomorphism problematic and difficult to corroborate. According to Deloria, despite selective anthropomorphism of various mythical personages, many Lakotas objected to the personification of natural phenomena in Walker's myths. For instance, Edgar Fire Thunder tells Deloria, "We had tales treating of *Ikto, Iya*, the Owl Maker, the cold wizard, the old woman or witch, coyote, and these were personified as humans and besides them there was nothing" (in E. Deloria 1937). Asa Ten Fingers, rumored to be the son or grandson of Walker's exceptionally important consultant Finger, states, "I have never heard anyone likening the sun and stars to people and telling their acts" (in E. Deloria 1937). In any case, it is clear that from Lakota perspectives being a person did not necessarily imply being human. Nonhuman mythical personages certainly had distinct personalities and dispositions as conscious subjectivities capable of social interaction and relationship. But personhood transcended humanity.

Complicating the matter is the frequency of transformation in Sioux mythology (M. Beckwith 1930; E. Deloria 1932; Walker 1917, 2006; Wissler 1907a, 1907b). As Hallowell (1960, 35) notes, "Metamorphosis occurs with considerable frequency in the myths where other-than-human persons change their form." The realms of mythology, dreams and visions, and ritual were the domains of transformation par excellence, and there are strong generative relations between these virtual realities and religious belief in general (Jahner in Walker 2006, 26). Nearly all the characters in Lakota ohúkaką, human and nonhuman alike, were capable of transforming their physicalities while maintaining an enduring interiority. This meant that in practical everyday experience any life-form could in fact be a wakʻą́ nonhuman person deserving of respect and honor and capable of relationship and bestowing medicine, knowledge, or power.

Human beings, often those who have or acquire mysterious wakʻą́ power and abilities, such as Tʻokáhe 'First Man' and various *wicʻáša wakʻą́* 'holy men', *ȟmúǧa wicʻáša* 'sorcerers or wizards', and *ȟmúǧa wíyą* 'witches', also appear in Lakota mythical narratives. Ohúkaką generally feature two major types of protagonists: those miraculously born, such as Stone Boy, Blood-Clot-Boy, and White-Plume-Boy, and those poor and ragged types who gradually rise to prominence and tribal power through the help of their grandmother's spiritual powers or medicine and teachings, such as Pʽiyá (Jahner in Walker 2006, 106). The mythical personages of Iktómi, the trickster figure most frequently encountered in human form or as a spider or coyote, and Ptesą́wį 'White Buffalo Woman', also known as Wóȟpe 'the Beautiful Woman', the intermediary and bringer of the *cʽanų́pa wakʽą́* 'sacred pipe', are perhaps the most common characters peopling Lakota mythology.

Through an examination of some common Lakota myths and mythical personages and themes I shall now illustrate various aspects of new animist perspectives, utilizing insights from Hallowell, Descola, and others. Mythical virtuality provides vital avenues for human social interaction with powerful nonhuman persons. The descent into the virtual reality of myth to establish or renew human-nonhuman relationships, recharge wakʽą́ power or energy stores, and retool and reset the compositional structurating dynamics of cosmological, social, and psychological construction reinforces the ontological import of mythical virtuality in the midst of life's processes and actuality.

As a point of departure it is useful to recall that the foundation of much Sioux mythology and creation stories involves an original state of undifferentiation between humans and animals, a virtually universal American Indian notion noted by Viveiros de Castro (1998, 471). In particular, recall that most Lakota creation stories tell of a chthonic origin in which the Lakota people were undifferentiated from their relatives, the Buffalo People (Pté Oyáte). It was only after the human emergence onto the earth's surface that the two nations (oyáte) were distinguished and their divergent physicalities crystalized (Walker 1991, 229–30). Recall that the Buffalo People, like other nonhuman persons in Sioux culture, had the capacity to transform their physicalities. According to Walker's (1917, 91) Oglala consultants, the Buffalo People "have the power to transmogrify and may appear on the world as animals or as of mankind, and may mingle with the Lakota and become their spouses. They can transmogrify their spouses and take them to the regions under the world." The notion that nonhumans can transform their physicality, marry, and communicate and fornicate with humans is common in Lakota mythology (Wissler 1907a, 1907b).

The Four Winds are conceptualized as brothers, the sons of the Wind (Tʻaté). One myth articulates how they established the four directions of the universe, defining the Lakota cosmos in terms of their dwelling places. The Four Winds established both time and space and act as intermediaries between the people and the spirits. Understanding the importance of the Four Winds and the related four directions is part of the foundational unity in thought that prevails in the domains of Lakota mythology, dreams and visions, and ritual (Walker 1917, 2006; cf. Hallowell 1966, 275–76). The story of the Four Winds illustrates the ontological import of mythical virtuality in actuality, as do other familiar tales, most of which teach some lesson that explains distinctive features of the natural environment or of human or animal behavior, social organization, or physiology (Wissler 1907a, 130).

The Thunder Birds (Wakíyą 'Flying Ones') of the west represent another important personage and collective in Sioux mythical virtuality. Powerful and terrifying creator/destroyer figures, the glance of the Wakíyą is lightning and its voice thunder. They dwell in a nest atop a high mountain in the west. Unfortunate individuals who dream of the Thunder Birds live in constant fear of being struck by lightning until they publicly (re)enact their vision through the performance of the *heyókʻa wózepi*. These individuals are obliged to act as *heyókʻa*, living an antinatural lifestyle until various vision obligations are met, lifting the prescribed contrary behavior patterns (Dorsey 1894, 441–43).

The Wakíyą live and fly in the firmament and are usually veiled from human sight by thick storm clouds. They are primarily conceived as avian in form, but their physicality is not constant, and sometimes they manifest themselves in human form (Dorsey 1894, 441–42; cf. Hallowell 1966, 276). As Dorsey (1894, 441) explains, "By some of the wakan men it is said that there are four varieties of the form of their external manifestation [physicality]. In essence [interiority], however they are but one." This illustrates the ethnometaphysical core of Lakota conceptions of being: outward appearance or physicality, like clothing, is ephemeral. Although the Wakíyą, like other nonhuman persons, have distinctive attributes of their own, they have the same basic, enduring interiority as human persons. However, this inner essence is usually inaccessible to visual perception: what can be perceived visually by humans is only the aspect of being that has manifest form or, in other words, the physicality (compare to Hallowell 1966, 276).

Dorsey's words also illustrate another common Lakota theosophical position, namely, that multiple disparate forms or essences are in actuality hypostases of one singular underlying essence or interiority (see Walker 1991, 35, 73, 95, 98). According to Little Wound (in Walker 1991, 70), "*Wakan Tanka* are many. But they are all the same as one." Sword reiterates this common belief, explaining, "*Wakan Tanka* is like sixteen different persons; but each person is *kan*. Therefore, they are all only the same as one" (in Walker 1917, 153). Sword also observes, "There are many kinds of spirits (*nagipi*). All the spirits of one kind are the same as one spirit" (in Walker 1991, 98).

Recall that the Wakíyą Oyáte 'Thunder Bird Nation' was constantly at war with the Uktéȟi Oyáte 'Water Monster/Water Serpent Nation', another personage and collective common in Sioux culture.[6] Dorsey (1894, 442) writes, "The Thunderers are represented as cruel and destructive in disposition. They are ever on the war path. A mortal hatred exists between them and the family of the Unkteȟi. Neither has power to resist the tonwan [*tųwą́* 'emitted potency'] of the other if it strikes him. Their attacks are never open, and neither is safe except he eludes the vigilance of the other. The Wakinyan, in turn, are often surprised and killed by the Unkteȟi. Many stories are told of the combats of these gods." The Thunder Birds are associated with warfare and the power to destroy life. They gave the Lakotas their war implements and paints with which they can render themselves invulnerable to their enemies. Through these interactions human-nonhuman entanglements (Hodder 2011, 2012, 2014) are established—relationships of dependency and exchange characterized by reciprocal duties, obligations, and rights. Through the exchange of physical objects a convergence of interiorities is achieved. Sioux mythology credits the Thunder Birds, as creative nonhuman persons, with the creation of wild rice and bringing life-giving and life-sustaining rain, which purifies the earth (Dorsey 1894, 441–43).

The Thunder Bird Nation figures prominently in all three of the major virtual domains of Sioux life. Many offerings and sacrifices are made to propitiate and honor the Wakíyą and to avert their wrath. The social organization of the Thunder Birds is apparently similar to that of human beings, as explained by the Belgian Jesuit priest Pierre-Jean De Smet, whose missionary work took him through Sioux territory around 1840. Among the Sioux, writes De Smet, "the thunder is an enormous bird, and . . . the muffled sound of the distant thunder is caused by a countless number of young (thunder) birds. The great bird, they say, gives the first sound, and the young ones repeat it; this is the cause of the reverberations. The Sioux declare that the young thunderers do all the mischief, like giddy youth who will not listen to good advice; but the old thunderer or big bird is wise and excellent; he never kills or injures any one" (in Dorsey 1894, 443).

Animals also figure prominently in Sioux mythology. While they are conceived as older and more knowledgeable and powerful than human beings, capable of transformation and bestowing medicine, as we have seen they also have various traits in common with humans. Animal collectives live in much the same way as humans do, dwelling in villages, having families and kinship structures, courting, marrying and having children, dancing, feasting, going to war against other tribe-species, participating in ceremonial practices, and so on.

Dorsey (1894, 478–79; 1889b, 133–34) discusses instances of wolf-human interaction in Lakota mythology. In one example a wolf pities a human encountered in the wilderness, showing him the way to his camp, where the human is received and adopted into the wolf collective (oyáte). Thereafter, explains Dorsey (1889b, 133), "This man always remembered the wolf as a kind animal, and when he killed any game, he threw a portion outside of the camp, as an offering to the wolf." Such interactions and intersubjective experiences entangled humans and non-humans in relationships of dependency, exchange, and mutual respect and illustrate an interspecies adherence to common moral dictums. These entanglements figured in everyday realities, as illustrated by the man being moved to observe elements of animal ceremonialism, offering meat to honor the wolf and recognize the wolf's kindness, generosity, and kin relationship. Wolves and other nonhuman persons understood and participated in the underlying, unquestioned fabric of Lakota life and culture. They were appealed to and moved by pity, they spoke to humans, sang songs, knew and were skilled in certain wak'ą́ arts, and had special gifts and attributes.

Wolves, in particular, were associated with predation: destructive yet necessary male pursuits such as hunting and warfare. Wolves were known to be able to mysteriously alter or control the weather, causing wind and fog or mist, known as "a wolf's day," especially desirable by war parties and on horse-stealing expeditions (Wissler 1912, 90–91). In one myth a man happens upon a wolf den in the wilderness. When he digs into it to get the pups, the mother wolf comes barking. "Pity my children," she says to the man, who pays no attention to her. The mother runs for her husband, who arrives and sings a beautiful song, "O man, pity my children, and I will instruct you in one of my arts." At the end of the song the wolf howls, causing a fog. When the wolf howls a second time the fog disappears. The man, realizing the wolf has "mysterious gifts," then tears up his red blanket into strips and adorns the wolf pups with them, painting and honoring them, and returns them to their den. The grateful father wolf then agrees to thereafter accompany the man to war and bring whatever he desires to pass. The wolf becomes the friend and spiritual guide of the man in actuality, divining the outcome of war expeditions and sharing extraordinary powers (Dorsey 1894, 478–79). There are many examples of human-animal interaction in Sioux mythology and oral narrative. I have examined wolves as a case study, but many other animals figure prominently as well, including buffalo, bear, elk, deer, horses, and so on.

Another central personage in Lakota mythology is Ptesą́wį 'White Buffalo Woman'. The very origin of the Lakotas as an oyáte is related in the story of the gift of the sacred pipe, which provided the foundation for culture and society. In this story, during a time of famine when the buffalo were scarce, a nonhuman spirit person in the form of a beautiful woman appeared to the Lakota carrying a bundle containing the first pipe, the sacred buffalo calf pipe, sent to the Lakotas by the spirits as a means of prayer. Ptesą́wį was the intermediary between the people and the spirits, the humans and the nonhumans. The bringing of the pipe established (or reestablished) kinship between the buffalo and the Lakotas, so that when the people smoked the pipe the spirits would hear their prayers and send buffalo. Ptesą́wį also taught the people the principles of the Lakʿól wicʿóȟʾą 'Lakota way of life', including the sacred rituals. Entrusting the pipe to a designated keeper, Ptesą́wį left the people, transforming into a white buffalo cow before disappearing over the horizon (Black Elk in DeMallie 1984, 283–85; DeMallie 2001, 799–801; Lone Man in Densmore 2001, 63–67; Finger and Tyon in Walker 1991, 109–12, 148–50).

The story of Ptesą́wį and the gift of the sacred pipe illustrates a number of central themes related to new animism and Sioux ethnometaphysics. White Buffalo Woman, a nonhuman person capable of bodily transformation, establishes relationship between human and nonhuman collectives through the bestowal of a sacred object. The sacred pipe entangles the people in a relationship of dependency and exchange with the spirits, without which they could not survive and life movement would cease. The personality of White Buffalo Woman continues to be reinforced through phenomenological experience, as she is personified and her role (re)enacted at a crucial moment in the annual sun dance ceremonies of various contemporary Lakota ritual groups. The rituals taught by Ptesą́wį continue into the present, illustrating the interplay and ontological import of mythical virtuality vis-à-vis actuality.

Finally, the pipe itself is a key symbol in Sioux culture that functions to connect interiorities. Through communal prayer with the pipe humans can link their interiorities with those of other humans and nonhumans. The pipe is the basis of kinship, belief, and ceremony, and through it the minds, wills, spirits, or interiorities of persons are soothed and united, relating all beings-alive in the sacred hoop of existence (Sword in Walker 1991, 81). As Sword explains, "The spirit in the smoke [of the pipe] will soothe the spirits of all who thus smoke together and all will be as friends and all think alike. When the Lakota smoke in this manner, it is like when the Christians take communion. It is smoking in communion" (in Walker 1991, 83).

According to Walker (1917, 70, 136; 1991, 219), smoking the pipe ceremonially causes the potency of the pipe to harmonize the spirits of the participants, of both the invokers and the invoked, causing them to be as relatives. This is because the t'ų́ (spiritual essence, emitted potency) of Ptesą́wį, the mediator, is in the smoke of the pipe. Ceremonial communal smoking also predisposes the spirits in the people's favor, causing them to look upon a ritual favorably. As Sword explains, "The pipe is used because the smoke from the pipe smoked in communion has the potency of the feminine god who mediates between godkind and mankind, and propitiates the godkind" (in Walker 1917, 157). Communally smoking the pipe in the proper manner focused the will of the people, narrowing it down to one sacred center in the now or present continuous, framing a ritual space as the very center of the universe (E. Deloria n.d.f, 3). According to Vine Deloria, "In many Sioux practices, we can see similar experiences in which the entire universe is present in its fullest dimensions — and yet simultaneously concentrated into a single point" (2009, 86).

Through the medium of the pipe the Sioux could commune with the nonhuman spirit persons in the cosmos, uniting their interiorities in a gnosis-like mystical union, and learn their will, which was then actualized in everyday life, providing knowledge, medicine, power, inspiration, and direction. As Walker explains, this was a central focus of Lakota religious belief and practice: "The sacred mysteries of the Oglala holy men were certain rites to be done which would impart to them superhuman powers and enable them to hold communion with their deities and speak their will and by the aid of consecrated fetishes to do miraculous things" (Walker 1991, 46). The pipe, given to the people by Ptesą́wį, a nonhuman person and mythical character with real ontological import, operated as a conduit between subjectivities, a sacred center through which human and nonhuman interiorities could be united, and the ultimate symbol of kinship and relatedness. Many of the central themes and symbols relating to mythology obtain well in the next Sioux domain I shall explore, namely the realm of dreams and visions.

CHAPTER 7

Nonhuman Persons in Lakota Dreams and Visions

Like the Ojibwes, and many other Native American tribes, the Sioux were and are a dream-conscious people and firm believers in the prophetic nature of dreams as signs and omens (P. Beckwith 1889, 250; Black Elk in DeMallie 1984; Densmore 2001; C. Eastman 1971; M. Eastman 1995, 55–61; McFatridge 1937; Walker 1991). "Among all the superstitions," Tabeau wrote in the early nineteenth century, "confidence in dreams is most credited" (Tabeau 1939, 191). Among the Sioux, explains Vine Deloria (2009, 167), "dreams are critical to understanding cosmology, space and time, family structure, and relations with animals and the non-human world." Dreams and visions were key avenues for social interaction with nonhuman spirit persons, through whom humans acquired knowledge (wóslolye) and power (wówašʼake) in the form of medicine (pʻežúta). Through dreams and visions reciprocal exchange relationships and entanglements of dependency between human and nonhuman persons were established and renewed. According to Brave Buffalo, a Stone dreamer and prominent medicine man from Standing Rock Reservation interviewed in the early twentieth century by Densmore (2001, 207), dreams of animals were particularly desirable among the Sioux:

> I have noticed in my life that all men have a liking for some special animal, tree, plant, or spot of earth. If men would pay more attention

to these preferences and seek what is best to do in order to make themselves worthy of that toward which they are so attracted, they might have dreams which would purify their lives. Let a man decide upon his favorite animal and make a study of it, learning its innocent ways. Let him learn to understand its sounds and motions. The animals want to communicate with man, but Wakaŋ'taŋka does not intend they shall do so directly—man must do the greater part in securing an understanding. (Brave Buffalo in Densmore 2001, 172)

Experiences in dreams and visions were not demarcated but were continuous with the other accumulated experiences of the self and the collective. The secret to establishing interspecies relationships, writes Deloria, was "to regard dreams as having an equal status to that of the waking observations and to act on the basis that dreams were an important source of reliable information. A good bit of the animal relationship, then, originated in dreams in which the human was expected to obey the messages they received. The men and women who had received special consideration from the birds and animals were called 'dreamers,' which meant that they could call upon these animals for assistance" (V. Deloria 2009, 125–26). In a similar vein, but speaking of the Berens River Ojibwes, Hallowell (1960, 40) explains, "Self-related experience of the most personal and vital kind includes what is seen, heard, and felt in dreams. Although there is no lack of discrimination between the experiences of the self when awake and when dreaming, both sets of experiences are equally self-related. . . . And, far from being of subordinate importance, such experiences are for them often of more vital importance than the events of daily waking life." Hence there is continuity in terms of virtual domains and actuality and a mutually constituting relationship between the two.

Speaking of the Dakotas and describing the imaginal space/time of dreams and visions, Samuel Pond (1908, 428) writes, "In speaking of a past state of existence, they invariably used the word which signifies to dream, which might imply that the pre-existence was imaginary rather than real." In many respects the virtual reality of dreams and visions was privileged, seen as more real, vital, and significant than actuality.

Interiority trumps physicality as virtuality trumps actuality (E. Deloria n.d.g, 57; see Deleuze 1988, 55). Things that were "as clear as in a vision" stayed on the people's minds for all time, as Ella Deloria (n.d.b, 29) explains: "This is quite characteristic; not the actual physical sight of a thing, but the thing seen in a dream or in a vision after fasting, is taken as being most vivid and lasting and real to them." Deloria highlights both the phantasmagoric space of dreams and visions and the privileging of interiority over physicality in terms of identity and selfhood. Similarly, in the mid-twentieth century Black Elk said, "it is very often during sleep that the most powerful visions come to us; they are not merely dreams, for they are much more real and powerful and do not come from ourselves, but from *Wakan-Tanka*" (Black Elk in Joseph Brown 1989, 59). According to Joseph Brown, "In American Indian cultures the vision experience served in an especially forceful manner to render transparent to the individual some facet of the phenomenal world, revealing aspects of a spiritual world of greater reality underlying this world of appearances" (2007, 61–62). Discussing similar beliefs among the Ojibwes and highlighting the role of phenomenology, Hallowell writes, "The cultural emphasis given to dream experience helps to unify the world of the self through *experience*" (1955, 181; emphasis in original).

Dreams and visions were a major impetus for ritual, especially the types referred to as *lowápi* 'to sing' and *káǧa* 'to make' (Fletcher 1887a; Lynd 1889, 170; Neill 1890, 233–37; see Powers 1986, 106–9). Obligations conferred in dreams were binding, and disregarding such obligations was considered bad conduct (wówaȟtani), tantamount to disregarding and denigrating kinship and one's role in an ordered, living cosmos. Such disregard flew in the face of Lakota social and cultural values and was sure to incur disaster, often in the form of a stroke of lightning or some other catastrophe. According to Sword (in Walker 1991, 79), "When one receives a communication in a vision he should be governed by it, for otherwise *Wakan Tanka* will bring misfortune upon him."

The first step toward actualizing the virtual potentiality of a dream or vision involved "telling" or describing the vision in great detail to a medicine man, who aided in the sacred dream's interpretation. This was referred to as *hąblóglaka*. Next the vision was announced to the tribe through its public (re)enactment in a ceremony called a káğa 'to make, imitate, impersonate, (re)enact'. In such ceremonies every detail of the vision had to be scrupulously and faithfully reproduced, from the painting and regalia of vision personages to songs conferred and actions performed (E. Deloria 1998; V. Deloria 1999, 226–28; 2009, 194; Densmore 2001, 157).

Speaking of the Dakotas, E. D. Neill (1890, 233) writes, "They believe, same as do all other tribes, that their manitou [read wak'ą́, or spirit guardian] shows to the imagination everything they see in dreams, which they carry out exactly, believing they would die if they failed." In describing songs learned in visions the term used by the Lakotas is *hó uk'íya* 'to receive, learn a song; to call out to someone, to send a voice to someone' (Powers 1986, 52).[1] According to Vine Deloria, "a person who hears a voice responds through ceremonial means. He or she then receives special powers and is set aside from the rest of the tribe because of the ability to perform certain functions—although always in cooperation with the spirits—which could not otherwise be performed solely by human beings" (2009, 154).

Dreams and Visions among the Sioux

Among the Sioux dreams and visions had a real significance and determinative effect on everyday life, providing knowledge/power (medicine), revelations, and guidance. The content of dreams was immensely practical, often warning of danger, sharing medicinal or spiritual knowledge and techniques, or informing an individual about future events (V. Deloria 2009, 172). Dream experiences often defined an individual and his path for the rest of his life. For example, a dream might determine which dream society an individual belonged to, which nonhuman person(s) he was related to, from where he received power/knowledge or medicine, what career or role he would pursue in his community, and so on. Further, a dream was often the basis for one's personal name. As Vine Deloria explains, "Dreams . . . are always personal in the sense that they affect us directly and are not merely an abstract picture of other realities to which we have no responsibility or relationship" (2009, 170–71).

The dream world, like that of mythology, was one of pure immanence and pure interiorities in which nonhuman persons were seen, heard, and otherwise existentially and phenomenologically *experienced* (cf. Hallowell 1960, 41). The appearance of nonhuman personages from mythology in dreams was not as strangers or unfamiliar figures but as well-known living entities of the Lakota cosmos. Vine Deloria writes, "A Sioux child was born into a complex system comprised of personal parents, a kinship family, the extended community, a cultural collective, and the living presence of ancestors, all psychically present in powerful ways" (2009, 138).

The self was basically equated with the interiority. Dreams of the dead, for instance, were considered actual manifestations of that person, an actual visitation from the naǧí (soul, spirit) of a deceased individual. The interpersonal social relations between humans and nonhumans in dreams was not disassociated from the accumulated knowledge of nonhuman persons that already existed in other contexts. All such relations and experiences were interpreted as experiences of the self in a practical and holistic way. Speaking of the Ojibwes, Hallowell (1966, 279) writes, "Dream experiences brought the individual into intimate personal contact with particular other-than-human persons. Besides this, the role that this category of persons played in those experiences was culturally defined as immensely vital to the welfare of the individual."

Applying Hallowell's insights on the Ojibwes to the Sioux shows that the unconscious or virtual reality of the dream or vision was an important basis for Lakota adaptation to actuality or the conscious world of lived reality, society, and culture (Spiro in Hallowell 1976, 356). To repeat an earlier quote from Vine Deloria, "Indians consider their own individual experiences, the accumulated wisdom of the community that has been gathered by previous generations, their dreams, visions, and prophecies, and any information received from birds, animals, and plants as data that must be arranged, evaluated, and understood as a unified body of knowledge" (1999, 66).

Dreams and visions provided valuable opportunities for humans to interact, communicate, and establish relationships with nonhumans (Standing Bear 2006a, 204). When a human being is asleep and dreaming his interiority (naǧí or šicų́), which is the core of the self, may become disassociated from the physicality (tʿącʿą́), leaving the bodily envelope (há 'skin, outer casing') and traveling freely through space and time. Thus the self has greater mobility in space and time while sleeping. Yet the virtual space/time in which the self is mobile in dreams and visions is continuous with the earthly and cosmic space of actuality: the virtual is not separate from the actual; it is simply different (cf. Hallowell 1960, 41). As Kapferer explains, "The virtual of ritual [mythology, and dreams and visions] is a thoroughgoing reality of its own, neither a simulacrum of realities external to ritual nor an alternative reality. It bears a connection to ordinary, lived realities, as depth to surface" (Kapferer 2010, 232). Hallowell (1966, 279) writes, "Social relations with other-than-human persons are not metaphorical but intimately meshed in their thought and experience with interrelationships between human beings."

According to Luther Standing Bear, "While in the spirit condition the dreamer was in contact with the spirits of all things of the world" (Standing Bear 2006a, 215). As we shall see, this also applies to ritual. Standing Bear's notion of "the spirit condition" is nearly identical to views expressed by contemporary Lakota ritual leaders and participants in regard to the sun dance, vision quest, yuwípi, and other ceremonies. If we conceive of the nağí as the spirit, soul, ego, self, or interiority this phase or aspect of Lakota ritual may be thought of as the period in which the self is transcended, the line between conscious and unconscious blurred, during which the nağí crosses the threshold into the spirit realm, enabling communication between the living and the dead, human and nonhuman.

Rich Boyd, a contemporary Lakota religious practitioner, describes the effects of fasting and the latter phases of the sun dance, explaining that initially you look within and critically examine yourself but that the ultimate goal is to transcend ego or self, letting go of physical suffering in an induced catharsis. Boyd describes this phase as the transition from "the red day to the blue day," signifying spiritual transformations that occur through ritual performance. In effect, the interiorities of the ritual participants cross over into the spirit realm (ųmá wicʿóni 'other life, other world'), Standing Bear's "spirit condition," which is one reason why the common people and onlookers at sun dances and other rituals are not permitted to communicate with the dancers (Posthumus 2008–17; see also Kapferer 1979). But more on this later.

In dreams and visions nonhuman grandfathers addressed the dreamer using kinship terms and interacted with him in much the same ways in which humans would, although these experiences differed in fundamental ways from those of everyday reality (cf. Hallowell 1960, 41). According to Vine Deloria, "For the Sioux, the dream/vision is a wholly different experience than everyday life" (2009, 167). All this speaks to Kapferer's insistence that virtual realities are not separate or idealized representations of actuality. They are no less fully lived existential realities and part of actuality, despite being different from it. Although they are not actualized they are nonetheless real potentialities. Among the Lakotas and Ojibwes dreams and visions assume a special significance in terms of the overall functioning of the sociocultural system. Dream experience, the dynamic, intense, imaginal, phantasmagoric virtual space/time of dreams and visions, is interpreted as bringing the individual into direct existential contact and communion with nonhuman persons and becomes intimately linked with the motivation of individuals, traditional values, and social behavior (cf. Hallowell 1966, 280).

Contacts and relationships—entanglements—with nonhumans were highly motivated and actively sought by individuals as a means of achieving a personal life adjustment consonant with the characteristic values and ethos of Sioux culture. Dream and vision experiences were also important in terms of the social system and community life, in that they not only influenced behavior but also validated statuses, positions, and specialized services, such as leadership or curing roles. For instance, women who dreamed of the mythical Double Women ever after possessed extraordinary or mysterious (wakʻą́) abilities in the arts and crafts, in particular producing beautiful quillwork. This ability and status was conferred by nonhuman spirits encountered in dreams and visions. As Ella Deloria (n.d.d, 93) explains, "The trick comes ready learned; no human can teach it or learn it."

The Lakotas, particularly males, relied on the generosity and compassion of nonhuman persons who had a surplus of knowledge/power or medicine. From the perspective of the Lakota worldview, in which reciprocal sharing and generosity were central values, nonhumans were expected to share some of their abundance with their human relatives, as long as the proper ceremonial forms and reciprocal rights and obligations were observed. Persons of the nonhuman category were believed to be more or less oriented to the same values and motivated in much the same ways as humans, moved to compassion by the humility and pitiful nature of humans in need. Although a particular nonhuman person, as an entity with a distinctive personality, intentionality, reflexive consciousness, affective life, and knowledge, could be benevolent or malevolent in its interaction with human beings depending on context, the social life of animals and other nonhuman persons resembled that of humans and was sustained by the same sources: solidarity, kinship, exchange, and deference toward elders (see Descola 2013a, 5, 8, 14; Hallowell 1966, 280–82).

The major mechanism for establishing relationship with a nonhuman person and obtaining knowledge (wóslolye) and power (wówašʾake) or medicine (pʿežúta) was through the vision quest (hąblécʿeyapi), a ritual focused on the attainment of medicine through successfully inducing a wakʿą́ dream or vision. But not all dreams were considered wakʿą́. Linguistically there is no distinction between dream and vision, the stem for both being ihą́bla. The difference, if any, between dreams and visions may be productively conceptualized as a continuum. On one end are mundane dreams that lack great meaning or import. On the other end are powerful, sacred, or wakʿą́ dreams of great meaning and significance. The difference would be easily and intuitively recognized through experience by those enculturated in Lakota society.

Dreams were often interpreted metaphorically. The virtual reality of dreams provided access to the domain of nonhuman spirit persons, pure interiorities, where appearances were not always as they seemed. Physicalities were often transformed, so that an animal spirit might appear as a human or a plant, a human as an animal or plant, and so on. Animal spirits of various tribe-species were experienced in dreams as living in much the same way as humans. Often there was a moment of realization of the fact that a man was not in the presence of other men or women but rather in the presence of animal spirits. For instance, in his vision Brave Buffalo experienced a moment of realization that the people he was interacting with were actually elks (Brave Buffalo in Densmore 2001, 176–77).

This was also a regular occurrence in mythology and oral narratives. In Ella Deloria's Yankton deer woman text a man is out hunting when he is mysteriously approached by a beautiful young woman he recognizes from his village. According to the story, "the man was sad in his heart. 'How does it happen that this girl, usually so well guarded that it is impossible to get near her, is out in these wild parts by herself?'" (E. Deloria 2006, 165). The hunter is suspicious and stealthily looks at the young woman out of the corner of his eye. He notices that she is wearing many rings on her fingers. Then "he glanced at the shadow [nağí] she cast, and it was not a woman's outline, but a deer's, with the long ears in constant motion" (E. Deloria 2006, 166). In Lone Man's version of the gift of the sacred pipe he concludes by saying that Ptesáwį (White Buffalo Woman) "came out of the tent on the left side, walking very slowly; as soon as she was outside the entrance she turned into a white buffalo calf" (Lone Man in Densmore 2001, 66). Densmore (2001, 66n1) footnotes this, explaining, "It is interesting to observe that the identity of a dream object often is unrecognized until it turns to depart."

Ella Deloria recorded a narrative, full of common Lakota vision tropes and themes, describing the origin of various beliefs concerning mice. In it an Oglala man from Pine Ridge was fasting west of the Black Hills. Ella Deloria (n.d.e, 14–15) writes that "after four days a man led him away in the spirit to a tipi out west where a council of chiefs was in session. They sat in a semi-circle. . . . When this man realized he was in a conclave of mice, he walked out on them and returned home." Later these dreams were told (hąblóglaka) and interpreted, often metaphorically and under the guidance of a shaman, to render them productive to human use (cf. Descola 2014a, 270).[2] Hence the central significance of dream interpretation in Sioux culture operating as a device that, according to Kohn, "aligns the situated points of view of beings that inhabit different worlds" (Kohn 2013, 141).

So on one level the individual determined and interpreted the significance of a dream, whether it was a common dream or a sacred dream or vision, and the proper or necessary actions that must subsequently be taken. On another level ritual or ceremony distinguished the common dream from the sacred vision. Visions proper were purposefully and ceremonially sought, accompanied by fasting, sacrifice, and arduous "prayer" upon a lonely hilltop (E. Deloria n.d.e, 4–5, 26). In any case the semantic distinction between dreams and visions (iháblA) is minor, and both had the potential to be significant in terms of Sioux ethnometaphysics.

Ella Deloria describes a wak'ą́ dream or vision as a "communication of supernatural power" (Deloria n.d.e, 7). These sacred visions were purposefully induced via culturally established, methodical ritual dynamics and followed a normative formula or pattern. Vision fasting, writes Deloria (n.d.b, 64), followed "a certain routine: abstinence; purification; isolation; fasting; weeping and importuning; singing religious songs, and waiting. But nobody sees this take place. Each man knows his own experience."

According to the formula, a nonhuman person (A), the instructor or teacher, usually manifested in a human physicality, appears to the dreamer (iháblA).[3] This nonhuman proclaims that medicine is to be given to the human and then points out or conducts him to another nonhuman person(s) (B), who rarely speaks but also appears in human form. This second nonhuman is the actual medicine (p'ežúta) or power (wówaš'ake) to be bestowed. Then another person (C), the one requiring aid or to be overcome by medicine, such as a sick person or an enemy, is pointed out. As the dreamer looks on B is transformed into a plant or other physicality, and C now appears in a form suggestive of the sickness or condition to be overcome by the medicine. These plants or herbs are to be gathered and used as medicine according to the instructions of A. The dreamer turns back to A, which is now transformed into its characteristic animal physicality and runs away. This animal then becomes the spirit guardian and "totem" of the dreamer or initiate. Finally, the dreamer receives certain prayers and songs from A, whose interiority becomes infused with that of the dreamer, adding to his wak'ą́ power or strength (Wissler 1912, 81; Curtis 1908, 21, 62–63; Densmore 2001, 173–74, 177, 185, 251–52, 266).

Medicine here is to be understood in a broad sense, applying equally to the treatment of physical or physiological ailments and to psychological, psychosomatic, or spiritual conditions. In general, medicine is understood as spiritual or mystery (wakʿą́) power, the opposite of poison, negative energy, or "bad medicine." Much like spirits and wakʿą́ energy in its latent form, medicine may be positive or negative, good or bad, social or antisocial. It may be used to maintain and sustain or impede and terminate life movement. Medicine was rendered either good or bad in its direction by human beings and in terms of the subsequent use to which it was put through human agency and intentionality. In all cases medicine was considered powerful and hence dangerous (Curtis 1908, 61; E. Deloria n.d.c, 1; Posthumus 2015, 141–61).

In the context of dreams and visions medicine may be likened to knowledge and power. Attaining medicine gave an individual status and (access to) various forms of cultural, economic, social, and symbolic capital. According to Ella Deloria (n.d.c, 16–17), medicine may be conceptualized as having communication or relationship with the nonhuman or wakʿą́. Vine Deloria writes, "Knowledge was derived from individual and communal experiences in daily life, in keen observation of the environment, and in interpretive messages . . . received from spirits in ceremonies, visions, and dreams" (1999, 44). Speaking of ascribed medicine abilities, he continues, "A truly wise and gifted individual can appear to 'cause' things to happen because that person can participate in the emerging event in a way that rarely occurs in Western science. Thus it is that people are said to have 'powers,' which is another way of saying that their understanding of natural processes and their ability to enter into events are highly developed and sophisticated" (1999, 50). According to Edward Curtis in *The North American Indian*,

> The entire culture of the Sioux is based primarily on two concepts, first, that his "medicine," or supernatural occult power, is derived from the mysterious forces of nature, and secondly, his creed of a brave heart. The conduct and the effort of every Sioux throughout

life were so to strengthen his supernatural power that he could not only resist any harm threatening him from ordinary sources, but could become possessed of invulnerability to those imbued with like power. He desired this mystery-power to be stronger than any he was to encounter. Many a brave warrior has cried out to his people that his "medicine" was so great that no arrow or bullet from the enemy could harm him, and, singing his medicine-songs, has charged recklessly into the camp of the enemy and struck them right and left; and, strangely enough, they seem often to have proved their pretension to supernatural strength in that while they were shot at repeatedly at close range they escaped unharmed. (1908, 21)

Another reading of the wak'ą́ vision experience involves the elusive concept šicų́ or wašícų, which I have defined as the immortal aspect of the soul, the transferable nonhuman guardian or familiar spirit of a human, or imparted nonhuman potency or energy. As the Oglala Seven Rabbits explains, "*Wasicunpi* may be seen in visions. They may be anything. They are the guardian spirits of the Lakota" (in Walker 1991, 118). The semantic distinction between šicų́ and wašícų in this regard is minimal and insignificant. In some cases the term *wašícų* was used generally to refer to spirit beings or nonhuman persons (Walker 1991, 125). Recall that Finger describes šicų́ as the t'ų́ 'emitted potency' of a wak'ą́ or nonhuman spirit person. Táku Škąšką́, the creative life force and energy animating all things that move, selects a šicų́ from the stars and gives one to each human at birth, so that every human being has a given šicų́. But additional šicų́ may be acquired throughout the life cycle via the proper ritual channels (Walker 1917, 87, 156, 158–59; 1991, 72–73; Posthumus 2015, 103–39).

Medicine men accumulate *šicų́pi* (plural form of šicų́) mainly through multiple vision quests throughout the life cycle. In successful or correctly performed healing rituals the practitioner invests one or more of his šicų́pi or part of his collective šicų́ in the patient or an object. This is necessary in order to renew or make over the patient (*p'iyá* or *wap'íya*) and hence to cure (various forms of the stem *asníya* 'to cause to recover, to cause to be well'), restoring wellness or balance. Powers (1986, 173–75) equates curing, the primary function of Lakota ritual specialists, with the ritual cleansing of symbolic illness. Thus each time a practitioner successfully cures a patient he loses some of his power through the transfer of šicų́, which then remains in the container or person until death, at which time the šicų́ returns to the star(s) from whence it came, metaphorically understood as a great "pool" or reservoir of šicų́pi from which Táku Šką́šką́ selects spirits for newborn humans and from which medicine men obtain their power through the vision quest and other rituals (Powers 1986, 117–18; Posthumus 2008–17).

In wakʻą́ visions a particular šicų́—the potency or interiority of a nonhuman spirit person—often manifested itself in a characteristic human or animal physicality. The šicų́ itself, however, is a pure interiority, unbounded by and dissociated from a physicality, immaterial by nature. In Lakota, this immateriality is expressed using a reduplicated form of the stem tʻų́, which can be understood as emitted potency or potentiality. Hence tʻų́tʻųšni refers to invisible potency or influence or anything that lacks physical properties or physicality, what we might conceptualize as inorganic or intangible. The related tʻų́tʻųšniyą refers to anything that is invisible due to a lack of physicality. Both terms are tied to wakʻą́, agency, intentionality, and efficacy. According to Walker's consultants, "The mysterious (*wakan*) of anything is the *tontonsni*. The *tontonsni* is that which causes it to act on other things or on mankind. It is that which causes medicines to act on people. It is that which spirits act on the people when they are not present. It is that from which the shamans and medicine men get their power. It is that which the spirits get from things which are offered them" (Walker 1991, 106).

Yet wakʻą́ energy or potency (tʻų́, šicų́, etc.) requires a material form, container, physicality, medium, or conduit in order to manifest, interact, and relate with human beings on a phenomenological level. This is tied to the capacity for transformation associated with wakʻą́ power and nonhuman spirit persons. According to Raymond DeMallie and Robert Lavenda:

> *Wakan* is an infinite, ineffable, wholly "other" quality and quantity, which, however, has no independent existence without a locus.

Therefore, *wakan* is transmuted by the type of vessel in which it is found. Thus, *wakan* as manifested in a tree is different from the *wakan* found in a human. Further, within the category of human, the transmutation of *wakan* varies. In its most obvious form, the *wakan* of a warrior is physical prowess and invulnerability to enemies, while the *wakan* of a shaman is spiritual.

It follows from this idea of transmutation that *wakan* is personal insofar as it becomes an attribute of individuals and that it is not a neutral quality. As it exists in the world, it exists for good or for evil. It seems to us that this is a function of its transmutation by individuals. If *wakan* could exist by itself (and we emphasize that it cannot), it would be neutral in the same way that electricity is neutral. (1977, 164)

DeMallie and Lavenda's insights on the embodied, personalized nature of wakʿą́ energy are comparable to Viveiros de Castro's notion of perspectivism and how a person's physicality is a particular perspectival lens or habitus through which the cosmos is experienced and comprehended and existence and practice interpreted and articulated. The body is a social or relational entity with the capacity to engage with other bodies, affects, and the environment. This relationality between multiple physicalities and the environment is the tool or apparatus through which multiple realities or worlds are unlocked.

A šicų́ invested in an object and enclosed in a container of some kind—such as a sacred stone wrapped in sage and sealed in a buckskin pouch—is referred to as a wašícų. Likewise, a šicų́ acquired through a descent into the virtual reality of dreams and visions and ritual was embodied by an individual, becoming part of his interiority, and understood as an indwelling spirit (wówakʿą or wašícų). According to Curtis's *The North American Indian*, "The spirit or mystery-strength [interiority] of the animal that appeared to him in vision entered his body and became a part of his *waká^n* strength. He might fast many times and have many such tutelary spirits within his body" (1908, 21). These indwelling nonhuman spirits were essential to Lakota ceremonial or magico-medico-ritual practice. Bushotter tells of the exploits of Spat Upon, his father's cross cousin and a powerful Bear dreamer and healer who had "very potent medicines" (p'ežúta waštéšte yuhá). Once Spat Upon's indwelling Bear spirit made its presence felt during doctoring ceremonies they were sure to be successful. "And when it, the bear spirit, is so inclined,"[4] Bushotter explains, "out of the doctor's mouth a bear cub falls [ítqhą mat'ó c'įcála kį héc'a wą hiyú], and moves about, sitting and then walking by turns." While the cub was outside the practitioner's body, without his "sustaining power," Spat Upon "faints and swoons, and well-nigh dies [t'ekínica]" (Bushotter 1887–88, story 199).

At the heart of wak'ą́ vision experiences were relationship and exchange. As Ella Deloria's Santee consultant Starr Frazier explains, "Through dreams or some other means of communication . . . individuals . . . gained power from the supernatural and were in harmonious relation with it" (n.d.c, 7–8). Vine Deloria writes of "a clear and consistent tradition of receiving information from plants and animals, either in visions, or in unique daily experiences" (1999, 25). Through dreams and visions a human dreamer became entangled, establishing a special reciprocal, binding, and dependent relationship with a specific nonhuman person, his spirit helper or familiar (wašícu). The human was considered to be in league with that particular nonhuman collective or oyáte for the rest of his life, even to the point of complete identification, as when a Bear dreamer was simply referred to as "a bear," for instance. He had special medicine or knowledge/power on account of or in relation to specific nonhuman collectives, such as Buffalo callers having the ability to locate and attract or call buffalo, Bear dreamers having special abilities vis-à-vis treating wounds, Wolf dreamers having specialized warfare abilities, Stone dreamers having distinctive powers of divination, Thunder dreamers having the capacity to control or alter the weather, and so on. Dreamers of the same nonhuman entity generally banded together in dream societies (ihą́bla ok'ólakic'iye), groups of individuals who shared a common nonhuman visionary power source, the founder, leader, and symbol of the organization, and hence also shared similar medicines, songs, and prayers (Wissler 1912, 81–99).

When a human person was recognized by or experienced a particular manifestation of a nonhuman person or collective in the domains of mythology, dreams and visions, or ritual he then became an adopted human member or representative of that oyáte, wearing its specific emblems and accoutrements, painting in its characteristic manner, singing its typical songs, and performing its distinctive rituals. Through relationship and experience the human was bestowed, infused, and blessed with the potency (tʻų́ or šicų́) of the nonhuman person. In other words a convergence of interiorities was instituted, marking an enduring sacred bond and blending of subjectivities or identities that the human carried with him into actuality, having a determinative effect on him throughout the rest of his life. In effect, this relationship or covenant established between a human person and a nonhuman collective forever altered the human's (ritual) habitus, adjusting the structuring structure of dispositions and affects guiding perception, thought, and behavior. He became a member of another tribe-species and learned how to think and behave according to their culture, to see the cosmos from their perspective or worldview, and to get a feel for the game they played and the field they occupied. These insights also speak to notions of what has been called totemism.

Wakʻą́ dreams enabled young men to be successful in hunting and warfare, two major and important male pursuits, which also made them desirable as husbands. Dreams gave shamans their mysterious powers and abilities and generally gave men status and a seat in the council. According to Bad Bear, an Oglala from the Wounded Knee District at Pine Ridge, "The Oglalas believed that by due form and ceremony they could get communications from the supernatural powers relative to any matter, and there were men among them who professed to be able to get such communications at their will, in which the supernatural powers would reveal matters for the benefit of the people. These men were the shamans and they were entitled to seats in the council. Their communications from the powers were listened to with respect upon any subject. Anyone having a dream or supernatural communication relative to anything was entitled to relate it in the council" (in Walker 1982, 28). Dreams were and are considered by many Sioux to be a connection or portal to the spirit world. Along with the rituals that enabled human-nonhuman communication, visions operated as a technology that provided access to virtual self-related experience of great ontological import in actuality. Through the virtual reality of dreams and visions Lakota people could commune with animals, other nonhuman spirits, their ancestors, and Wakʻą́ Tʻą́ka (Posthumus 2008–17).

Bad Conduct and Sioux Disease Theory

Dreams and the nonhuman spirit persons encountered therein also figure prominently in conceptions of sickness, wellness, ethnomedicine, and disease theory. These connections are deep, transcending both time and Sioux tribal divisions. Referring to the Lakotas of the Upper Missouri circa 1803–4 Tabeau explains, "As among the Sioux . . . there prevails no natural sickness, as all illness is either the result of the vengeance of some angry spirit or a succession of evil deeds of a magician, diviners are the only recourse. They are called *medicine men*, which signifies supernatural power. . . . Often the doctor, . . . if after songs and invocations, the illness persists, he is convinced that it is the moral disposition or sorcery which opposes the cure" (1939, 183–84). Tabeau's account addresses issues that will be more fully explored below, in particular, the interrelated notions of bad conduct and the disease sanction.

According to the Oglala holy man No Flesh (in Walker 1917, 161), "Evil spirits cause all diseases." In particular, he attributes many illnesses, such as boils, maggots, and festering wounds, to the malevolent family of spirits known as the Uktéȟi, the terrifying spirits of the waters (No Flesh in Walker 1917, 162). Sword substantiates No Flesh's claims, explaining in 1901 that "disease is caused by the *wakan* (mysterious), or it may be caused by the mysterious-like (*wakanla*). The evil mysteries may impart their potencies to the body and this will cause disease. Poisons and snakes and water creatures cause disease in this way. A magician can cause disease by his mysterious powers. A holy man can cause disease by his songs and ceremonies" (in Walker 1991, 91). Illness could be caused by either offending a more neutral spirit person or by the direct intervention of those spirits in the Lakota universe who tended to interact negatively with human beings, such as Íya, Gnaškíyą, Uktéȟi, Anų́gite, Iktómi, and so on.

Arthur E. McFatridge was a day-school teacher and inspector in He

Dog's Oglala camp in the Cut Meat District of the Rosebud Reservation from 1898 to 1905. His description of the habits, customs, and characteristics of He Dog's Oglalas substantiates No Flesh's claim, particularly the notion that all sickness and death was caused by malevolent spirits (McFatridge 1937). According to Curtis's *The North American Indian*, "The medicine practices of the Lakota are inseparable from their religious rites. Disease is evil, brought on by some malign influence, and naturally the treatment is in no case by pharmacy alone. In fact, such medicinal plants as are used are those revealed to the individuals during their fastings, and are therefore *wakáⁿ*" (1908, 61).

According to Williamson, the Dakotas suppose "every object, artificial as well as natural, to be the habitation of a spirit capable of hurting or helping them, and that all diseases were caused by some one or more of these spirits taking possession of a part or the whole of the body of the patient" (1869, 435-36). Riggs substantiates Williamson's claim that the Dakotas believed that disease ultimately came from the spirit world, adding, "The gods are offended by acts of omission or commission, and the result is that some spirit of animal, bird, or reptile is sent, by way of punishment, and the man is taken sick" (1893, 216). Mary Eastman's account of the Eastern Sioux near Fort Snelling in the 1840s further corroborates the basic assumption that much sickness, both physical and psychological, was caused by evil spirits (1995, 19, 26-28, 55-61). The foregoing accounts demonstrate the pervasive, intertribal scope and diachronic persistence of these beliefs among the various Sioux groups.

It is likely that these beliefs concerning disease theory refer mostly to aboriginal or culture-bound sickness: symbolic illness that predates the arrival of the whites and is distinctively indigenous and/or Sioux. Powers, citing Mary Douglas (1970), describes symbolic illness as representative of "the ritual acting out of the drama of life and death.[5] Symbolic illness also marks a larger category, that of social disorder in general, further symbolized in terms of aches and pains, or personal anxieties related to the individual's transgression of social regulations, that is, the commission of error or sin" (Powers 1986, 177). Powers's "transgression of social regulations" and "commission of error or sin" parallel Hallowell's (1955) interrelated notions of bad conduct, disease sanction, and confession among the Ojibwes, as well as Elizabeth Grobsmith's (1974) understanding of *wakúza* as "supernatural retribution" underpinning a system of social control and Bushotter's translation of *wókuze* as an observance or rule imposed by a spirit being (1887–88, story 109). But more on this later.

In any case symbolic illness marks the category that subsumes all forms of social disorder or disequilibrium that, if left unchecked, would lead to complete social disintegration. Today symbolic illness may take the form of alcohol or drug abuse, physical aches and pains, anxiety, "heartsickness," PTSD, and other psychological conditions. It may be compared to "Indian sickness," as opposed to "white man's sickness" (see Powers 1986, 178). Most Lakotas today seek treatment for physical ailments at Western medical facilities, although this type of treatment is frequently paired with traditional magico-medico-ritual treatment through traditional religion and ritual or the Native American Church. Consequently, much contemporary Lakota religion and ritual focuses on symbolic illness or "Indian sickness" in terms of general physical and mental health and spiritual equilibrium.

This notion of spiritual equilibrium, harmony, or balance is well documented in historical accounts. According to Charles Eastman (1980, 75), the Dakota "medicine-man possessed much personal magnetism and authority, and in his treatment often sought to reestablish the equilibrium of the patient through mental or spiritual influences—a sort of primitive psycho-therapy."[6] Hence the term *wap'íya* 'to renew, make anew, make over, repair, fix', used in reference to healing or doctoring (see Tyon in Walker 1991, 161–63, 170–71; Black Elk in DeMallie 1984, 102, 139; Curtis 1908, 63; Densmore 2001, 245). Recall that historically sickness was usually conceptualized in terms of disease-object intrusion: as pollution or "matter out of place" in Mary Douglas's terms (Douglas 1966, 44; see also Powers 1986, 173–79). While usually sickness and death were ascribed to the agency of malevolent spirits, human behavior was also a catalyst for this negative nonhuman intervention in human affairs, whether in actuality or in the virtual domains of visions and ceremony (see Posthumus 2015, 162–86).

Particularly vivid, powerful, or significant dreams often resulted in the prescription or proscription of various behaviors or practices, often in the form of taboos (*wógluze, wót'ehila*) and animal ceremonialism (Sword in Walker 1991, 78; Riggs 1869, 79–81). According to Charles Eastman, "The Indian loved to come into sympathy and spiritual communion with his brothers of the animal kingdom, . . . and while he humbly accepted the supposed voluntary sacrifice of their bodies to preserve his own, he paid homage to their spirits in prescribed prayers and offerings" (1980, 15). Later Eastman explains,

> Every act of his [the Indian's] life is, in a very real sense, a religious act. He recognizes the spirit in all creation, and believes that he draws from it spiritual power. His respect for the immortal part of the animal, his brother, often leads him so far as to lay out the body of his game in state and decorate the head with symbolic paint or feathers. Then he stands before it in the prayer attitude, holding up the filled pipe, in token that he has freed with honor the spirit of his brother, whose body his need compelled him to take to sustain his own life. (1980, 47)

Walker describes Lakota beliefs tied to animal ceremonialism that substantiate Eastman's Dakota account: "To have game animals submit to their fate and become food for mankind, a Shaman should explain to a captured one that this is its destiny, then decorate it as a mark of friendship, and, freeing it, bid it tell its kind what he said and did to it. A man may so offend game animals that they will escape from hunters, and if so a Shaman should penalize the offending one by making taboo to him some portion of the offended animals" (Walker 1917, 92).

Breaches of dream obligations, vows (*wóiglakapi*), and taboos (wógluze, wót'ehila) were considered a form of bad conduct (wówahtani 'wrongdoing, sin, transgression or violation of a tribal law, custom, or religious taboo') causally linked to sickness. According to McFatridge (1937), He Dog's Oglalas of the Cut Meat District "believe in a doctrine of sin and punishment, [but] their idea of sin is vastly different from those who adhere to the Christian religion." Unfortunately McFatridge does not elaborate on this Sioux "doctrine of sin and punishment," aside from casually observing that "one of the greatest sins among the tribes would be to let a little child go hungry and homeless. . . . It being a religious duty to care for the orphans of the tribes" (1937). McFatridge does, however, explain later that "they believe a happy man is a healthy man. When a person sorrows or is in trouble he is sick.⁷ A happy man is happy and content. To be ill is a sure sign you have committed some crime against nature and are being punished by the Sun God. And if the crime is unpardonable you will die" (1937). Just how much this theosophy was influenced by Christianity and other intrusive nonnative sources we can only speculate, and McFatridge's use of the term *Sun God* is problematic, although the Sun (Wí) certainly plays an important role in Sioux mythology, ontology, religious belief, and ritual practice. In any case McFatridge's account emphasizes the holistic understanding of Sioux disease theory, medicine, and treatment, in which the mind, body, and spirit are conceptualized as an integrated and interconnected whole, all of which must be accounted for.

In many ways Sioux notions of disease theory, bad conduct, medicine, and treatment parallel those of the Berens River Ojibwes as described by Hallowell, who explains that

> interpersonal relations between human and other-than-human beings involve reciprocal rights and obligations, in the same way that social relations between human persons do. And these obligations are reinforced by the same sanctions that apply to social relations between human beings. Failure to fulfill them, in either case, is one variety of "bad conduct," bad conduct being culturally defined as any unpredictable or deviant conduct that fails to conform with the traditional normative standards of interpersonal relations. The penalty for bad conduct is illness. Any kind of bad conduct on my part is said to "follow me." I will inevitably become ill, or my children may get sick, or my wife may die. The fear of becoming ill and the anxiety engendered by any serious sickness is the major sanction of the Ojibwe sociocultural system. What is particularly characteristic is the fact that the bad conduct of human beings is believed to be the major source of illness. Consequently in every case of serious sickness an individual must reflect upon what kind of misdeeds he may have been responsible for in the past. Even in cases of sorcery the reputed act of the sorcerer is interpreted as retaliation for some previous bad

> conduct on the part of the victim in his interpersonal relations with the sorcerer. (1966, 280)

Recall that the notion that bad conduct follows an individual or his or her relatives, even intergenerationally, is very common among the Sioux. Grobsmith writes, "The native system of logic—if you make mistakes, you pay for them—applies equally to non-Indians living in the Indian community. My own loss of several objects within a single week was explained as a warning by the spirits of some improper event in my life. Most of my friends suggested a supernatural explanation for my personal misfortune" (1981, 79). Combining insights from Douglas, Powers, Grobsmith, and Hallowell, we might posit that the bad conduct of human beings is the major source of symbolic illness among the Sioux and that the fear of becoming ill is the major sanction (the "disease sanction") in the traditional Sioux sociocultural system.

Elaborating on bad conduct and the disease sanction among the Ojibwes, Hallowell writes,

> Disease situations of any seriousness carry the implication that something wrong has been done. Illness is the penalty. Consequently, it is easy to see why illness tends to precipitate an affective reaction to a culturally defined danger situation. Furthermore, a closer examination of the dynamics of Saulteaux society reveals the fact that fear of disease is the major social sanction operative among these Indians. In this society, certain classes of sexual behavior (incest, the so-called perversions in heterosexual intercourse, homosexuality, autoerotism, bestiality), various kinds of aggressive behavior (cruelty to animals, homicide, cruelty toward human beings, the use of bad medicine to cause suffering, rough or inconsiderate treatment of the dead, theft, and a number of ego injuries like insult and ridicule, failure to share freely, etc.), behavior prescribed by guardian spirits, the acquisition of power to render specialized services to others (i.e., curing or clairvoyance), all fall under a disease sanction. (1955, 268)

The disease sanction operates to deter bad conduct in social relations between persons, ensure that dream obligations are carried out, and encourage individuals to be responsible for their conduct, despite the fact that the disease sanction in and of itself is not in any real sense religious (Hallowell 1955, 272, 421n27). Hallowell writes, "Fear of illness in this life is a controlling factor of much greater importance than any fear of unhappiness in the life after death. In former times, customs with a 'disease-sanction' were undoubtedly those followed with maximum stringency" (1955, 157). McFatridge's (1937) account parallels Hallowell's almost verbatim: "The Indian does not believe in a future punishment for their sins. They believe they will be punished here on earth for their many sins while yet they are living, and that such punishment is brought upon them by their Medicine men as a curse." While McFatridge's account emphasizes why the common people fear and respect ritual practitioners, we must remember that the ultimate source of human power is nonhuman or spiritual, hence the underlying assumption that the disease sanction is upheld and reinforced by the pervasive belief in the ubiquitous nature and unlimited power of the spirits and what Grobsmith (1981, 78) calls "supernatural retribution."

The agentive force (and enforcer) behind the Sioux disease sanction is ultimately the spirits, and this connection is well-documented among the various Sioux tribes. Speaking of the Minnesota Dakotas circa 1834 Samuel Pond writes,

> They did believe in a superintending righteous Providence. Although this belief was vague and undefined, it was real and universal, and so strong as to exert great influence over their conduct.
>
> Evil deeds which provoked this unknown power to anger were not always of the same class with those which were punished by the gods of the wakan-men, but were transgressions of the divine law, what we call sins; and they believed that by this power individuals, families, nations, were punished for their iniquities. They sometimes said that they had been restrained from carrying out some wicked purpose by the fear of Taku-wakan; and they told of many individuals and families who had been destroyed by this mysterious power because of their wickedness. It was believed that whole bands were sometimes destroyed for their misdeeds. (1908, 425)

Grobsmith, who conducted fieldwork among the Lakotas at Rosebud Reservation in the 1970s, documents similar beliefs vis-à-vis the spirits and social control:

> The belief in supernatural spirits is an integral part of Lakota belief. Spirits are believed to be everywhere and can appear at any time, whether ritually summoned or not. To most individuals, these spirits appear as flashing white or blue lights, often accompanied by high shrieking sounds that are deafening and extremely frightening. These spirits have boundless power. . . . These spirits play an important role in social control. Many individuals believe in a system of immanent justice or supernatural retribution effected by spirits. It is people's belief in supernatural controlling agents that may dissuade them from committing an act of wrongdoing. Some Indian people feel that, despite the ineffectiveness of law enforcement, social order is maintained because individuals fear supernatural retribution from spirits if their conduct is at all improper. So spirits are perceived as a mechanism that, ultimately, protects them against potential harm. (1981, 78)

Spirits are believed to know when rituals are performed improperly and, much like humans, can be vindictive and punitive against transgressors or when offended or antagonized. "Spirits, then," writes Grobsmith (1981, 79), "are not only blamed when things go awry; they are also credited with keeping things morally in order and seeing that human beings, in their mortal errors, do not make too big a mess of things."

Bad conduct is tied to what Grobsmith refers to as wakúza,

> the attempt to use supernatural spirits to effect a particular outcome of some event. This may take the form of casting a hex or curse on an individual either as a threat to, or as punishment for, malicious or dangerous behavior, or it may take a positive form, that is, summoning spirits to help an individual. In the event of a wrongdoing, the victim utters a hex in Lakota to the effect that any person causing evil or unjust events will be punished drastically, perhaps by death. Even if a hex is not cast, infraction of the moral order will still be punished by spiritual forces. It is people's knowledge of this system

of divine retribution that acts as a deterrent against more crimes being committed than are already. Many Indian people regard certain dangerous events as warnings, and, recognizing them quickly, correct their behavior before a serious tragedy befalls them. (1981, 78)

Grobsmith goes on to give a number of examples illustrating the pervasive Lakota belief in supernatural interventions as warnings by spirits. Among them is one in which a woman on the Rosebud Reservation in the summer of 1973 was afraid and unable to sleep at night because she kept hearing mysterious sounds. After consulting her grandmother it was determined that the woman was being punished by the spirits: that her fear and inability to sleep were a warning from the spirits that she had done something wrong or committed some kind of bad conduct. The woman enlisted the aid of a holy man, who held a yuwípi meeting for her, at the conclusion of which he gave her a sacred stone and instructions to pray with it to relieve her anxiety. After the ceremony and receiving the sacred stone the woman's fears were allayed (Grobsmith 1974, 131).

The notion of ritual or moral bad conduct among the Sioux is a significant causal link between behavior, sickness, misfortune, death, and other inauspicious consequences and effects that disrupt or terminate life movement. In Lakota these negative results are usually expressed using various forms of the terms *wótʻehi* 'difficulty, trouble, hardship, misfortune, woe, sorrow, tragedy, dread, anxiety' (from the stem *tʻehí*), *wóakʻipʻa* 'tragedy, misfortune, trauma' (from the stem *akʻípʻa*), and *wahtáni* 'to transgress or violate a taboo, tribal law, or custom, fail to perform a vow'.[8]

Further, as Hallowell points out in reference to the Ojibwes, bad conduct could follow an individual—manifesting itself in space and time removed from the here and now or present continuous—and could also potentially affect (or infect) the relatives rather than or in addition to the offender. In other words, sickness, resulting from bad conduct, could be transmitted intergenerationally,[9] as discussed by Ruth and Wilson Wallis (1953, 435), who conducted fieldwork among the Canadian Dakotas in 1914 and 1951–52: "The concept of sickness caused by an ancestor's sin seems to be deeply rooted in Canadian Dakota belief and to be universally accepted on the two Reserves studied.[10] It is certainly not less emphatic among the least acculturated persons, a fact which suggests that the concept is aboriginal among Dakota or in some other group with which they have had contacts."

Sickness was associated with improper social or kinship interactions, ritual misconduct, desecration of sacred traditions or things, breach of taboo, and other actions that offended or antagonized spirit persons. Wallis and Wallis (1953, 432) write, "Sins that cause illness in descendants are of at least three types: ritual transgressions, torture or mockery of animals, crimes against a person or against the group."

The most common form of bad conduct was apparently ritual transgressions. Discussing the creation of new ceremonial forms, Walker's Oglala consultants cautioned that "not many dare to attempt to do this. Only very old and very wise men would attempt to do this, for if one should do such a thing wrong the spirits would be displeased with it and punish such a one in some way" (Walker 1991, 104). Speaking of ritual, Black Elk explains, "If things are not done in the right way, something very bad can happen" (in Joseph Brown 1989, 45–46).

Included in the category of ritual or spiritual transgressions were interdictions relating to sexuality and gender (Wallis and Wallis 1953, 432–33). DeMallie writes, "The Sioux believed that everything relating to sexuality was imbued with great power (*wak'aŋ*) and was therefore to be treated circumspectly. For Sioux men, engaging in sexual relations was at odds with the culturally defined warrior ethos. Men valued continence as proof of their bravery" (1994, 134). Female power conflicted with male power, so that men going to war or on hunting expeditions were obliged to abstain from sexual relations. This gendered division also applied to the magico-ritual realm. As DeMallie explains,

> A woman's blood was said to be a very powerful substance, and, during menstruation, harmful to men—not because it was polluting but because it was a specifically female power, at odds with or "blocked" by the power of men.[11] A menstruating woman absented herself from the household and stayed alone in a small dome-shaped structure apart from the camp circle. Men's belongings were zealously

guarded against contact with menstruating women. In general, sexual relations were considered detrimental to a man's power. Therefore, sexual intercourse was not engaged in immediately before ceremonial activities, warrior society meetings, or war expeditions, for it could render a man's sacred power temporarily impotent. (1994, 134)

Apparently anything deemed wakʻą́ or sacred was subject to the disease sanction, and disregarding or desecrating such things was sure to result in disaster. For instance, referring to the sacred tree that is central to the Lakota sun dance, Walker (1917, 103) writes, "This tree is thereby made the Sacred Tree and its *nagila* endowed with extraordinary potency so that it can bring disaster on anyone who profanes it by treating it as other trees are treated." Discussing taboo and bad conduct among the Eastern Sioux, Samuel Pond (1908, 422) writes, "Many things were forbidden on the ground that they were wakan, that is, the doing of them would be followed by some calamity. . . . Indeed, a thousand things that were considered dangerous or improper were wakan." Discussing the role of bad conduct and divination in Dakota doctoring practices, Gideon Pond (1889, 247) writes, "The doctor ascertains the sin which has been committed, and the particular god which has been offended and inflicted the disease. Then he makes an image of the offended god, which he hangs on a pole and which is shot by three or four persons in rapid succession. As the image falls the spirit of the god which is in the doctor leaps out, and, falling upon the spirit represented by the image, kills it."[12] No Flesh (in Walker 1917, 163) describes Oglala conceptions of the relationship between animal ceremonialism, breach of taboo, and sickness: "If one has dedicated an animal or part of an animal according to his vision and then such a one should eat that animal or part of the animal before the dedication runs out, then the thing that it was dedicated to, will bring some kind of sickness upon such a one."

Fletcher describes comparable beliefs among the Santees:

The implicit faith in the careful performance of rituals should never be lost sight of, as a distinctive characteristic of Indian religious ceremonials and as exercising a marked influence on the thought and action of the people. A woman whom I knew, and who was suffering from a nervous affection which made it almost impossible to walk, was hopeless of treatment, and her husband, also, because she had failed once in some of the minutiæ of the observances at a religious festival, and she was thus consequently punished. Every ill of life is supposed to be traceable to some such sin or omission, the people reasoning from the analogy of the relation of one person to another, or one tribe to another, where breaches of etiquette might lead to disastrous results. (1887c, 293n10)

Fletcher also describes similar dynamics among the Oglalas. Once a ghost lodge keeper neglected his duties at a sun dance and took his six-year-old daughter in his arms. This was a grave ritual breach that incurred a severe penalty. Two weeks later the little girl lay sick and dying. The heartbroken father accepted the girl's fate as punishment for his bad conduct, and the mother was equally hopeless. Fletcher writes, "To every inquiry I made as to the cause of the child's illness, cold, fever, or the like, the invariable answer given by relative or acquaintance was: 'Her father forgot and took her in his arms.' It was impossible to present to the people any natural cause for the child's illness, from that which was so clearly another evidence, supernaturally given, of the sanctity and power of their religious ceremonies" (1887c, 298n2). Apparently bad conduct in the form of ritual transgressions was subject to the disease sanction among all the Sioux tribes.

Fur trader Rufus B. Sage describes an example of bad conduct as it relates to the torture of animals.[13] Traveling the West from 1841 to 1844, Sage spent a great deal of time with the Brule Lakotas. In the dead of winter Sage and his companions unearthed a den of thirty-six large snakes in the bank of a river. As the snakes were in a torpid state due to the cold, Sage and his Euro-American companions were able to place them into a hole and pour scalding water on them, causing the snakes to reanimate suddenly before expiring. "The Indians were much shocked on seeing this," writes Sage, "and expressed their astonishment at our reckless presumption by their deeply accented 'tula,'—turning away from the spot with evident emotions of terror. On inquiring the cause, I learned in answer, that the various Indian tribes in the vicinity of the mountains are accustomed to regard the snake with a kind of superstitious veneration, and consider the act of killing it a sure harbinger of calamity. In the observance of this singular notion, they are scrupulously exact" (1857, 114).

The needless destruction or torture of animals, especially those held to be particularly wakʻą́, was a moral transgression and an example of bad conduct (wówahtani) causing sickness and subject to the disease sanction. All varieties of bad conduct led to wakų́za 'supernatural retribution', as discussed by Grobsmith (1974, 1981), or more generally wótʻehi 'difficulty, trouble, hardship, misfortune, tragedy', and were conceptualized as bad omens (wówaglece or wakų́za). Recall that the notion of wakų́za as supernatural retribution was linked to a strong belief that an individual's actions followed him and would come back to him: that you pay for your transgressions. This belief is still strong among many Lakotas today.

However, seeking the advice of a medicine man and undergoing various prescribed ceremonies of purification and sacrifice cleansed ritual impurities or spiritual pollution and reestablished spiritual equilibrium and psychological unity or balance disrupted by bad conduct. Recall that in many respects curing symbolic illness is functionally equated to ritual cleansing or purification. Hence the term *wapʻíya*, from the stem *pʻiyá* 'to make over, make anew, mend, fix, renew', refers to doctoring or curing and to a shaman, medicine man, or traditional healer. The nominalized form *wapʻíyapi* refers to a doctoring or healing ceremony (DeMallie 1984, 102n3). Individuals who experienced mysterious or powerful dreams often consulted with practitioners who interpreted the dreams, ascertained the symbolism, and diagnosed or prescribed the proper course of action to subsequently take. This method has been compared to psychoanalysis (see V. Deloria 2009), and the end result often entailed the imposition of a taboo or prescription of a ritual performance. According to Vine Deloria,

> From those animals and their relationships some tribes have developed tremendous systems of psychoanalysis, better and more accurate, I think, than astrology or Jungian psychology or anything else the West

has developed. They can look at people and intuitively pick out what medicine animal that person has, or what animal would approach that person and develop a relationship of medicine exchange. From the characteristic of that animal, and how it behaves in its natural environment, the human personality of that person takes on certain parallel or similar aspects. In extremely traditional Indian societies, people finally come to the realization through vision quest or training that they have the medicine of the deer, or the badger, or the antelope, or the raven. That realization opens a whole new avenue of human development through observation of animal adjustments to other life-forms and adjustments of the human personality to the life-forms with which he or she must deal.

The medicine animals become very close kin with human animals. (1999, 227–28)

Through dreams and visions human persons established and maintained relationships, entanglements of dependency, with nonhuman persons and vice versa. In these reciprocal relationships of medicine exchange humans offered propitiation, honor, and sacrifice in exchange for knowledge (wóslolye) and power or strength (wówašʼake), often collectively glossed as 'medicine'. In Sword's text on the vision quest this exchange is characterized in terms of the human lamenter agreeing to look upon or behold (based on the stem wąyą́ka) the nonhuman spirit person in exchange for certain demands and, ultimately, medicine (Sword 1938). These relationships of medicine exchange gave a human special knowledge and abilities vis-à-vis a particular nonhuman person, but these powers remained dormant as virtual potentialities until they were activated and actualized through public performance in various ceremonies, such as the various forms of the wakʻą́ ką́ǧa 'sacred imitation or [re]enactment'. In many cases revelatory visions were the major impetus for ritual action (Fletcher 1887a; S. Pond 1908, 415). Ella Deloria (n.d.b, 62) explains that many Lakota ceremonies were "dependent on dreams and visions, and upon the particular spirit with which a performer was in league."

As a segue into the next chapter on Lakota animist beliefs and personhood in ceremonial contexts I present this lengthy quote describing the vision of Little Moon, a Hunkpapa consultant of Ella Deloria's from Standing Rock Reservation. In particular this quote demonstrates common animist Lakota vision tropes and themes; the connection between dreams, symbolic illness, and the disease sanction; and the continuity between both the actual and the virtual and dreams and ceremony:

> Little Moon dreamed one day while grazing his horses, when he lay down in the afternoon, on a hillside for a moment. He was led to a tipi by a messenger and there was an altar, covered with feathers in motion [down], as most altars were. But at the four corners, there were clusters of things. On closer inspection they proved to be snakes of all species, who had bored through the ground and lay with their heads exposed in tight clusters at each direction. And from the four corners, in long green streamers reaching to the top where the poles were tied together, were those green worms one sees in the trees, doubling up as they advance. They covered the streamers and caused it to be in continuous motion. The man who invited him there was a screech owl.
>
> He heard them saying outside, "Now has One-with-horns-of-Black-Plum-tree Woman arrived," and "Now has One-with-horns-of-First-ranking-Pipe Woman arrived." He ran out to see. A host of elks were arriving. When he woke up, he did not try to interpret any mystery into the vision. All he did was, on the birth of his first two children, girls, to name them respectively, "He Kʻątʻúhu Sápewį," and "He Tʻacʻą́nųpa Tʻokáhewį."
>
> But that was not enough. The supernatural [wakʻą́] was not satisfied that he did not follow up this lead, so he had a second dream, during a nap again, and a woman approached from the west, carrying a hoop covered with fuzzy worms such as stay on sagebrush leaves. And she hurled the hoop at him calling him a heedless person, and he came down with a terrible malady as a punishment for ignoring the visions.
>
> Little Moon's two grandmothers, past the change of life, so that they were not in danger of hurting the medicine by their flow, were expert doctors, and one of them drew several feather-like pieces from perforations in his chest made by an awl in the hands of the other

one. These extractions were really fuzz from the worms, and had been hurled as projectiles by the woman from the west.

Had he heeded the call, which was an honorary one, since he was not seeking it, then he would have doubtless been a grand medicine man with the snakes and reptiles and creeping things for his control. (E. Deloria n.d.e, 33–34)

CHAPTER 8

Nonhuman Persons in Lakota Ritual

So what lessons can we learn from Little Moon's visions? Had he followed up and (re)enacted and actualized his initial vision, imitating and hence bringing to life the nonhuman personages therein and performing his vision publicly,[1] he would have surely become a powerful shaman. However, his disregard of the vision, an example of bad conduct subject to the disease sanction, brought disaster in the form of a mysterious and debilitating sickness. Ceremony, descending into ritual virtuality, was the only way to reset Little Moon and make over (wap'íya) the disharmony and distortion he had engendered through his reckless neglect. Only through ritual could spiritual, psychological, and physiological equilibrium and wellness be renewed. Hence his grandmothers drew out the feather-like disease objects from Little Moon's chest, which were, of course, fuzz from the worms shot as bad medicine by the dream woman from the west as punishment for Little Moon's bad conduct. Here we see a clear example of the power of the virtual to transform and impact actuality, as well as the dialectical and generative relationship between dreams and visions and ritual. This chapter examines the nineteenth-century Sioux animist ontology in relation to ritual dynamics.

Among the nineteenth-century Sioux ritual structured and informed life, providing a creative and (re)generative dynamic space where identity, ethnicity, and worldview were (re)affirmed, (re)enacted, and (re)negotiated. Although it was a constant sociocultural foundation, ritual itself was fluid, characterized by innovation and practical adaptation. The role of individualism and human agency must not be underestimated. Lakota ritual practice may be understood in terms of Ninian Smart's (1987, 17–18) notion of "syncretistic realism": the idea that religious belief, ritual performance, and worldview are born from hybrid ideologies. The Great Plains, in particular, was a veritable melting pot of ideas, practices, and technologies, alternately diffused and indigenized by the various tribes occupying the region in an endless dialectical process. Lakota religious belief and ritual practice were heavily influenced both directly and indirectly by Eastern Woodlands, Subarctic, and Great Basin tribes, as well as neighboring Plains peoples.

Sioux interaction with nonhuman spirit persons, and much ritual behavior in general, often occurred during inauspicious times and was motivated by hardship (*wótʿeȟika*), misfortune (*wóakʿipʿa*), uncertainty, suffering (*wókakiže*), sickness (*wówayazą, wókʿuže*), and death (*wičʿúŋtʾe*). As Clifford Geertz (1973, 103) suggests, the "problem of suffering" is one of central importance, as the two main loci of tribal religions are sickness and mourning.[2]

Recall that according to nineteenth-century Sioux disease theory the spirits or mysteries (wakʿą́ and wakʿą́la) were ultimately the cause and inflictors of misfortune, suffering, sickness, and death (Riggs 1869, 92–100; Tabeau 1939, 183–89). Sickness was the result of spirits imparting, projecting, or otherwise introducing their potencies (tʿų́, tųwą́, or šicų́) or some other disease object into the body (Walker 1917, 161–62; 1991, 91, 119). However, although spirits were the agents inflicting sickness, human behavior was the ultimate cause: there was and is a normative postulate in Lakota culture that misfortune, sickness, death, and other negative, inauspicious effects could be the direct result of bad conduct, particularly behaving without respect toward the wakʿą́, such as violating one or more of the interdictions surrounding objects or persons from which power is derived or in which it is contained (cf. Hallowell 1955, 268; 1966, 280; Basso 1970, 45).

This malevolent intervention of spirit beings in human affairs necessitated various forms of propitiation (honoring [yuónihą] and respect [wóohola]): "prayer,"[3] incantation, chants, music and song, dance, offering and sacrifice, rites of affliction, and other ritual actions aimed at mitigating and influencing spirit behavior. However, not all ritual was performed after the fact to appease offended spirits and renew respectful, unhostile relations between humans and nonhumans. In this chapter I focus mainly on the vision quest ceremony to demonstrate the usefulness of a Descolian animist approach as a lens with which to read nineteenth-century Sioux ethnography, although many other ceremonies could be productively read (or reread) from this perspective.

I also apply Kapferer's notion of ritual as virtuality in an attempt to extend the reach of the new animist framework into various virtual realities. In particular I hope to demonstrate the mutually constituting, (re)creative, and (re)generative function of ritual in a dialectical relationship with ontology. The virtual of rite is intimately linked to the dynamics of cosmological, social, and personal construction, entering directly within the individual and collective ritual habitus and adjusting its parameters (Kapferer 2010, 232, 245). According to Kapferer (2010, 245), "The virtual of rite is a means for engaging immediately with the very ontological ground of being." Experiences of the self in virtual realities support, (re)affirm, and vitalize animist hunter-gatherer ontologies, giving life and character to nonhuman persons and substance and meaning to human-nonhuman interaction and relationship.[4]

The vision quest or hąbléc'eyapi (literally, 'to cry for a vision') involved an exacting, progressive series of what Kapferer (2006b, 2010) calls ritual dynamics,[5] various techniques aimed at framing a sacred space, positioning and conditioning the self or one's ritual habitus within that space, and inducing physiological changes in the brain that produce psychological alterations of the mind or consciousness. This emergent process, characterized by a reflexive and discursive interplay between agency and structure, is the descent into the virtual, which may be likened to a kind of collective unconscious, the foundation of which is culture and a specific worldview and distinctive ethnometaphysics. These domains constitute an interrelated dialectic, and nonhuman spirit beings are ontologically as real as human persons. Nonhuman persons are well-known through mythology and oral tradition. They are also phenomenologically experienced in ceremony. This provides the input and fuels interactions between humans and nonhumans in dreams and visions, which, in turn, determines how nonhumans are portrayed or imitated (brought to life) and (re)enacted in ritual.

This descent into virtuality is accomplished through a number of common Sioux ritual dynamics or ritemes, such as separation or isolation, banishing, purification, incensing or smudging, fasting, prayer, music and song, drumming, dancing, invocation, consecration, propitiation or adoration, visualization, various techniques of thought control and methods of concentration of the mind or will (wac'į), various techniques of bodily control, offerings, sacrifice, self-torture, and ultimately identification. These largely invariable dynamics basically functioned as cathartic techniques learned by shamans and passed down through the generations (E. Deloria n.d.b, 64; Walker 1991, 75, 81, 85). They composed a tested and reliable technology for purposefully inducing altered states of consciousness, allowing for a descent into the virtual and a dissociation of the interiority from the physicality. In other words, properly executed ritual dynamics allowed the ritualist to project his interiority, to cross over, so to speak, into the spirit world composed of the eternal essences (interiorities) of all things.[6]

Recall Standing Bear's words: "While in the spirit condition the dreamer was in contact with the spirits of all things of the world" (2006a, 215). Similarly, John Neihardt writes in *Black Elk Speaks*, "Crazy Horse dreamed and went into the world where there is nothing but the spirits of all things. That is the real world that is behind this one, and everything we see here is something like a shadow from that world" (2008, 67). Although I focus on the vision quest in this chapter there were many ways to communicate with the spirits and receive visions, guidance, and medicine. The purposeful inducement of altered states of consciousness and the dissociation of interiority from physicality via Sioux ritual dynamics was common across Sioux tribal divisions and throughout history, occurring in the vision quest, circle dance, sun dance, and yuwípi ceremonies, to name a few (Riggs 1893, 225–26). Lame Deer, a Minneconjou, provides a contemporary example of the spiritual and material migrations across time and space that regularly occur in Sioux ritual. Speaking of the yuwípi ceremony, he explains that once the practitioner is tied and placed in the center of the sacred area "he is now as one who is dead. He does not exist anymore. While the *yuwipi* lies on the floor in his star blanket, his spirit could be hundreds of miles away in the far hills, conversing with the ancient ones" (Lame Deer and Erdoes 1972, 204). In ritual practice many of these common and deep animist ontological orientations surface, as we shall see in the following analysis of the Sioux vision quest.

Hąbléc'eyapi 'Crying for a Vision'

In 1896 the Oglala holy man George Sword explained, "*Hanble* (a vision) is a communication from *Wakan Tanka* or a spirit to one of mankind" (in Walker 1991, 79).[7] In similar terms, Ella Deloria describes a wak'ą́ dream or vision as a "communication of supernatural power" (n.d.e, 7). The vision quest, according to Sword, was a means for "learning the will" of a nonhuman spirit person: "*Wowihanble* is something told to a man by something that is not a man. It is what the white people call a holy dream (vision). God tells his will to man by *wowihanble*. . . . In former times if a man wished to know the will of his God he sought a vision" (in Walker 1991, 81, 84). Essentially the aim of the vision quest was gnosis: mystical enlightenment; spiritual insight; attaining direct knowledge of the esoteric, unseen, or spirit world; and obtaining occult or mysterious powers and medicine through the establishment of relationship with nonhuman spirit persons. Charles Eastman writes, "That solitary communion with the Unseen which was the highest expression of our religious life is partly described in the word *hambeday* [*hąblé* in Lakota], literally 'mysterious feeling,' which has been variously translated 'fasting' and 'dreaming.' It may better be interpreted as 'consciousness of the divine'" (1980, 6). By attaining this superior knowledge via direct and immediate communion with one's spirit guardian or helper (wašícų) a human could be liberated from his entanglement with the world of physicalities and the senses.

A boy usually cried and fasted for his first vision when his voice changed, but visions were sought throughout the life cycle to obtain power, knowledge, guidance, and direction for matters both trivial and of great import. According to most sources, historically the vision quest—and ceremonial pursuits in general—was largely a male enterprise. However, today many women also seek visions in the traditional manner for guidance, medicine, and to become female ritual practitioners (Posthumus 2008–17). As Black Elk (in Joseph Brown 1989, 44, 46) explains, "Every man can cry for a vision, or 'lament'; and in the old days we all—men and women—'lamented' all the time.... Our women also 'lament,' after first purifying themselves in the *Inipi* [sweat lodge]; they are helped by other women, but they do not go up on a very high and lonely mountain. They go up on a hill in a valley, for they are women and need protection." Successfully acquiring a vision was an important basis for Sioux adaptation to actuality and facilitated a truer understanding of the self and a balance or reconciliation between what we might call free will and destiny or fate, agency and structure (Walker 1991, 79–86).

Nonhuman persons did not differ from humans in terms of structure. For both categories the interiority was the enduring vital essence, equated with the self, while the physicality differentiated various collectives. Rather, the difference was in degree: it was a qualitative difference in terms of knowledge, power, or medicine.[8] This qualitative or hierarchical difference in knowledge, power, or medicine applied not only to humans in relation to nonhumans but also in relations between nonhumans. In this way we see again that spirit behavior and interrelationships mirror those of humans. According to the Oglala holy man Ringing Shield,

> There are a great many spirits. They control everything; and they know everything. They can make a man do anything they wish. They can make animals and trees and grass do as they wish. They can talk with animals and they can make animals talk with men. The spirits go about in the world all the time and they make everything do as they please. Some spirits may want things done one way and others may want them done differently. *Then the strongest spirits will overcome the weaker. Some spirits are very powerful and others are not so powerful. Any spirit is more powerful than a man.* (in Walker 1991, 113; emphasis added)

Likewise, in 1896 Sword explained, "The *wakan* beings are the superior beings, that is, they are superior to ordinary mankind. They know what is past and present and what will be" (in Walker 1991, 84).

A key indexical attribute of power was the capacity for transformation, especially when volitionally induced. The wakʻą́pi, or spirits, were also considered to be immortal. According to the Oglala holy man Finger, "The *Wakan* have no father or mother. Anything that has a birth will have a death. The *Wakan* were not born and they will not die" (in Walker 1917, 156). This distinguishes the spirits from humankind and also explains why the term waną́ǧi 'ghost' is used only in reference to the spirits or interiorities of deceased humans (cf. Hallowell 1955, 179–80).[9]

The vision quest was the standard means by which an individual interacted with nonhuman spirit persons and obtained a familiar, spirit helper, or guardian (wašícu). As all people, especially males, required power in order to be successful in all undertakings, and the only source of that power was nonhuman persons, the vision quest was an essential link between human and nonhuman that enabled intercollective relationship and exchange. Dependency defined the relationship between the Lakota individual and the spirits, which explains a great deal about ritual dynamics, especially the centrality of sacrifice and the evocation of aid or pity (ų́šika or ų́šila). Sacrifice is a central indexical ritual dynamic (Kapferer 2006a) expressive of the ultimate relationship of exchange between humans and nonhumans. Speaking of aid or pity, based on the stem ų́šika/ų́šila, White Hat writes, "*Ųmašike* means, 'I have a particular need, and I need help with that need.' If I come to you and say '*Ųšimalayo*,' all I'm saying is that I need help with a particular need. The church took that word and translated it as 'I'm pitiful; have pity on me.' Today probably 90 percent of our people think of that as the meaning. Translations like this were very powerful and have contributed greatly to our people being conditioned to dependency on higher, or outside, authority" (2012, 75n3).

Humans relied on the generosity of nonhumans and their willingness to aid or pity humans, act according to kinship expectations and obligations, and share their abundance of power. Individuals became extremely attached to their spirit helpers, referring to them in possessive terms (*mitʿáwašicų* 'my spirit helper' or *tʿawášicų* 'his or her spirit helper'), even to the point of complete identification or union of interiorities. Brown notes similar beliefs in regard to animal ceremonialism. The quest for game, he explains, was "a religious activity to be prepared for and concluded by ritual. The quarry was an eminently sacred or power-bearing being. Hunting is a quest, Black Elk insisted, which requires preparatory prayer and sacrificial purification. The diligently followed tracks are steps in the ritual, while final contact or identity with the quarry is the ultimate goal" (Joseph Brown 1997, 10).

Further, humans who obtained power from nonhumans, often demonstrated through transformation, were seen as closer on the continuum of power to the spirits themselves. They were superior to their fellow humans in this regard and hence were respected and feared (Posthumus 2015; G. Pond 1889; cf. Hallowell 1955, 180, 182). In reference to the Dakotas of Minnesota in the mid-nineteenth century Gideon Pond writes, "As regards the medicine man as a doctor, or exorcist, or juggler, it is not only believed that he can cure diseases, but that he can inflict them at his pleasure, on any person who may dare to offend him. It only requires a *purpose* on his part. They are feared, if possible, more than the gods themselves, for *they are present* in the camp and in the lodge" (1889, 251–52; emphasis in original). In 1896 Sword explained that a Lakota shaman "is feared by all the people. . . . The oldest or wisest shamans are the most respected" (in Walker 1991, 80). According to Ella Deloria, "Mystics are lonely. Among all peoples they reach out ahead of the masses, and here too that was true. 'Lonely is the man with vision'" (1998, 58).

In sacred dreams or visions, as in myth and ceremony, the interiority could disassociate from the physicality and experience increased mobility in time and space, as evidenced by Oglala holy man Nicholas Black Elk's vision in which he traveled in the spirit back to his home at Pine Ridge while he was in England with Buffalo Bill's Wild West show (DeMallie 1984, 252–53). Ella Deloria writes that a common vision quest trope involved the lamenter being led by a spirit person in human form "through the air or over land and sea, resting at last at some spot not to be found on earth where he would receive his revelation" (1998, 59).

Numerous additional examples of this phenomenon could be cited (see, for instance, Bushotter 1887–88, story 12). Frequently (combinations of) Sioux ritual dynamics or ritemes—such as isolation, fasting, smudging, incantations, chants, music, dance, sacrifice, self-torture, and so on—functioned to facilitate this separation of interiority from physicality, thus revealing the underlying, fundamental interiorities of all things, which were privileged in Sioux culture, and allowing for the free movement of the interiority through time and space and for communion and covenants between human and nonhuman interiorities. In Sioux ceremonies the physicality is purposefully neglected and put aside so that the interiority may move unfettered in the spirit world.

Tųwápi is an important yet problematic concept in Sioux ethnometaphysics (see Posthumus 2015). It may be understood as a centrifugal aspect of the interiority, akin to Husserl's intentionality or object-directed consciousness, but the concept is not well documented in the literature. According to Gideon Pond, the Minnesota Dakotas in the mid-nineteenth century understood tųwápi as an emitted or projected wak'ą influence: a missive potency or capacity to act, purposefully directed (*ó* or *yeyá* 'to shoot or send') by agentive and powerful human and nonhuman persons. The ability to shoot tųwápi is common to all the Táku Wak'ą or sacred nonhuman spirits and is infused in medicine bundles through the proper ceremony. Once tųwápi is infused in a medicine bundle the bundle itself is equated with the spirit whose potency it contains and is then capable of projecting or shooting tųwápi into other objects or people, as in the Dakota mystery dance. Lightning (wakíyą tųwápi) is the emitted potency or tųwápi of the Wakíyąpi or Thunder Birds (G. Pond 1889, 219–20, 224–26, 228; cf. Walker 1991, 80, 95–96, 186).

As Sword (in Walker 1917, 153) explains, "We do not see the real earth and the rock, but only their *tonwanpi*." Sword's statement substantiates Pond's earlier claims and is instructive in multiple ways. Tųwą́ (literally, 'to stare, glare') in this sense basically means emitted spiritual or nonhuman potency: a shot or manifestation of projected wak'ą energy. Adding the suffix *-pi* indicates the animate plural, highlighting how "inanimate" objects, such as the earth and rocks, had the capacity for personhood in Sioux ethnometaphysics. So we can interpret Sword's statement from a Platonic perspective as saying that the *real* earth, rock, and so on is the eternal, underlying essence or interiority of these phenomena, not their physicalities. What we actually see with our eyes in the physical world or actuality is merely a projection or manifestation of the enduring essence or interiority. Black Elk expresses a similar notion as he stands at the "center of the world" in his great vision:

> And while I stood there I saw more than I can tell and I understood more than I saw; for I was seeing in a sacred manner the shapes of all things in the spirit, and the shape of all shapes as they must live together like one being. And I saw that the sacred hoop of my people was one of many hoops that made one circle, wide as daylight and as starlight, and in the center grew one mighty flowering tree to shelter all the children of one mother and one father. And I saw that it was holy. (in DeMallie 1984, 97)

Black Elk's words corroborate many of the themes explored in this study.

In virtual domains time also operates differently in that it is immanent, relative or specific to rite, and circular, akin to the present continuous or Nietzsche's eternal return or time as totality, wherein all time, past, present, and future, intersects and aligns (Kapferer 2013a, 2014b). Kapferer writes, "Following Nietzsche it might be said that ritual aims to re-situate (re-originate, re-birth) its participants within time so that the past is stopped from becoming its future—indeed the past and its effects being overcome through the machinery of rite in which, effectively, a new past is created through the future rather than vice versa. . . . Within ritual participants can be conceived as entering into time in itself from which all existence (Past, Present, and Future) can be conceived as being emergent" (Kapferer 2013b, 6). On the virtual plane both time and space operate differently, and in such spaces humans had access to knowledge, power, and persons they did not normally have access to. This explains how in yuwípi conjuring ceremonies rock or yuwípi spirits are capable of miraculously traveling great distances in both time and space, reporting back to human shamans and informing them of the location of lost people, animals, and objects or foretelling the future (see Powers 1982b;

Fugle 1966). These spirits dwell in the virtual plane where all time and space converge.

Brown describes it thus: "Intercepting the horizontal dimension to the world of appearances [physicalities], there is always, for the Oglala mind, the vertical dimension of the sacred [interiorities], and in this sacredness there is the sense of 'mystery' [wakʻą́]" (Joseph Brown 1997, xii). DeMallie (in Walker 1982, 113) addresses this topic as well, explaining that the Lakota "past is preceded, accompanied, and followed by an ever present, sacred dimension which is outside the realm of human time. Here the gods and spirits are the relevant participants, who sometimes intrude into the flow of human history but are not dependent on it." Vine Deloria (2009) also addresses the relativity of time and space in Sioux belief and ritual. To the Sioux, nonhuman persons and powers, like the rest of the cosmos, were alive: immanent potentialities capable of growth, transformation, movement, intelligible speech, relationship, and free to intervene in the human sphere or actuality at their will (cf. Basso 1970, 42).

Where these two planes or dimensions meet is the ritual "center of the universe/world," a common vision and ritual trope described by Black Elk (in DeMallie 1984) and Vine Deloria (2009), among others. Much of the goal of preliminary Sioux ritual dynamics or ritemes, such as the creation of an altar or sacred space and the pipe (offering) ceremony, is to ritually center the individual in time and space and call the attention of the spirits to this centering. Where Brown's two axes meet constitutes a doorway (tʻiyópa) or portal between the actual and the virtual, the material world of physicalities and the spirit world of interiorities. At the center many mysterious things are possible: humans can encounter nonhuman interiorities or nonhumans can manifest in various guises and communicate with humans, as when the ghost of a deceased human or an animal spirit manifests itself in actuality. In contemporary Oglala yuwípi ceremonies the altar is likened to a portal between the human world and the spirit world. The altar allows for intercollective communication and relationship, as when a conjuror enlists the aid of his rock spirit helpers. The shaman is truly in a liminal space, on the precipice of death, between the world of physicalities and interiorities. Further, the interiorities of celebrated historical figures, such as Crazy Horse, Sitting Bull, and famous medicine men, manifest their presence in ceremonies, giving aid and guidance to the people from the spirit world through ritual virtuality.

Purposefully inducing an altered state of consciousness and the descent into the virtual, a plane of pure immanence and interiorities with unlimited potentialities, has a (re)constitutive and (re)generative effect on the individual and collective in actuality. In the virtual planes of mythology, dreams and visions, and ritual nonhuman persons were existentially and phenomenologically experienced: they were seen, heard, felt, and communed with (cf. Hallowell 1960, 41). In such spaces humans gained access to knowledge, power, and persons they did not normally have access to.

According to Sword (in Walker 1991, 86), "If one has a vision, he sees something. It may be like a man or it may be like an animal or a bird or an insect or anything that breathes, or it may be like a light of some kind or a cloud." Speaking of vision encounters with a particular spirit the Oglala Thunder Bear (in Walker 1991, 131) explains, "It may come to him in the form of a man, an animal, or a bird or it may come as a voice only or only in his thoughts. When it comes, it will tell him something which will be a knowledge of some medicine or what to do in the future or a warning against some evil or to make another quest or to cease from seeking a vision. The communication is apt to be ambiguous and require an interpretation." For up to four lonely days and nights a human, usually clad only in a breechcloth and moccasins, cried and starved for a vision, for a visitation from a nonhuman person and a chance to interact with the spirits and obtain wakʻą́ knowledge and power.

Creating a sacred space or center (*hócʻoka*, ową́ka, *ową́gkağapi*), commonly referred to in English as an altar, and isolating oneself from other humans were essential preliminary Lakota ritual dynamics. Prolonged isolation relaxes the automatic mechanisms that drive us and allows for the dissociation of the interiority from the physicality. After purifying oneself, smudging the sacred space, and other preliminaries, the vision quester or lamenter went to the place where he would seek his vision, far away from human habitation, and cleared a space of every living thing that breathes or grows. This is done because the altar is sacred and there should be nothing on it that is not acceptable as an offering to the spirits (Walker 1917, 69; 1991, 132–33). "At the altar," writes Ella Deloria (1998, 59), "usually on the edge of a remote butte, the man took his place, there to remain all alone on the hallowed plot until someone came to lead him into the *wakan* realm. There he hoped to see something supernaturally significant that would help him become a worthwhile man: a good hunter, a good warrior, an effective and true medicine man, a diviner, or whatever. He wanted power to be useful in his tribe."

Sword (1938) describes a similar notion using the phrase *wicʻácʻeȟpi icáȟtake šni* 'never having touched human flesh' in reference to acceptable offerings to the spirits. Apparently the idea is that human beings in their natural state are impure or common (*ikcéka* 'common', as opposed to *wakʻą́* 'sacred') and hence unacceptable or unworthy to the spirits.[10] This explains the centrality of purification in Sioux ritual dynamics as a preliminary and persistent riteme. According to many early observers (see Dorsey 1894, 436–37; Lynd 1889; Riggs 1869; Walker 1917, 1991), purification, alongside sacrifice, is the most prominent and ancient feature of Sioux religious belief and ritual practice. Purification, explains Riggs (1869, 82), "is the preparation for the highest forms of sacrifice." According to Ringing Shield, "If one wishes to talk with the spirits he must purify his body" (in Walker 1991, 113). The usual way to purify the body was through the *inípi* or sweat lodge ceremony, an essential preliminary ritual performed as a ceremony in its own right and also in preparation for all other ceremonies (see Sword in Walker 1991, 79, 85; Bucko 1998).

Once purified and established in a sacred space, isolated from human contact, the lamenter begins a repertoire of various ritual dynamics aimed at inducing psychological alterations of consciousness allowing for the descent into the virtual. Fasting is one essential element, the lamenter going without food or water for the duration of the ceremony. According to Ella Deloria, "He ate and drank nothing; he only had his pipe. After he had fasted a long time, having begun at home of course, his head became light and his senses became so delicate and acute that even a little bit of stick pricking him was unbearably intensified. If a bird called, he might hear a message from the spirit world. If an animal approached him, he might see it as a man to guide him to his vision" (1998, 59; see also Tyon in Walker 1991, 152).

Various verbal techniques, such as "prayer" (wac'ékiya), incantations, chants, and singing (waálową), are also employed. Importantly, various concentration and visualization techniques for controlling and focusing the mind or will (wac'į or t'awác'į) are also utilized. According to Sword, "If a man is alone and speaks to no one and neither eats nor drinks anything and thinks continually about the superior beings, he may have a vision. The usual way to seek a vision is to purify the body in an *Initi* by pouring water on hot stones and then go naked, only wrapped in a robe, to the top of a hill, and stay there without speaking to anyone of mankind or eating, or drinking, and thinking continually about the vision he wishes" (in Walker 1991, 85). Reporting on the instructions given by shamans to initiates, lamenters, or vision seekers (*wóle*), Walker (1991, 133) writes, "When you have entered on this place, you should meditate only on seeing a vision. You may invoke the spirits in words or song and you must always address them in a reverential manner." As Ella Deloria (n.d.e, 4) explains, "To have power you must give your entire concentration and confidence to your subject." Similarly, Black Elk reports that a vision seeker "may remain silent with his whole attention directed to the Great Spirit or to one of His Powers. He must always be careful lest distracting thoughts come to him, yet he must be alert to recognize any messenger which the Great Spirit may send to him, for these people often come in the form of an animal, even one as small and as seemingly insignificant as a little ant. . . . All these people are important, for in their own way they are wise and they can teach us two-leggeds much if we make ourselves humble before them" (Black Elk in Joseph Brown 1989, 58).

Another key Lakota ritual dynamic is sensory deprivation and overload. An example is total darkness, characteristic of the sweat lodge, yuwípi, and other evening healing and divination ceremonies. Tied to this is the imagination and the notion of seeing with one's spirit or interiority, what Joseph Brown (1989, 42) claims Black Elk called "the eye of the heart" or c'ąté ištá: "It is the wish of *Wakan-Tanka* that the Light enters

Fig. 3. Depiction of the vision quest, by Lakota artist Amos Bad Heart Bull. Reproduced from Bad Heart Bull and Blish (1967, 275), by permission of the University of Nebraska Press.

into the darkness, that we may see not only with our two eyes, but with the one eye which is of the heart [Chante Ishta], and with which we see and know all that is true and good." While Brown's notion of the eye of the heart was influenced by his own reading of the teachings of his spiritual mentor Frithjof Schuon (see Joseph Brown 1989, 42n2), and hence Brown's work in general is problematic and must be read critically, there are corollaries from other sources in the literature.

Discussing the vision quest, Ella Deloria explains that a man seeking a vision often closed his eyes: "It was the rule not to open the eyes, but to take in facts through the mind's or spirit's eye" (n.d.c, 44). Visions were frequently experienced through the mind's or spirit's eye. A similar dynamic operated in yuwípi performances, a ceremony held in complete darkness in which the practitioner was carefully tied up and wrapped in a bison robe or blanket. Attached to the outside of the robe was a small circular mirror, symbolic of an eye and light (Fletcher 1887a, 277, 284; Wissler 1907c, 40–43). "The mirror was fastened to the spot opposite their forehead," writes Ella Deloria (n.d.e, 43), "where the mind could

Fig. 4. Depiction of the vision quest, by Stephen Standing Bear. Courtesy of Buechel Memorial Lakota Museum, Photo Archives, St. Francis Mission, St. Francis SD 57572.

look through and see in the distance the thing taking place as it would in a little while, or see the lost horse or man, lying or standing as he would be found." The mirror, like a receptacle of water, congealed blood, or other reflective surface, also figured prominently in divination (see Posthumus 2015, 248, 325, 334, 337–39), allowing the practitioner to see with his mind's or spirit's eye, beyond the limits of sight allowed by his physicality, into the world of interiorities through a descent into ritual virtuality.

The mind, will, or willpower (wacʻį or tʻawácʻį) is an important concept for understanding Sioux religious belief and ritual.[11] DeMallie (1984, 116n7) describes it as "the power of mind—which is not merely passive, but creative—that is enriched ('made wise') by the vision experiences." The wacʻį 'mind/will' may be likened to the consciousness, personality, disposition, mental or cognitive faculties, intentionality, or object-directed subjectivity, the dynamic aspect of the self. It is a functionally distinctive aspect of the interiority. Receiving and activating visionary powers bestowed by nonhuman spirit persons required clarity of understanding (*waábleza*), a focusing of the mind/will on the psychic or spiritual gifts of the spirits. Mastery of a vision required great effort and study, discipline, and a focusing or sharpening of one's mental faculties (see Densmore 2001, 85; Joseph Brown 1989, 64n5; DeMallie 1984, 116n7; cf. Fletcher 1897).

The following lengthy quote from Dorsey demonstrates a number of important themes and ritual dynamics discussed herein:

> If a Dakota wishes to be particularly successful in any (to him) important undertaking, he first *purifies* himself by the Inipi or steam bath, and by *fasting* for a term of three days. During the whole of this time he *avoids women and society*, is *secluded* in his habits, and endeavors in every way to be *pure* enough to receive a revelation from the deity whom he *invokes*. When the period of *fasting* is passed he is ready for the *sacrifice*, which is made in various ways. Some, passing a knife through the breast and arms, attach thongs thereto, which are fastened at the other end to the top of a tall pole raised for that purpose; and thus they hang, suspended only by these thongs, for two, three, or even four days, *gazing upon vacancy, their minds being intently fixed upon the object in which they desire to be assisted by the deity, and waiting for a vision from above*. . . . A third class pass knives through the flesh in various parts of the body, and wait in silence, though *with fixed mind*, for a dream or revelation. . . . Still another class practice the haŋmdepi without such horrid *self-sacrifice*. For weeks, nay, for months, they will *fix their minds intently upon any desired object, to the exclusion of all others, frequently crying about the camp, occasionally*

> *taking a little food, but fasting for the most part, and earnestly seeking a revelation from their god.* (1894, 436–37; emphasis added)

In reference to similar ritual dynamics in the Dakota sun dance Lynd (1889, 167) writes, "The mind of the worshipper is fixed intently upon some great desire that he has, and is, as it were, isolated from the body. In this state they are said to receive revelations from the sun, and to hold direct intercourse with that deity." In 1896 Sword (in Walker 1991, 79) explained, "To seek a vision one should *Inipi* [purify one's self in the sweat lodge], and then remain alone as much as possible, thinking continually of that about which he desires a vision. While doing this he should eat no food nor take any drink, but he may smoke the pipe."

The writings of Beede, based on his discussions with Northern Lakotas from Standing Rock Reservation in the early 1900s, help us grasp the complexities of Sioux understandings of human interiorities. Discussing the "geocentric" nature of Western Sioux cosmology and mythology, Beede writes,

> A man's mind (tawacin), and soul (wicanagi), is all-around the man, and reaches a great way off. When a man is intently using his mind for something he calls to the use nearly all of his mind, but still it is extending far away in every direction. When a man is not using his mind it goes on journeys far away. Sometimes a man's mind nearly all of it leaves him and goes away on a far journey so that the man is "nearly-the-same-as-dead" (tanunse), but the mind has not left him. His mind and soul needs him as much as he needs his mind and soul, and so the mind and soul come back, however far they wander. . . . The mind (tawacin), as the child grows into a man learns to stretch himself far and wide. Thus the mind and soul (towacin [sic] wicanagi kici) may stretch himself far away while a man is asleep, or in a wihanble (a sort of vision), and behold many things; and may even travel to the home of the Great Spirit. The mind and soul grows (icage) and becomes the ruler as the child grows into a man, but it all begins with the child, who has its body before it has much mind and soul, and the child begins with its mother. The child's body is its mother's body. A man's heart is his mother's heart and her heart

is his heart (heart meaning mind and soul plus decision and choice, as it seems), especially so when from decision and choice a fixed disposition and inclination has been formed. In the same way Holy Mother Earth has grown from childhood to maturity. Her mind has grown and stretched himself (this mind of earth is regarded as primarily masculine, though the element of the feminine inheres in it), far and wide in all life forms. They regard "wiconi," in one aspect of its meaning at any rate, as meaning the totality of life-forms, as in the phrase "Wiconi, na wicasa he e sni, mdotahunke ece," a Hunkpatina Sioux saying. The Hunkpatina are much like the very Western Sioux. This saying indicates that it is life in all life-forms, and not solely or chiefly in man, which is leader in the forward moving caravan of all creatures. Among the Western Sioux I find no indication of opinion that the man-form is the fixed or chief or superior form. (Western Sioux Cosmology 1912, 18–20)

As an aspect of the interiority the mind, like the soul, is conceptualized as an intangible or spiritual essence or energy. It is not bounded by the physicality but rather transcends it in both time and space. In virtual realities various ritual dynamics are voluntarily and consciously employed to facilitate the dissociation of the interiority from the physicality. Clearly the wacʻį́ as mind/will or consciousness is not conceptualized as a physical object, contained within the skull of a person. Lakotas refer to that sense of mind as *nasúla* (brain, cerebrum). Beede's insights illuminate our discussion of the role of the interiority in Sioux ritual dynamics and virtuality, particularly in relation to the vision quest.

Most visions generally followed a normative pattern or formula composed of a common core stock of cultural symbols, yet in detail they varied considerably. According to the general pattern a nonhuman person in human form appeared to the human dreamer.[12] The nonhuman was a manifestation of šicų́ (potency, immortal aspect of the human soul; the interiority of a wakʻą́, sometimes glossed as 'familiar' or 'guardian spirit') and a representative of a particular oyáte or collective who acted as an instructor. In this way the nonhuman representative was akin to the

Fig. 5. Dream or Spirit Elk. Reproduced from Bad Heart Bull and Blish (1967, 199), by permission of the University of Nebraska Press.

"owner" or "master" Platonic spirit of a particular collective.[13] Without getting into great detail, the nonhuman was the key to the human's attainment of medicine (pʻežúta) or power (wówašʼake). Usually the nonhuman would point out a plant that would then be used in actuality by the dreamer as medicine. At some point in the vision the instructor would transform into his characteristic animal physicality and run off. This animal thereafter became the spirit helper or familiar (*wašícų*) of the dreamer. Last the dreamer received certain prayers and songs from the instructor, whose interiority became infused with that of the dreamer, adding to his wakʻą́ power or strength. Essentially the human was adopted into the nonhuman collective. Often a šicų́ thus acquired was either localized in a ritual object or embodied by an individual and understood as an indwelling spirit (wówakʻą or wašícų) (Wissler 1912, 81; Curtis 1908, 21, 62–63; Walker 1991, 129–32, 150–53; Densmore 2001, 184–88, 274–75; E. Deloria 1998, 58–62; cf. Hallowell 1955, 179–80).

Dreams and visions, obtained through the ritualized vigil or retreat, were a major impetus for ceremony and had a real significance and determinative effect on everyday life. Dream experiences often defined an individual for the rest of his life (Bad Heart Bull and Blish 1967, 275; Fletcher 1887a; Lynd 1889, 170; Neill 1890, 233-37). Through dreams reciprocal relationships, what Ian Hodder (2012, 2014) refers to as entanglements of dependency, between human and nonhuman persons were established and renewed. Visions entangled humans and nonhumans in relationships of exchange and dependency and came with binding obligations tied to the disease sanction. Recall that obligations conferred in dreams were binding, and disregarding them was sure to incur misfortune, hardship, or disaster in some form (E. Deloria 1998, 104-5; Densmore 2001, 157).

The most common vision obligation was a required public ritual performance known as a káǧa.[14] According to Helen Blish (in Bad Heart Bull and Blish 1967, 200), "Such performances are given in response to someone's dream or vision in which he is told to test his medicine and the guardianship of the particular animal seen in vision." These ceremonies were detailed (re)enactments of vision experiences that (re)created and actualized virtual potentialities, activating the powers exchanged in visions and proving that one had received a vision and medicine. In mimetic fashion these performances publicly reflected the virtuality of the vision onto actuality. Whereas in the vision itself a convergence of interiorities was achieved, in the káǧa physicalities were brought in line so as to induce transformations. This is similar to what is referred to as "remembering" one's spirit guardian. The details of the virtual experience were (re)created and (re)enacted in exact detail, from the actions to the songs and the regalia to the distinctive painting, demonstrating the constitutive and generative power of the virtual in actuality. For this reason each káǧa was unique, based on individual visionary experiences, despite drawing from a pool of common religious symbols and motifs. This obsession with detail and the exactitude of operations was linked to the disease sanction (Fletcher 1887a, 277, 285n9; 1887b, 289n2, 293n10; E. Deloria n.d.d, 89; Kapferer 2010, 245). The phenomenological experience from the perspective of the onlookers or ritual gathering

(Rappaport 2000) was a union of virtuality and actuality: a mirror image or reflection of the former in the latter. According to Viveiros de Castro,

> To put on mask-clothing is not so much to conceal a human essence beneath an animal appearance, but rather to activate the powers of a different body. The animal clothes that shamans use to travel the cosmos are not fantasies but instruments: they are akin to diving equipment, or space suits, and not to carnival masks. The intention when donning a wet suit is to be able to function like a fish, to breathe underwater, not to conceal oneself under a strange covering. In the same way, the "clothing" which, amongst animals, covers an internal "essence" of a human type, is not a mere disguise but their distinctive equipment, endowed with the affects [capacity to affect and be affected] and capacities which define each animal. (1998, 482)

During certain ritual performances the human *became* the nonhuman. These transformations were accomplished through a conscious, purposeful blending or convergence of physicalities and various ritual dynamics (Kapferer 2006a), such as symbolic identification, imitation, (re)enactment, and various aesthetic dynamics. These dynamics induced ritual transformations and unions of interiorities, the descent into the virtual, as when a shaman donned the clothing or skin (há) of a bear or the tail of a buffalo, painted himself in the characteristic way of a particular nonhuman, performed specific songs and dances, recited particular prayers or incantations, and so on. Essentially the distinctive properties and qualities of animals and medicines were transferred to the object or person to which they were ritually affixed, achieving a merger of interiorities through a convergence of physicalities. As proof of this transformation a shaman imitating a specific animal spirit often left the tracks of that animal, rather than human footprints, demonstrating his efficacy and relationship or kinship with a particular nonhuman collective (Bad Heart Bull and Blish 1967; E. Deloria n.d.a, 32; n.d.e, 18; Wissler 1912, 88, 91–92, 96, 98).

According to Descola (2013a, 136), "Conversion from animal to human and from human to animal is a constant feature in animist ontologies: the former process reveals interiority, while the latter is an attribute of

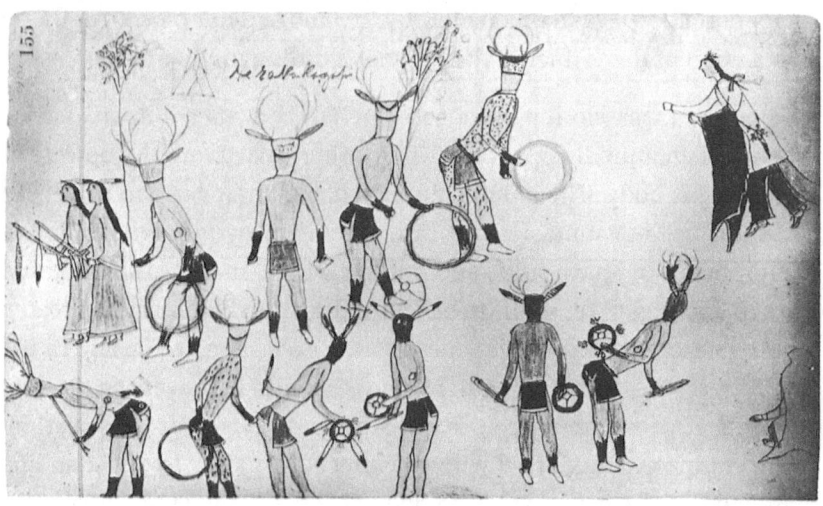

Fig. 6. Deer and Elk dreamer ritual performance (*káǧa*). Reproduced from Bad Heart Bull and Blish (1967, 274), by permission of the University of Nebraska Press.

the power with which certain particular individuals (shamans, sorcerers, specialists in ritual) are credited, namely the power to transcend at will the discontinuity of forms and adopt as their vehicle the body of some animal species with which they maintain special relations." Elaborating on the notion of transformation in animist societies Descola (2013a, 138) writes that the "visitor," in this case the human shaman, "assumes a position that puts him on the same footing as his hosts, for this is necessary if he is to establish communication, and this he does by adopting the same costume as those he is addressing. Nonhumans reveal their interiority by taking on the form of human physicality; humans abandon their own physicality in order to take on that of a nonhuman or so as to move freely within the world of interior forms."

Based on his work with Bushotter, Dorsey describes a Lakota man who was capable of transforming himself into a grizzly bear. The ritual gathering camped in a circle, in the center of which was erected a special lodge. The onlookers sang grizzly bear songs while the man sat with a grizzly bear hide over his shoulders. As the ritual gathering looked on the man began to make the distinctive sounds of the bear (*matʻó hotʻúpi*) and soon was transformed into a grizzly, chasing and scattering the terrified people. "He overtook one man," writes Dorsey (1889b, 137), "tore him to pieces, and devoured the body, leaving only the bones. This made all the spectators wail, but they were not afraid to gather up the bones in a blanket, which they took back to the tent of the slain man. Once more the bear was walking around the circle, and this time he was growling. All at once the slain man was restored to life!" The Bear man shook a plum tree placed in the center of the circle, causing plums to fall to the ground, and hit the earth with his paw, pulling up wild turnips. Finally the Bear man resumed his human physicality (Dorsey 1889b, 137–38).

Tyon describes a four-day Bear healing ceremony in which all the Bear doctors or "Bear men" from the camp congregated with their medicines (*pʻežúta*) in a specially designated "Bear tipi" where the patient was placed. At the dramatic height of the ceremony, as the Bear dreamers sang and the people looked on expectantly, the leader of the Bear society performed the Matʻó kága 'Bear imitation', in which he ritually became (*áya*) a bear, growing wild (*gnaškíyą*) and running amok (Tyon in Walker 1991, 157–59). Completely covering his head with a bear skin, the leader burst out of the Bear tipi, grunting and growling ferociously, making the characteristic sounds of a bear. Pawing the earth, he mysteriously produced prairie turnips from it. Large canine teeth miraculously descended from his jaw as he shook plum trees in imitation of a bear. He chased people, and if a hapless stray dog happened to cross his path while he was in such a state he literally tore it to pieces with his bare hands, devouring parts of it raw. The people fled from him in fear until he was ritually soothed by other members of the Bear society, often through the singing of Bear songs (Curtis 1908, 63–64; Bushotter 1887–88, story 199; Walker 1991, 158–59). In this altered ritual state the Bear dreamer might also become bulletproof or stab people with his knife and subsequently heal them. He often explained that he was "going hunting" (Walker 1991, 159). Figure 7 is George Catlin's depiction of a Lakota Bear dance, first sketched near Fort Pierre in 1832.

Samuel Pond describes similar dynamics of imitation and transformation in a nineteenth-century Dakota ceremony known as the raw fish feast:

Fig. 7. *The Bear Dance, Preparing for a Bear Hunt* (1844), by George Catlin. Courtesy of Wikimedia Commons.

> This feast ... was celebrated only when it was revealed to someone that it was absolutely necessary, which was not very often. ... The chief actors, those who devoured the fish, represented beasts and birds of prey. Some personated wolves, bears, foxes, etc.; and others hawks, cormorants, and other rapacious birds. ... Each assumed the appearance and imitated the manner, as well as he could, of the beast or bird which he represented. They also attempted to imitate their voices, and in this some of them succeeded very well; for it is part of their craft, as hunters and warriors, to learn to mimic the voices of birds and beasts. ... It was as beasts, not as men, that they ate the raw fish. (1908, 415–16)

Gideon Pond witnessed a Dakota raw fish feast at Shakopee, Minnesota, in the summer of 1852. In the ceremony the pike devoured raw by the ritual performers was painted with vermilion and adorned with swan's down. "The dancers," writes Pond (1889, 241), "who were naked, except the breech-cloth and moccasins, were fantastically smeared with pigments of various colors, and otherwise ornamented with down, white and red.... The dancers claimed to be inspired by the cormorant." It is likely that this ceremony was actually referred to as a *hų́tka káǧa* 'cormorant imitation or [re]enactment' in Dakota.

Recall that the virtual realities of mythology, dreams and visions, and ritual were mutually constituting and generative, continuous with other cumulative self-related experience. Consequently virtual experience was in a dialectical relation with ontology and worldview. Transformation was a hallmark of the person category, especially in virtuality. Lakota culture privileges experience and participation as foundational to ontological and epistemological understandings, what Ingold (2004, 35) refers to as a "condition of engagement" or "the primary context of their active, perceptual engagement within an environment."

Imitation (káǧa 'to represent, enact, imitate, perform') functioned to bring nonhuman spirits to life and was also conceptualized as a "prayer" or invocation of relationship to secure the aid or protection of a particular spirit person and to activate and manifest the powers and attributes associated with its distinctive bodily apparatus (Wissler 1905, 258–59).[15] Imitation is prayer, and prayer is imitation. Wissler (1905, 268) writes, "The way to realize a condition in nature according to this philosophy is to put one's self in the attitude of the men or animals who do accomplish what seems desirable." Exemplifying this ritual convergence of physicalities, one of Ella Deloria's consultants described a "buffalo-man," the shamans who typically conducted buffalo ceremonies:

> He wore a flat piece of pte-hį́ pahpa, the fur that moults [sic] in sheets from the buffalo, on his head. In all ways he was designed to be a buffalo-bull. He looked fierce and wakʻą́. He didn't seem human.... He was made to look like a buffalo; he wore horns on his head. He was painted, and looked fierce. His tail hung limply behind; he crawled on all fours, from his tipi, towards the ceremonial tipi. He was very wakʻą́. He growled as he advanced, and shook his head angrily from side to side, just like a bull. (n.d.a, 30, 36)

The káǧa was akin to another type of ceremony described by Ella Deloria as "remembering" one's spirit guardian (1998, 60–61). The major means for humans to acquire medicine, that is, nonhuman wakʻą́ knowledge and power, was through appealing to the generosity of nonhuman spirit persons in dreams and ritual. Through visionary experiences humans could accumulate power, analogous to a reservoir or wellspring, which they could then tap into through various ritual dynamics, descending into the virtual in times of anxiety, strife, sickness, danger, and so on. Power incantations, songs, techniques, and objects originated through human-nonhuman communication and exchange in virtual space/time (Fletcher 1887a, 278, 280; Wissler 1907c, 30; 1912, 53). Fasting for a vision, writes Fletcher (1887a, 278), was "believed to be strengthening to the man, by laying up a store of experiences which are drawn upon for succor in the day of battle, or of trouble. At such times, or when on missions of importance, the man recalls his vision and sings its songs thus appealing to his god."

Focusing the mind/will and remembering one's vision allowed an individual to travel in the mind and spirit into the spirit world of interiorities. The willed, purposive focusing of the mind/will simultaneously recognized a human-nonhuman relationship, invoked a particular spirit, and actualized and activated various mysterious or nonhuman powers and abilities. According to Ella Deloria (n.d.b, 67; n.d.h, 192), this sense of remembering, common in the Sioux literature, means that an individual recalls his identification with a particular nonhuman spirit person or collective and so *becomes* that nonhuman for the time being: "It means, or implies, that the man in question has at some previous time been promised help by the animal mentioned. He is therefore privileged to draw power from that animal. He may so far never have had to avail himself of the right, but now it is necessary. So he 'remembers his beaver.' The translation is faulty here. His beaver does not mean a specific beaver which he owns, but rather, his *beaverhood*, if you will; at any rate, it means he recalls his right to a connection with beavers as a medium of power" (E. Deloria n.d.e, 18).

This line of thinking also clarifies elements of what has been termed contagious magic in Sioux ethnographic accounts. By attaching an eagle feather to one's physicality, for instance, one embodies the characteristic attributes and bodily apparatus of the eagle and hence temporarily *becomes* an eagle. The same could be said of a wolf skin or buffalo tail. But such transformations were considered exceedingly dangerous (wókʻokipʻe), because the potential that one would be unable to reverse the transformation and return to one's characteristic physicality was always present. This is why many contemporary Lakotas caution of the dangers of remaining in the virtual plane or spirit world for too long in ritual performances (Posthumus 2015, 98; 2008–17; Wissler 1912, 90–91).

The Ethnometaphysics of Sioux Medicine Bundles

Similar dynamics operated in the beliefs and practices associated with ceremonial bundles, commonly referred to as medicine bundles. Also called wašícų, ceremonial bundles were objects ritually infused with nonhuman interiorities or šicų́pi, similar to the embodiment of a šicų́ in each human being at birth. Medicine bundles were localizations of wakʻą́ power containing the tʻų́ or spiritual essence of a nonhuman person and were often made to physically resemble and symbolically represent that animal or spirit (see Posthumus 2015, 112–39). As James R. Walker explains,

> Most of the Gods can emit their potencies and when so emitted their potencies become *sicunpi*. Such a *sicun* can be imparted to material things by a proper ceremony correctly performed by a Shaman. A *sicun* so imparted must be clothed by proper wrappings about the material It pervades. The wrappings may be in the form of a pouch, bag, bundle, or any receptacle that will cover and hide the material. The wrapping, the material, and the *sicun*, all together make a *wasicun*. A *sicun* is operative only when It is a part of a *wasicun*.[16] The Oglala concept of a *wasicun* is most nearly expressed in English by the word Fetish, and this word will be so used hereinafter. While a Fetish may be operative independent of the source of its potency It must be treated with the veneration due to the God that emits its *Sicun*, for in all Its properties It is as that God. . . . The contents of a medicine bag may be either the material, the spirit-like of which is the potency, or material to which potency has been imparted. . . . If the potency of any God abides in anything that thing should be the

material enclosed in the wrapping of the Fetish pertaining to that God. . . . The functions of a Fetish are to serve Its possessor with Its supernatural powers which are effective when properly invoked. When preparing a Fetish, the Shaman devises a formula which must be repeated to invoke Its powers. (1917, 87–88)

Ceremonial bundles were associated with specific prayers or ritual formulae and songs. According to Sword, "The holy man prays to his ceremonial bag. He must know the song that belongs to it and the right words to say in praying to it. Then when he sings this song and says these words, the bag will do as he bids. It is not the bag which does this but that which is in the bag. This is called *sicun* in Lakota. The bag is called *wasicun*" (in Walker 1991, 92). Walker (1991, 224) writes, "A shaman's fetish is a material that has a supernatural potency imparted to it and the bag or wrappings about it. By proper invocation, the potency of the fetish may be exercised as the shaman wills. The fetish has been called a medicine bag, which is a misnomer as it has nothing to do with medicines."

Recall that a wašícų was closely identified—even equated—with the spirit being or šicų́ it contained and from which it was created. It was in every respect considered to be a wak'ą́ life-form in its own right and capable of various forms of mysterious agency. Like the spirits themselves there was a qualitative hierarchy of šicų́pi in terms of power and ability or efficacy. Hence not all *wašícųpi* (sacred bundles) were created equal. In 1905 Walker's Oglala consultants explained, "Anyone may invoke his *wasicun* by repeating the correct formula or singing the right song. . . . When one invokes his *wasicun*, it will do as he wishes. . . . A *wasicun* can do only what the God can do. . . . A more powerful *wasicun* will prevail against a less powerful" (Walker 1991, 96).

Like humans and spirits one's wašícų could be temperamental and capricious, easy to offend and antagonize. Not only would an offended bundle be ineffective, but it might also bring disaster onto the one giving offense. According to Walker (1917, 87), a šicų́ "may be pleased or displeased with its possessor and may be operative or inoperative according to its pleasure."

Táku Škąšką 'Sky' (spirit of animation and movement), who gave each human a šicų at birth, taught the Lakotas about ceremonial bundles and the injunction that they be made according to dream or vision specifications, reverenced, and never disrespected or profaned (Walker 1991, 117). Disrespecting a sacred bundle was considered a form of bad conduct subject to the disease sanction. According to early Dakota sources—and some Lakota sources (see Dorsey 1894, 440; Walker 1991, 112, 118, 122)—Uktéȟi, the horned water spirit responsible for floods, drowning, and other accidents and misfortunes relating to water, is most closely associated with medicine bundles, particularly in relation to the mystery dance (G. Pond 1889, 219–20; Riggs 1869, 90–92; 1880). Apparently this shift in prominence from water spirits (Uktéȟi) to sky spirits (Táku Škąšką and Ptesąwį or Wóȟpe) occurred gradually as the Lakotas migrated westward throughout the seventeenth and eighteenth centuries, leaving behind the hybrid riverine/woodlands lifestyle in the lake country in and around present-day Minnesota and adopting the fundamental elements of the plains lifestyle.

A ceremonial bundle successfully manufactured was reverenced, smudged, prayed and made offerings to, and in every way equated with the spirit whose interiority was infused in it. In every respect it *was* that spirit person and was considered to be very holy and treated accordingly as a living life-form with great mysterious power and autonomous agency, moods, whims, and even personality (Walker 1991, 73, 80, 95; E. Deloria n.d.c, 27; cf. Graeber 2015, 29). In 1896 Sword (in Walker 1991, 80) tellingly referred to a ceremonial bundle as a "thing of power." Red Cloud, Meat, and No Flesh (in Walker 1991, 117) describe it as "the place where good is."

A man's wašícų 'ceremonial bundle' was often the same as—or at least linked to—his wót'awe 'war bundle or war medicine'. Riggs, in his *Dakota-English Dictionary* (1992), defines wašícų as "a familiar spirit" and wót'awe as "armor; weapons consecrated by religious ceremonies; whatever is relied upon in war." However, according to the Oglala interpreter Thomas Tyon, "That which is called the *wotawe* and whatever is the *waxicun* [wašícų] (war bundle) are really the same" (in Walker 1991, 264).

A man's sacred war implements were commonly referred to as his wótʻawe, using possessive language (from the stem tʻáwa). A wótʻawe empowered individuals and members of men's societies to perform brave deeds in battle and on raiding parties, giving them superhuman agency or a mysterious power to act and the ability to perform otherwise miraculous or impossible feats (Walker 1991, 303n8). According to Lynd and Riggs, a Dakota wótʻawe 'war bundle' usually consisted of a spear, an arrow, a small bundle of paint, swan's down painted red, and occasionally some herbal medicines used for treating wounds. It was given to an initiate by an established zuyá wakʻą́ 'sacred war leader', along with esoteric teachings and certain protocols to be observed. These included a knowledge of which animal or nonhuman person the bundle represented—and hence was—and often a taboo (wóhduze, wógluze), sacred injunctions, prescriptions, and proscriptions associated with the bundle and tied to notions of sacrifice (waų́yąpi, wóšnapi) and animal ceremonialism. The initiate ever after held the bundle and the nonhuman it represented as wakʻą́ and was never to harm or kill it unless the injunction was lifted through the proper ritual (Lynd 1889, 161–63; Riggs 1893, 219).

The following lengthy quote from Riggs provides significant ethnographic detail on Dakota beliefs vis-à-vis war bundles. A man's war bundles or "sacred armor" were

> given by an older man, who was believed to have power over spirits, and who had, in the act of consecration, made to inhere in them the spirit of some animal or bird, as the wolf, the beaver, the loon, or the eagle. Henceforth these, or rather the one which became each one's tutelary divinity and his armor god, were sacred and not to be killed or eaten until certain conditions were fulfilled. . . . The reception of the wo-ta-we, or armor, by the young man places him under certain pledges which he must, if possible, redeem in after life. It taboos or consecrates certain parts of an animal, as the heart, the liver, the breast, the wing, etc. Whatever part or parts are tabooed to him he may not eat until by killing an enemy he has removed the taboo. (Riggs 1893, 219–20)

Lakota accounts are consistent with Riggs's description of Dakota beliefs concerning sacred war bundles. Tyon describes a wótʻawe as regalia and various war implements, namely a *wahúkʻeza* 'spear' and *wápaha* 'lance, war standard'. Different individuals and men's societies had different types of wótʻawe. For instance, a kit fox skin was the sacred regalia of the Kit Fox society and a crow skin represented the Omaha society (Tyon in Walker 1991, 265–66). As Tyon explains, "Each society has different regalia in their lodges and they make it for war. The regalia that they make are made to be *wakan*. Therefore nobody is allowed to laugh. It is considered very *wakan*. It is the same as what they call *wotawe*" (in Walker 1991, 268). Standing Bear also discusses Lakota conceptions of war medicine:

> There was no tribal charm that worked safety for all the people, nor did every warrior have a medicine. However, before going on the war path, many of the warriors went to a medicine-man and got a *wotahe*, a charm in which he could have faith for his protection. Some of the warriors made their own charms and planted them in the earth as an offering to the Great Mystery. These offerings were little sticks sharpened at one end so they could be stuck in the ground, to the tops of which were fastened little buckskin bags filled with tobacco and an eagle feather or, perhaps, a *wacinhin* or hair-feather. As the warrior planted his offering, he often prayed, "Grandfather, help me." (2006a, 154)

Lakota accounts also emphasize the notion that the proper ceremony consecrates a person or object, rendering a ceremonial or war bundle wakʻą́ and potent (Walker 1991, 46, 90). In 1896 Sword described the process of consecration in relation to preparing the smoking material for a pipe ceremony. The preparer, explains Sword, "should sing a song or pray to a God while preparing the smoking material" (in Walker 1991, 75). This was done, explains Tyon, because "the spirits were pleased with invocation properly made" (in Walker 1991, 119). This almost obsessive attention to detail in consecration and ritual in general—and the accompaniment of song and "prayer"—was common in most ritual undertakings, whether preparing smoking material or consecrating a sacred pipe or bundle. Walker's Oglala consultants also note that a medicine bundle could be prepared and consecrated only by a shaman or holy man (Walker 1991, 105).

Jaw or Okíc'ize-t'àwa 'His Battle', a Northern Lakota of Hunkpapa and Sans Arc ancestry who spoke with Densmore in 1913, substantiates many of the basic elements and beliefs associated with war bundles, providing evidence of continuity among the Dakotas and Northern and Southern Lakotas. His war bundle was a hide pouch containing wasé (vermilion or red paint mixed with grease) for painting his face and body when he went to war or to raid enemy horses. Jaw also wore a wolf skin and carried an eagle-bone whistle and a wooden bowl, common paraphernalia in both war and ceremonial affairs. To the whistle Jaw fastened his medicine bag, which contained a mixture of four herbs, dried and powdered, which could be used singly or in combination (Densmore 2001, 387–89). Jaw's medicine bag was a veritable pharmacopeia of useful herbs used to remedy various ailments one might face living a nomadic lifestyle.[17] According to Densmore, Jaw's war medicine was a combination or synergy of the four herbs and "had power as a charm in addition to its efficacy as a curative agency" (2001, 389).

This notion of a potent synergy brought about by the combination of disparate elements in a ceremonial bundle was also common among the Dakotas of Minnesota, particularly in reference to the mystery dance. According to Gideon Pond, Uktéȟi, the spirit of the waters, instituted the mystery dance and gave the Sioux the medicine sack. Uktéȟi determined that the medicine sack

> should consist of the skin of either the otter, the raccoon, the weasel [sic], the squirrel, the loon, one variety of fish, and of serpents. It was also ordained that the sack should contain four species of medicines, of wakan qualities, which should represent fowls, medicinal herbs, medicinal trees, and quadrupeds. The down of the female swan represents the first, and may be seen at the time of the dance, inserted in the nose of the sack. Grass roots represent the second, bark from the roots of trees the third, and hair from the back or head of a buffalo, the fourth. These are carefully preserved in the sack.

> From this combination proceeds a wakan influence so powerful that no human being can, unassisted, resist it. (G. Pond 1889, 223)

Through the proper ritual Ųktéȟi infused each medicine sack with tųwą́, the missive influence or nonhuman potency later shot at candidates for membership in the mystery dance society, symbolically killing them, later to be reborn as members of the society (G. Pond 1889, 220, 224).

Demonstrating deep similarities in terms of beliefs associated with what I call the (medicine-)bundle complex, Ringing Shield, one of Walker's Oglala consultants from Pine Ridge, discusses the contents of ceremonial bundles in startlingly similar terms vis-à-vis Gideon Pond's Minnesota Dakota account. Ringing Shield explains that plumes, down, and red paint belong to Ųktéȟi, who gave the wakʻą́ medicine bag to the Lakotas, along with the teachings and traditions associated with it. "This must be made of the skin of an animal or bird," says Ringing Shield, "as it is shown in the vision. It must contain something of an animal and of a bird and of a reptile and of the vegetables" (in Walker 1991, 112). In this way, and similar to the filling of the pipe in the pipe offering ceremony, the entirety of the universe is represented and ritually centered or focused in the medicine bag (see Black Elk in Joseph Brown 1989).

The relationship between an individual's familiar or tutelary spirit, taboo, and consecration is vague. In effect, Lynd and Riggs equate the tabooed entity with the familiar spirit. Further, Riggs equates taboo with consecration. Essentially consecration involved the infusion of nonhuman potency, šicų́ or tʻų́, into a human or nonhuman physicality through the properly performed ritual. Henceforth the sacred bundle was equated with the nonhuman spirit whose potency it contained and was therefore subject to the disease sanction (see Walker 1991, 234). The Sioux warrior cherished his war bundle, which explains Sword's use of the Lakota term *wótʻeȟila* for taboo: an object of love, literally, 'something adored, cherished, loved, valued, or treasured'. According to Sword,

> An offering is always *wotehila* (taboo) to the one who makes it, except offerings of food or drink. One may make an offering of these by throwing on the ground a bit, and then eat or drink the remainder.

A Lakota may be forbidden to do anything. The thing he is forbidden to do is *tehila* (taboo) to him. To secure the favor of *Wakan Tanka* a man may vow to taboo something. Or to placate *Wakan Tanka* or a spirit he may make such a vow. Or a shaman may forbid one to do something and then that is a taboo to the one forbidden. Or *Wakan Tanka* may in a vision forbid one to do something, and then that is taboo to that one. . . . If one does that which is taboo for him *Wakan Tanka* will be displeased, and will bring some misfortune on such a one. (in Walker 1991, 78)

Again we see the (re)generative and (re)constitutive power of virtual experience in actuality played out in beliefs and behaviors associated with the ceremonial bundle complex. "Frequently they form images of this animal and carry [it] about with them," explains Lynd (1889, 162), "regarding it as having a direct influence upon their every-day life and upon their ultimate destiny—a thing supernatural, all-powerful, and sacred." Tabeau likens the wašícų to a "familiar spirit": a "guardian angel . . . whose power and protection work every day supposed miracles that affirm and strengthen the superstition" of the Indians of the upper Missouri River (1939, 187, 190). Speaking of his Dakota people Charles Eastman writes, "Ever seeking to establish spiritual comradeship with the animal creation, the Indian adopted this or that animal as his 'totem,' the emblematic device of his society, family, or clan. . . . The sacred beast, bird, or reptile, represented by its stuffed skin, or by a rude painting, was treated with reverence and carried into battle to insure the guardianship of the spirits. The symbolic attribute of beaver, bear, or tortoise, such as wisdom, cunning, courage, and the like, was supposed to be mysteriously conferred upon the wearer of the badge" (1980, 76–77). George Catlin describes similar beliefs vis-à-vis sacred bundles (see Catlin 1973, 1:36–37).

Riggs (1869, 471–72) describes ritual songs addressed to the "mystery sack" (*wópʻiye* or *cʻątóžuha*) sung by Dakota members of the mystery dance (wacʻípi wakʻą́) in the mid-1800s. In the song the medicine bundle is addressed as grandfather (tʻųkášila), equated with the quadruped it represents or symbolizes (they are considered as one), and honored by having its face stroked, that is, the customary stroking motion of the hand over the face, expressing adoration and ritual supplication. Recall that Dorsey describes this as an essential element of "prayer": the practice of yuwįtapi 'to stroke or rub something with the hands', as in ité yuwįtapi 'to stroke the face', a gesture of gratitude, respect, and honor (Dorsey 1894, 373, 435).

Similar to beliefs concerning ghost bundles, sacred bundles in general were reverenced and treated as sentient beings or persons. Further, they liked the things that humans liked, for instance, good weather, to be smudged, and offered food and drink (E. Deloria n.d.c, 27; Riggs 1893, 219–20). Gideon Pond writes that a young male Dakota receives from a war prophet (blotáhuka)

> the implements of war, as the spear and tomahawk, carefully constructed after a model furnished from the armory of the gods, painted after the divine prescription, and charged with the missive virtue—the tonwan—of the divinities. From him also he receives those paints which serve as an armature for the body. . . . The weapons thus received are preserved by the Dakota warrior . . . sacredly. . . . They are carefully wrapped in cloth, together with sacred pigments, and in fair weather are every day laid outside of the lodge, and may never be touched by an adult female. (1889, 244–45)

The relationships or entanglements of dependency and exchange that developed between humans and particular nonhumans, demonstrated by the vision quest and the ceremonial bundle complex, are akin to Lucien Lévy-Bruhl's (1926) notion of (mystical) participation, later developed by C. G. Jung (1959, 1971).[18] According to this theory humans establish convergences with nonhuman persons and objects through a type of dual projection or transference, a psychological connection that leads to a unification of subject and object, human and nonhuman. Participation is tied to notions of correspondence and immediate affective associations between humans and nonhumans to the point of identity and consubstantiality, implying both a physical and mystical or spiritual union. In participation, two formerly disparate entities are united and participate in the existence of each other. This amounts to a direct relationship and often total identification between the two parties (see Tambiah 1990, 84–90, 105–10; Hanegraaff 2003, 373; Evans-Pritchard 1965, 85–86, 91; Greenwood 2005, 9, 89–92; cf. Sahlins's discussion of consubstantiality as the distinctive quality of kinship, in Sahlins 2013).

(Mystical) participation is an example of nonrational, nonlogical, mystical, or magical thought, which operates in opposition or relation to rational, logical, or scientific thought in all societies. Usually context determines when one form of thought predominates over the other, but in any case both have been extremely important in human life and development (see Evans-Pritchard 1965; Kapferer 2002; Greenwood 2005). According to Tambiah, participation can be represented as occurring when "persons, groups, animals, places, and natural phenomena are in a relation of contiguity, and translate that relation into one of existential immediacy and contact and shared affinities" (Tambiah 1990, 107). Participation uses the language of solidarity, unity, holism, and continuity in space and time, while also engendering a sense of encompassing cosmic oneness (Tambiah 1990, 109; Greenwood 2005, 9). In other words participation parallels the fundamental elements of a relational ontology. In Descola's terms, participation entails a convergence of interiorities: a relation that links human and nonhuman identities in a deep and profound way and has generative implications in actuality. The theoretical connections between Lévy-Bruhl's notion of participation or the principle of correspondence and mitákuye oyás'į and the relational interpretive principle characteristic of Sioux thought call for further exploration.

This ultimate expression of united identity and relationship is vividly demonstrated in an esoteric Lakota ritual expression. In preparation for a ceremony or going to war a Lakota shaman or warrior ritually activated the wakʻą́ potency of his ceremonial bundle, smudging, praying, and singing the characteristic songs associated with the nonhuman spirit whose interiority was infused in the bundle. These songs were usually transmitted from nonhuman to human through visions (see Densmore 2001, 54, 59–60). Much like ceremonial pipes, bundles, sacred stones, and other ritual paraphernalia, songs received as gifts in visions from nonhumans were palpable, concrete connections—symbols of relationship and consubstantiality—between human and nonhuman, actual and virtual. They were technologies for invoking or summoning nonhumans for aid and existential manifestations of spiritual energy and established relationships (cf. V. Deloria 2009, 95, 157–58, 162–64). Standing Bear writes, "Since song was the usual method of keeping the Lakota in touch with his Wakan Tanka, it formed a large part of all ritual. Many songs were dreamer songs received while in communion with spirits of beings personified as humans. Some of the dreamers who brought songs to the people were the Elk, Duck, Thunder, Hawk, Wolf, Spider, Fox, Crow, and Stone. The wisdom of these beings was given to the dreamer in song and he in turn sang them to help his people" (2006a, 214).

As part of this ritual activation process and invocation the individual laid hands on and reverently stroked the bundle, which was equated with the spirit itself. Concentrating his vision, mind, will, consciousness, and entire being on the bundle, he uttered the incantation "I am you, you are me," poetically epitomizing the total identification between and unification of subject and object, human and nonhuman (Posthumus 2008–17).[19] The underlying ontological assumptions of participation, correspondence, and mitákuye oyás'į were essential to the maintenance and perpetuation of both individual and collective life movement ("that the people may live"), the theme of the final chapter.

CHAPTER 9

The Dynamics of Life Movement

Sioux culture and worldview were—and continue to be—elaborated with emphasis upon kinship and the interaction of persons, both human and nonhuman, in a society composed of many collectives (oyáte) that was cosmic in scope and symbolized by the pipe and the circle. Relationship and participation or consubstantiality were central interpretive and experiential frameworks through which the Sioux perceived their world and acted within it. The agents in this society, human and nonhuman persons, manifested differential physicalities (which were capable of transformation), characteristics, attributes, and power. They played various roles but were unified by a similarity of interiorities and traditionally established sets of reciprocal rights and obligations, interspecies covenants and moral responsibilities grounded in notions of human kinship. These mutually beneficial relationships were essential to living respectfully in a moral universe characterized by its unity.

According to Hallowell, the central goal and motivating force of traditional Ojibwe life was expressed by the concept pimadaziwin, meaning life in the fullest sense, the good life, or life in the sense of longevity, health, and freedom from illness, hunger, and misfortune. Pimadaziwin was at the very root of Ojibwe ontology and worldview and could not be achieved without the help and cooperation of both human and nonhuman persons, in conjunction with one's own individual efforts. Without the "blessings" bestowed by the grandfathers or nonhuman spirits, the medicine or power/knowledge exchanged in virtual space/time, humans with their limited powers had little hope of achieving pimadaziwin, little hope of living the good life free of illness, hunger, and misfortune (Hallowell 1960, 45, 1966, 281–82; cf. Pflüg 1996).

However, being a good relative and upholding one's end of the reciprocal obligations, duties, and rights in relation to nonhuman persons was as important as successfully securing medicine. Ella Deloria eloquently illustrates this point in relation to the Sioux:

> I can safely say that the ultimate aim of Dakota life, stripped of accessories, was quite simple: One must obey kinship rules; one must be a good relative. No Dakota who has participated in that life will dispute that. In the last analysis every other consideration was secondary—property, personal ambition, glory, good times, life itself. Without that aim and the constant struggle to attain it, the people would no longer be Dakotas in truth. They would no longer even be human. To be a good Dakota, then, was to be humanized, civilized. And to be civilized was to keep the rules imposed by kinship for achieving civility, good manners, and a sense of responsibility toward every individual dealt with. (1998, 25)

Beede's (1912, Western Sioux Cosmology) Northern Lakota consultants describe Deloria's civility as *tąyą́ ų́pi* 'well-being or civilization', and clearly the "individuals" Deloria mentions were both human and nonhuman. In a similar vein Hallowell writes of the Ojibwes, "It was as essential to maintain approved standards of personal and social conduct as it was to obtain power from the 'grandfathers' because, in the nature of things, one's own conduct, as well as that of other 'persons,' was always a potential threat to the achievement of *pimadaziwin*. Thus we find the same values are implied throughout the entire range of 'social interaction' that characterizes the Ojibwe world; the same standards which apply to mutual obligations between human beings are likewise implied in the reciprocal relations between human and other-than-human 'persons'" (1960, 46).

The entire psychological field and world within which the Ojibwes lived was unified through their understanding of the role of persons and the sanctioned moral values and responsibilities that guided human-nonhuman social interaction, relationship, and exchange. In other words, kinship. Within that intricate web of social relations or kinship network the individual Ojibwe strove for pimadaziwin, or life in the fullest sense. If an individual failed to live up to his kinship obligations, broke sacred taboos, disregarded the sanctions imposed by animal ceremonialism, and so on he could not expect to achieve pimadaziwin on account of his bad conduct, which was subject to the disease sanction and invited the wrath of the spirits (Hallowell 1960, 48; 1966, 274, 288).

In this concluding chapter I demonstrate the usefulness and intuitiveness of a Descolian animist approach to Sioux ontology in a comparison of the Ojibwe concept pimadaziwin with the Lakota goal of attaining wicʻózani 'health, wellness' and striving to live in harmony with the wakʻą́ or wóniya, the collective spirit or generative, animating life-breath of the universe. Applying the major themes and findings of this study I also utilize Jeffrey Anderson's concept of life movement, that is, "the aim to generate long life, blessings, and abundance for self, others, family, and the tribe" (2001, 5), in order to gain a more complete and nuanced understanding of nineteenth-century Sioux ethnometaphysics and worldview. The notions of pimadaziwin, wicʻózani, wóniya, and life movement are collectively expressed and encompassed in the common Lakota ritual phrase *hécʻel lená oyáte kį nípi kte* 'that the people may live' and are grounded in the Lakota relational ontology exemplified by the axiom mitákuye oyásʼį 'all my relatives'.[1]

In nineteenth-century Lakota life and culture notions of personhood permeated cognitive processes, guided strategies, and motivated behavior. Kinship and the ontological role of persons was the foundation of a distinctive Lakota worldview. Within this intricate web of human-nonhuman social relations the Lakota individual strove to live in harmony with wóniya, the collective life-force and spirit of the universe, comparable to the abstract sense of wakʻą́ 'sacred, mysterious, holy' and similar to the Ojibwe concept pimadaziwin, both of which are akin to Anderson's notion of life movement, the maintenance and perpetuation of which was the major concern and goal of Lakota life.

Wóniya is a noun meaning spirit, life, breath, or breath of life, based on the stem *niyá* 'life, breath, life-breath'. According to the Oglala Good Seat (in Walker 1991, 70–71), the presence of wóniya distinguishes a living human from a dead one. According to Beede's (1912, Western Sioux Cosmology) Northern Lakota interlocutors, the Western Sioux thought of wóniya as nearly identical to Wakʻą Tʻąka, the Great Mystery and totality of all wakʻą power or energy in the universe, commonly glossed as 'Great Spirit'. Wóniya was believed to have no origin and to be omniscient, omnipresent, and fundamental in all things, including human and nonhuman persons.

Walker's Oglala consultants equate wóniya with Táku Škąšką 'Sky', the great spirit of the air responsible for all locomotion. Further, Táku Škąšką is also equated with Wakʻą Tʻąka or conceived as one of the major emanations or manifestations of Wakʻą Tʻąka: "*Woniya Tanka, Skanskan*, who is the *Wanagi Tanka* [literally, 'Great Spirit']. He gives the breath of life [niyá] and the spirit [nağí] to every child that is born alive" (Walker 1917, 161). The notion that multiple spirit persons are really one or manifestations of the same power is common and apparently ancient in Lakota theosophy (see Joseph Brown 1989, 27, 77, 79, 92; G. Pond 1889, 232; Walker 1917, 57–58, 79–81, 152–55; 1991, 31–32, 35, 50–51, 93–96, 107, 140, 271; 2006, 10). In Descola's terms, multiple physicalities essentially share the same interiority, grounded in a culturally established logic of correspondence (cf. E. Deloria 1998, 58). According to Little Wound, "*Wakan Tanka* are many. But they are all the same as one" (in Walker 1991, 70). Sword (in Walker 1917, 152) concurs, explaining, "The word *Wakan Tanka* means all of the *wakan* beings because they are all as if one. *Wakan Tanka Kin* signifies the chief or leading *Wakan* being which is the Sun. However, the most powerful of the *Wakan* beings is *Nagi Tanka*, the Great Spirit who is also *Taku Skanskan*; *Taku Skanskan* signifies the Blue, in other words, the Sky."

Wóniya was vast, invisible, and intangible; the term was used by early Christian missionaries in their translations of the Bible to designate the Holy Spirit. Pertinent to both the emphasis on interiority in animist ontologies and Lévy-Bruhl's notion of participation and the related indifference to secondary causes or intervening mechanisms (see Tambiah 1990, 86), Beede explains, "So fully did the Western Sioux conceive of all things and the whole world as actually *being*, fundamentally, mind, intelligence, reason, spirit, that there was no room for . . . conscious symbolism" (1912, Western Sioux Cosmology; see also Posthumus 2015, 148–50).

Vine Deloria addresses this issue as well, arguing that instead of *symbolize*, in which one thing stands for another, the proper term is *represent*: "Representation means that there are spiritual presences in attendance in the same way that people represent an interest group or institution. It does not mean representation in terms of images or communication. Rather, the spirits are here—present—ready to participate" (2009, 192). Thus Deloria's notion of representation is intimately linked to experience and participation: through the dynamics of representation humans, animals, birds, stones, plants, and other nonhumans all collectively engage and become active participants in ceremonies, each representing their particular collective, or oyáte. The individuals and collectives experienced by the Sioux in virtual space/time, as in the vision quest, were not merely symbolic: "It is not that the Sioux people did not use symbols," explains Deloria (2009, 193), "but that in this spiritual context, we are talking about real experiences rather than borrowed or transferred meanings."

The combined notions of a living cosmos, participation, and representation speak to various significant elements in Sioux ceremonial belief and practice. For instance, in Lakota ritual contexts when a religious practitioner says aloud, "The Earth and the Rock and the Buffalo are in the lodge," they are literally understood to be *in* the lodge: invoked and manifested by the speech act itself (Walker 1917, 131). They are not merely symbolic or, reduced to psychology, suggestive projections of the human mind. These nonhumans are *present* through invocation and various other ritual dynamics, existentially experienced, and ready to participate. The same is true of calling songs that function to call and invite spirits into the lodge at the beginning of a ceremony and closing songs that send the spirits back to the spirit realm (see Posthumus 2015, 148–53).

Wóniya was understood as universal spirit or life, and, like wak'ą́, it transcended human understanding. All power in the universe, whether manifested in human or nonhuman forms, flowed from wóniya. "Spirit (Woniya)," explains Beede (1912, Western Sioux Cosmology), "is the author and source of all 'force and energy' in all things, or rather persons, for the entire world, to them, consisted of persons." Wóniya was conceived of as both feminine and masculine, never aggressive, and not in any sense a Creator figure. According to Beede (1912, Western Sioux Cosmology), "It does not bother the Western Sioux Indians to think of all space as being replete with invisible living, conscious, intelligent beings, persons, though not in man-form, and they do not think such persons, or any other persons or beings, have any power independent of and apart from Woniya."

The spiritual goal and fundamental aim that dominated and directed Lakota life was essentially gnosis or spiritual enlightenment and knowledge through direct communion with nonhuman spirit persons. The Lakota individual strove to piously and pitiably approach, understand, and become attuned to wóniya, gaining the correct attitude of the mind and soul toward this universal life-force, energy, or power.[2] According to Beede, "The mind, intelligence and spirit [interiority] of each [person or life-form] is privileged to range through and blend with totality by gaining a right attitude toward Woniya (Spirit). . . . They believed also that each being, including man, was eventually to become like Woniya, so that each could share the intelligence and all the characteristics of Woniya, which was the desire of all worship" (1912, Western Sioux Cosmology). Wóniya was often compared to a light guiding the spirit of humans down the correct path in life, today referred to as the good red road.[3] Human beings sought knowledge of and relationship with wóniya so that their minds, bodies, and spirits could achieve peace and loving-kindness (wac'ą́tkiyapi) (Beede 1912, Western Sioux Cosmology).

Sioux life, and particularly religious belief and ritual, dealt largely with maintaining spiritual, psychological, and physical equilibrium, harmony, well-being, and health. This may be compared to the conscious striving to live in tune with wóniya discussed by Beede. Anderson's concept of life movement is also relevant here, combining at least two core Lakota religious values. The first and most fundamental value is wicʻózani 'health'. The stem, zaní 'to be healthy, well, whole', refers to both physical and psychological health and well-being and is related to the stem of wóniya, namely, niyá. Sioux people value health very highly and pray for it for themselves, their relatives, friends, and tribe as a whole. Another important religious value encompassed by the concept of life movement is wicʻóicʻağe, the generations, life, growth, and longevity, which captures the idea of continuing health and prosperity for the people into the future and throughout the generations and time (DeMallie and Parks 1987, 211).

The notion of life movement is connected to movement as a general indexical attribute of persons in Sioux ethnometaphysics. It is also tied to the notion of life as a process of transformation and continuous birth, growth, and development, expressed in Lakota by various forms of the multivocal term tʻų́, which means spiritual potency or its transmission or emittance but also refers to the process of giving birth. As Finger (in Walker 1917, 155) explains, "When the people say *ton* they mean something that comes from a living thing, such as the birth of anything or the discharge from a wound or a sore or the growth from a seed. Only shamans speak of the *ton* of the *Wakan*. Such *ton* is *wakan* and the shamans only know about it. The people are afraid to talk of such *ton* because it is *wakan*."

According to Beede, "With the Western Sioux Indians 'miracle' is life-transformation-process (not life-process). . . . The word 'wakan' connoted a life-transformation-process always, as Indians understand. And Great Spirit (Wakan-tanka), whatever the origin of the term, is, to them, the Being Who is the Master of, or Lord of, or Source of, or Totality of the total life-transformation-process in the entire world or species or groups" (1912, Western Sioux Cosmology). Ingold draws a similar conclusion in his discussion of the animacy or personhood of stones: "Movement is not an outward expression of life, but is the very process of the stone's staying alive, its 'continuous birth.' The same could be said of trees" (2004, 38). Vine Deloria notes that in a living universe time is understood as a growth or transformation process, the end goal of which is maturation, and that we are all responsible as (co-)creators to participate in the continuing generation of reality (1999, 46–57). Clearly the ethnometaphysics of life as a process of transformation or morphogenesis and continuous (re)generation among the nineteenth-century Sioux people was complex and profound.

Paving the way for future studies, Kapferer, in his discussion of a Sinhala Buddhist antisorcery rite called the Suniyama, explores the connection between ritual virtuality and the processual (re)creation and (re)generation of life, what I have here referred to as life movement:

> Participants located in the imaginal space of the rite re-embody its processes as essential to the ongoing generation of life in all its chaotic actuality. The Sinhala Suniyama rite also is explicitly concerned with descending inside space/time dynamics, repositioning participants within such processes and bringing forth their capacity to constitute unselfconsciously dimensions of ordinary life, to move unhindered through its various orders and processes. Within the virtual space of the rite, participants engage in exercises of structuration of relations (via the dynamics of the gift) and of consciousness (via the practice and power of language . . .), regaining their composure with the flows of actuality. (Kapferer 2010, 246)

Kapferer's insights, albeit concerned with a people very different from the Sioux, are certainly relevant to an exploration of Sioux ontology as it unfolds and is essentially continuously (re)created and (re)generated through ritual practice, the major aim of which is the maintenance and perpetuation of life movement and the continuation of the life-transformation process embodied in the concept of wóniya.

As Vine Deloria explains, "The world is constantly creating itself because everything is alive and making choices that determine the future" (1999, 46). This is exactly what ritual taps into: this (re)generative, (re)constituting dynamic, this life-transformation process or force known as wak'ą́ or wóniya. The past and present are linked to the future through life and agency (language, intentionality, mind/will, growth, movement, transformation, choice, etc.), and, in particular, the conscious, intentional actions of human and nonhuman persons.

Lakota tradition itself may also be conceptualized as a dynamic, participatory process, constantly in a state of flux, (re)creation, and (re)generation (see DeMallie 1991; Posthumus 2015). In discussing Lakota tradition Raymond Bucko (1998) and others have been inspired by the work of Morris Foster, who utilizes Edward Shils's (1981) conception of tradition to great effect in his influential study of Comanche identity (Foster 1991). Foster's definition of tradition is interactive, participatory, and processual: "The pattern of repeated interaction constitutes the tradition in each community. The modes of subsistence, the social units, the cultural frameworks, even the languages used in any one period are instrumental rather than fundamental to this pattern of tradition" (1991, 172–73). Foster's work reflects Lakota definitions of tradition as continuously (re)constituted and (re)produced by and through practice, participation, and communal action. Tradition is an essential part of the preservation and perpetuation of both individual and collective Sioux life movement.

The common Lakota ritual phrase "that these people may live" captures this focus on sustaining and perpetuating life movement so critical to Lakota religious belief and magico-ritual practice. Religion, ceremony, and a spiritual relationship with the universe and the spirit persons who inhabit it are among the central features of Lakota traditionalism. Religion or spirituality, expressed in belief and ceremony, is vital to Lakota identity and ethnicity, governing and centering the traditional life of the Lakota people since time immemorial (DeMallie 1991, 8). Religion is ensconced beside history at the very heart of Lakota tradition, pumping precious lifeblood into the entirety of the Lakota nation and allowing for the perpetuation of collective or ethnic life movement. And at the very center of Sioux spirituality, both past and present, is a distinct relational ontology centered on kinship and the role of human and nonhuman persons as volitional, sentient life-forms capable of communication, relationship, movement, growth, reciprocity, and exchange.

This study has demonstrated the usefulness of the new animist framework, as exemplified by Descola, in a reinterpretation of the ethnohistorical literature on the Sioux while highlighting Hallowell's pioneering role in ontologically inflected anthropologies. It also suggests some possible new directions for ontological and new animist approaches by applying Kapferer's insights to extend their reach, specifically into various virtual domains, such as mythology, dreams and visions, and ritual. But beyond the scope of anthropological interest, why is this important? Without being too melodramatic or sentimental, is there a lesson we can take away from this study that can potentially improve our lives and relations with other people and species and help to restore balance and health to the world in which we live and ensure its continued growth and development?

Here again I am inspired by the writings of Vine Deloria, who speaks of a moral universe, kinship, and the associated obligations and responsibilities we all share as human beings living collectively with a myriad of other life-forms on this earth. Using the familiar analogy of the road, common in many Native American traditions, Deloria explains, "This colorful image of the road suggests that the universe is a moral universe. That is to say, there is a proper way to live in the universe: There is a content to every action, behavior, and belief. The sum total of our life experiences has a reality. There is a direction to the universe, empirically exemplified in the physical growth cycles of childhood, youth, and old age, with the corresponding responsibility of every entity to enjoy life, fulfill itself, and increase in wisdom and the spiritual development of personality. Nothing has incidental meaning and there are no coincidences" (1999, 46). Together we are all responsible for our conduct and for the maintenance of the earth. Further, writes Deloria, "In the moral universe all activities, events, and entities are related, and consequently it does not matter what kind of existence an entity enjoys, for the responsibility is always there for it to participate in the continuing creation of reality" (1999, 47).

In the American Indian context this principle of relatedness appears most often in the ceremonial realm, in which interpersonal, intercollective, and interspecies relations are emphasized, established, renewed, and mended. Among the Sioux this principle of relatedness is exemplified by the ritual phrase mitákuye oyás'į 'all my relatives', which is the title of this study. Yet, according to Deloria, this phrase has much more to teach us about ourselves and our world: "'All My Relatives,' believed by many people, including many Indians, to be merely a devout religious sentiment, also has a secular purpose, which is to remind us of our responsibility to respect life and to fulfill our covenantal duties. But few people understand that the phrase also describes the epistemology of the Indian worldview, providing the methodological basis for the gathering of information about the world" (V. Deloria 1999, 52).

Two key interrelated concepts in Deloria's work are relevant here: respect and the notion of the covenant. According to Deloria, "Respect in the American Indian context does not mean the worship of other forms of life but involves two attitudes. One attitude is the acceptance of self-discipline by humans and their communities to act responsibly toward other forms of life. The other attitude is to seek to establish communications and covenants with other forms of life on a mutually agreeable basis" (V. Deloria 1999, 51). Mutual respect is at the heart of Deloria's notion of a covenant. "The idea of the covenant, clearly articulated in the Old Testament theology of the Prophets," writes Deloria, "is an early and important concept for tribal peoples. . . . A covenant places responsibilities on both parties and provides a means of healing any breach in the relationship" (1999, 51–52). A covenant involves not only mutual respect and responsibility but also the acknowledgement of our common kinship: that we are all related. Covenants also have an inherent mechanism for healing or mending temporary ruptures in times of stress, crisis, and trauma. Without this ability to heal we would be unable to mature as human beings and maintain and perpetuate individual, collective, and global life movement and growth.

We are all related, a truth articulated in animist ontologies through the belief in a common interiority shared by all life-forms. If we are to perpetuate our existence and ensure our planet's future, mutual respect is a crucial requirement, not just among human beings of various races and ethnicities but also between humans and nonhumans. Developing self-knowledge and self-discipline is essential in this ongoing participatory process (see V. Deloria 1999, 50–51). Deloria insists that maturity, tied to the attainment of self-knowledge and self-discipline, is the ultimate goal of human existence from the American Indian perspective: "Maturity, in the American Indian context, is the ability to reflect on the ordinary things of life and discover both their real meaning and the proper way to understand them when they appear in our lives" (V. Deloria 1999, 13–14; see also V. Deloria 2012). Striving for maturity entails a processual personal and collective development from classifying stimuli or information inputted through perception to knowledge to wisdom, wisdom understood as learning or knowing the right way to live, to walk the good red road. Wisdom and maturity can be achieved through virtual and ceremonial experience and their pragmatic application in actuality.

Too often we moderns fail to reach or even seek maturity and wisdom. One of the roots of our troubling contemporary situation is the self-imposed separation of humanity from the rest of the universe: the dichotomization of nature and culture characteristic of the naturalist ontology of the West, according to which all life-forms share a common physicality—we are all made of the same stuff—but not a common interiority—only humans (or certain groups of people) have the capacity for soul or spirit. Exacerbating this alienation is our obsessive focus on information, theory, and technology—on objects or things without spirit or soul—that often limits us to a disenchanted life and a world without joy, magic, or healthy mysteries (see V. Deloria 1999, 15; Descola 2013a).

Throughout his life C. G. Jung was bothered by this secularization and split between the Western psyche and nature. He writes, "No wonder the Western world feels uneasy, for it does not know how much it has lost through the destruction of its numinosities. . . . Its moral and spiritual tradition has collapsed and has left a worldwide disorientation and dissociation . . . Nothing is holy any longer. Through scientific understanding our world has become dehumanized" (Jung in V. Deloria 2009, xi). Jung attributed this dehumanization of Western society to the loss of immediate communication with nature (see V. Deloria 2009, xv–xvi).

We too often forget that we are all related as human and nonhuman beings, sharing our experiences and our world. Sioux theosophy and other American Indian traditions have much to teach us about relationship, respect, responsibility, and maturity. As Deloria explains, "Now that many species are tragically gone or facing extinction, the Western mind is gradually coming around to an appreciation of other forms of life, recognizing that these creatures may well teach us something significant about time, space, psyche, and a cosmology based upon relations with other beings in the universe" (V. Deloria 2009, 131). Unfortunately the division is deep, and we are running out of time to right the ship or get back on the right road.

Ella Deloria expresses this unsettling dehumanization and disconnect in terms of kinship. Contrasting the traditional Sioux economic system based on kinship with that of the modern West, she writes, "The two systems in question are irreconcilable. They go counter to each other. One says in effect: 'Get, get, get now; all you can, as you can, for yourself, and so insure security for yourself. If all will do this, then everyone will be safe.' And it depends on things, primarily. The other said: 'Give, give, give to others. Let gifts flow freely out and they will flow freely back to you again. In the universal and endless stream of giving this is bound to be so.' And that system depended on human beings—friends, relatives" (E. Deloria 1998, 120). The naturalist ontology of the modern West goes hand-in-hand with the irresponsible and unbounded capitalist-consumer culture of our times. It not only undergirds and legitimizes the mistreatment and destruction of the environment but also justifies the genocide in the colonization of the "New World" and elsewhere: it eases and enables the dehumanization and domination of others, both human and nonhuman, by positing an inherent separation and difference vis-à-vis a discontinuity of interiority or soul. If we are to reach maturity we must rethink this destructive way of being-(alive)-in-the-world.

Aside from the potential to enrich our relations with the world around us and to enhance our understanding of historical indigenous cultures and traditions, the Descolian animist lens can also broaden our understanding of important contemporary issues. In a recent panel discussion at the University of South Dakota about the opposition to the construction of the Dakota Access Pipeline in Cannon Ball, North Dakota, Lakota educator and elder Gene Thin Elk articulated the conflict in a particularly powerful way. He sees it as a struggle between two sets of competing values or ideologies. On one side the indigenous "water protectors," mainly Lakotas, acknowledge the life and spirit in all things, while the other side acknowledges only the life and spirit of (a select group of) human beings (and perhaps corporations). *Mní wic'óni* 'water is life', as the Lakota rallying cry goes, is a natural extension of the foundational principle mitákuye oyás'į 'we are all related' and exemplifies the key features of Descolian animism discussed herein.

Thin Elk's analysis coincides with Descola's distinction between animist and naturalist ontologies. The former is characteristic of many indigenous peoples, who make few sharp distinctions between nature and society and relate to other life-forms as subjectivities with common interiorities worthy of respect. The latter ontology, characteristic of the West, sees human beings as superior to all other life-forms and objectifies and exploits the natural world. The naturalist assumption that only humans possess souls reduces nature to little more than a lifeless repository for human consumption.

Perhaps it is the legacy of animism and a relational ontology that has allowed Native American spirituality to flourish in a modern world in which many other religious traditions are threatened or endangered. Perhaps this legacy has allowed native peoples to escape the spiritual disenchantment and secularization characteristic of much of the West,[4] which paradoxically motivates many Westerners to seek spiritual succor and fulfillment through participation in native ceremonial traditions. All speculation aside, in an era of increasing polarization, ethnic conflict, sectarian violence, and ecological crisis this study demonstrates just how much we all can learn from Sioux philosophy and spirituality in terms of abolishing the destructive and shortsighted nature/culture dichotomy and living respectfully with other life-forms in a multispecies world.

GLOSSARY OF LAKOTA TERMS AND PHRASES

akíc'ita: messenger, representative, lieutenant, scout; soldier, warrior; camp police
ak'íp'a: for something to befall one, suffer (as problems), to be afflicted with (misfortune)
Anúġite: Double Face, Double Woman, Double Women
asníya: to cause to recover, to cause to be well
áya: to become, to grow into a new state of being, to become gradually, to be changing
blotáhuka: war leader, lieutenant; may also refer to a war prophet or sacred war leader
c'ašt'ų́: to name someone or something, to give a name to
c'agléška wak'ą́: sacred hoop
c'ąnáġi: tree spirit, tree interiority
c'ąnúpa iyáhpeyapi: to ceremonially offer the sacred pipe
c'ąnúpa wak'ą́: sacred pipe
c'ąté: heart, feelings, emotions
c'ąté ištá: eye of the heart
c'ątóžuha: mystery sack, sacred bundle; a tobacco pouch, pipe bag
c'ąyáka: heartsick; groaning or moaning in pain
c'ékiya: to pray to someone or something, beseech, entreat; to cry, weep, wail to/for someone or something; to address someone or something using the proper kinship term (*c'ékiyapi* is the nominalized form 'prayer')
c'éya: to cry, weep, wail
gnaškíyą: wild, crazy
Gnaškíyą: Crazy Buffalo
há: skin, hide, bark, outer casing or shell of anything; clothes, clothing, physicality
hąblápi: vision quest, vision fast
hąblé: a vision or dream

hąbléc'eya: to cry and fast for a vision
hąbléc'eyapi: vision quest, vision fast
hąblóglaka: to relate one's vision or spiritual experience
Hąwí: Moon
héc'el lená oyáte kį nípi kte: that the people may live
heȟáka: elk, male or bull elk (*heȟákapi* is the plural form)
Hé K'ąt'úhu Sápewį: One-with-Horns-of-Black-Plum-Tree Woman
Hé T'ac'ánųpa T'okáhewį: One-with-Horns-of-First-Ranking-Pipe Woman
heyók'a: contrary, sacred clown
heyók'a wózepi: *heyók'a* ceremonial performance
hóc'oka: sacred space, altar; camp circle
hókawiȟ: outside the camp circle
hó uk'íya: to receive, learn a song; to call out to someone or something, to send a voice to someone or something
Hunúp: Bear
hunúpa: two legged
hutópa: four legged
hųká: adopted relative; making of relatives ceremony (also refers to an individual who has been honored in this ceremony)
hųkátakuya: friendship, adoption
hų́tka káǧa: cormorant imitation, (re)enactment

ȟeyáta: back in the hills, out in the country, in remote areas
ȟmúǧa wic'áša: sorcerer, wizard
ȟmúǧa wíyą: sorceress, witch
ic'áǧa: to grow, spring up, mature, develop, turn into; growth, development
iȟą́bla: to dream, have a dream or vision
iȟą́bla ok'ólakic'iye: dream society
iȟą́blapi: dreams, visions; dreamer
iȟpéyapi: offerings
ikcéka: common, ordinary
Iktómi (Iktó): Spider (the Trickster of Lakota myth and oral tradition)
iníȟą: to be afraid of someone or something, to be in awe of
inípi: sweat lodge ceremony, purification ceremony
init'i: sweat lodge
itąhą mat'ó c'įcála kį héc'a wą hiyú: out of the doctor's mouth a bear cub falls
ité yuwį́tapi: to stroke the face
it'ą́c'ą: chief, social or civil leader
Íya: Giant Eater, Cannibal (the giant cannibal of Lakota mythology)
iyótą wak'ą́: most holy, sacred, mysterious; supreme object of worship
íyą: rock, stone (*Íyą* may also refer to rock as a spirit being or nonhuman person)
Íyą Hokšíla: Stone Boy

íyą t'aníya: the breath of rocks or stones (as manifested in the sweat lodge)

káğa: to make something, create; to represent (a certain spiritual power in enacting one's vision), to enact a character, impersonate, imitate, (re)enact, to perform (as a certain ceremony)

káğapi: ceremonial (re)enactments of vision experiences and sacred imitations of nonhuman spirit persons performed publicly

kağí: to avoid someone or something out of respect, fear, or in awe; to respect and hold in esteem or reverence

k'okíp'a: to fear or be afraid of someone or something

k'olá: friend, ally

k'olátakuya: friendship

-la: diminutive suffix

Lak'ól wic'óȟ'ą: Lakota way of life, Lakota traditions, Lakota culture

Lak'óta: friend, ally; the people; the Sioux; the Lakota (*Lak'ótapi* is the plural form)

lekší: uncle, my uncle

lową́: to sing

lową́pi: sing (a type of healing ceremony)

mak'á: earth, dirt, country

manítu: wilderness, uninhabited regions

mat'ó: bear (*mat'ópi* is the plural form)

mat'ó hot'úpi: the characteristic call or cry of the bear

mat'ó káğa: bear imitation, (re)enactment

mitákuye oyás'į: all my relatives, we are all related

mit'áwašicu: my spirit helper

mní wic'óni: water is life

nağí: spirit, soul, ghost (one aspect of the human soul or interiority); may also refer generally to spirits (*nağípi* is the plural form); shadow, shade

nağíla: like-a-spirit, like-a-soul, interiority-like; may also refer to the soul or interiority of a nonhuman thing (*nağílapi* is the plural form)

nağípila: spirits-ish

nasúla: brain, cerebrum

ní: life, breath, vitality; to live (*nípi* is the plural or nominalized form)

ní ų́: to be alive, to be living

niyá: life, breath, life-breath (literally, 'that which causes life'); ghost, the animating soul of the body (one aspect of the human soul or interiority) (*niyápi* is the plural form)

ó: to shoot and hit someone or something

ohóla: to respect someone or something (*ohólapi* is a nominalized form)

ohų́kaką: myth, mythology

oíc'aǧe: make, class, type
Okíc'ize-t'àwa: His Battle, Jaw (a Northern Lakota of Hunkpapa and Sans Arc ancestry who spoke with Frances Densmore in 1913)
ókiya: to help someone or something, assist, aid
ómakiya yo/ye: help me
onámaȟ'ų wo/we: hear me
oníya: life, breath, life-breath (literally, 'that which causes life')
oúc'aǧe: form, likeness, shape, appearance, image, look, resemblance; growth
oúye: one's habits or way of life, lifestyle; one's situation or condition; one's nature
owáǧkaǧapi: altar, sacred space
owáka: altar, sacred space
oyáte: people, nation, tribe
-pi: animate plural suffix
p'eȟúta: medicine
p'eȟúta waštéšte yuhá: to have very potent medicines
p'iyá: to renew, make over, repair, mend, make something better; to treat someone, cure someone, make someone well
P'iyá: personage in Lakota myth
pté: buffalo, American bison (generic term)
ptéȟcakapi: buffalo, American bison (generic term)
pté hį́ paȟpá: the fur that molts in sheets from a buffalo's head

Pté Oyáte: Buffalo Nation, Buffalo People, Buffalo Tribe
Ptesą́wį: White Buffalo (Cow) Woman
p'ó: steam, vapor
sįtésapela: black-tail deer
šayápi: to ceremonially paint someone or something red to honor and consecrate it
šicú: soul, spirit, imparted nonhuman potency, familiar, spirit guardian, the interiority of a *wak'ą́* (spirit being, nonhuman person) (one aspect of the human soul or interiority that is of nonhuman origin and given to each human being at birth by *Táku Škąšká*; other *šicúpi* [plural form of *šicú*] can be acquired throughout the life cycle in various ways); the *t'ų́* (potency) of a *wak'ą́* (spirit being, nonhuman person)
šiglá: to resent someone or something, feel resentful, feel offended or insulted, have one's feelings hurt
šiná wóųye: prayer flags, cloth offerings
Šiyáka: Teal Duck (a Sioux elder from Standing Rock Reservation interviewed by Frances Densmore in 1912)
šką́: to stir, move, move about, act
šųgmánitut'ąka: wolf
šų́kawak'ą: horse
táku: thing, something

táku ní ų́ cikcístina: little living things, little living persons (literally, 'little things that are alive or living')

táku šką́ką́: sacred pebbles or stones utilized in the *yuwípi* ceremony

Táku Šką́šką́: Sky, That Which Moves, Moving Spirit (the spirit or aspect of Wakʿą́ Tʿą́ka that controls all movement and locomotion; sometimes referred to as Šką́ or Šką́šką́)

táku tʿókeca: something different, strange, or anomalous

táku wakʿą́: holy things, sacred things; nonhuman spirit persons

táku wínihą: something causing fear, excitement, or awe

takúye: relative

tąyą́ úpi: well-being; civilization

Tobtób Kį: The Four Times Four (a term used in reference to the sixteen manifestations of Wakʿą́ Tʿą́ka)

tʿącʿą́: body, form, physicality

Tʿaté: Wind

Tʿatúye Tópa: Four Winds, Four Directions, Four Brothers

tʿatʿą́ka: buffalo, male or bull buffalo (Tʿatʿą́ka may also refer to buffalo as a spirit being or nonhuman person)

tʿáwa: his, her; something is his or hers

tʿawácʿį: mind, will, intellect, reason, disposition, understanding

tʿawácʿį wicʿánaǧi kicʿí: human mind and soul

tʿawášicų: his or her familiar or spirit helper; his or her sacred or ceremonial bundle

tʿehí: trouble, hardship, misfortune

tʿehíla: taboo; to love someone or something, adore, cherish, hold dear

tʿiwáhe: family, household

tʿiyópa: door, entrance, doorway

tʿiyóšpaye: lodge group, tipi group, band, extended family

tʿóka: enemy

Tʿokáhe: First Man

tʿókeca: to be different, strange, weird, anomalous

tųwá: emitted potency; to stare, glare, open the eyes, look about (*tųwápi* is the plural form)

tʿų́: emitted nonhuman potency; the *wakʿą́* aspect or element of anything; spiritual essence; the power or ability to do "supernatural" or mysterious things

tʿųká (yatápika): sweat lodge stones or rocks; rock or stone understood as a spiritual entity

tʿųkášila: grandfather (also a kinship respect term commonly used to address male spirit beings or nonhuman persons)

tʿų́tʿųšni: invisible potency or influence; anything that lacks physical properties or physicality, inorganic

tʿųtʿųšniyą: anything that is invisible due to a lack of physicality

t'ekínica: near death, to almost die, faint, swoon

ų́: to be, exist, live

ųcí: grandmother (also a kinship respect term commonly used to address female spirit beings or nonhuman persons)

Ųktéȟi: Horned Water Monster Spirit (*Ųktéȟipi* is the plural form)

Ųktéȟi Oyáte: Horned Water Monster Nation, Horned Water Monster People, Horned Water Monster Tribe

ųmáni: altar

ųmašike: I have a particular need, and I need help with that need

ųmá wic'óni: other life (often used in reference to the spirit world)

ų́ši ic'íc'aǧa: to humble oneself, make oneself poor (idiomatically, 'to humiliate oneself hoping thereby to be pitied or to invoke another's good will')

ų́šimala yo/ye: pity me

ų́šika: to be poor, pitiful, destitute, helpless, needy, miserable; to have pity or mercy on someone or something; to be kind to someone or something

ų́šila: to be poor, pitiful, destitute, helpless, needy, miserable; to have pity or mercy on someone or something; to be kind to someone or something

wa-: indefinite object marker

waábleza: clarity of understanding, to comprehend

waálową: singing

wac'ą́tkiyapi: peace, loving-kindness

wac'ékiya: to pray to or for, to cry to or for; to address someone or something as a relative; to ceremonially smoke the sacred pipe

wac'į́: mind, will, intellect, consciousness

wác'įhį: plume, down or soft feather

wac'į́k'o: to pout, sulk for a long time, be out of humor

wahį́heya: mole (*wahį́heyapi* is the plural form)

wahúk'eza: spear

waȟtáni: to transgress or violate a taboo, tribal law, or custom, fail to perform a vow; sin

waȟúpa: winged

waíc'išpapi: flesh offerings

wakáǧapi: effigy

Wakąka: Old Woman, the mythical Witch

wakíc'aǧapi: a giveaway or redistribution ceremony that occurs at the end of the ghost-keeping ceremony

wakíȟtani: to bring evil or misfortune on someone or something by violating a taboo, religious rule, or tribal law

Wakíyą: Thunder Being, Thunder Bird, Winged One, Flying One (*Wakíyąpi* is the plural form)

wakíyą hot'ų́pi: thunder; the characteristic call or cry of the Wakíyą

Wakíyą Oyáte: Thunder Being Nation, Thunder Being People, Thunder Being Tribe

wakíyą tųwápi: lightning; the stare or glare of the Wakíyą

wakúza: supernatural retribution

wak'ą́: sacred, sacrality, mystery, mysterious, holy, power, powerful, incomprehensible, energy, 'medicine'; may also refer to a spirit being or nonhuman person

wak'ą́la: wak'ą́-like; to deem someone or something sacred, holy, mysterious

wak'ą́lapi: to be considered wak'ą́

wak'ą́pila: wakans-ish

wak'ą́yą: in a wak'ą́ or sacred way, sacredly, mysteriously, mystically

wak'ą́ ką́ǧa: sacred imitation, impersonation, or (re)enactment

Wak'ą́ T'ą́ka: Great Mystery, Great Mysterious, Great Spirit

wak'ą́ wac'ípi: mystery dance, medicine dance, holy dance, sacred dance, medicine lodge ceremony

wak'ą́ wic'óȟ'ą: sacred acts, mysterious acts; a sacred ceremony, ritual, or rite

wak'ą́ wóec'ų: ceremony, ritual, rite; sacred activity, action, doing, event, performance, undertaking, work

wak'ą́ wóhąpi: mystery feast, sacred feast

wak'úwa: hunter

walúta: down painted with sacred red earth paint

wamák'anaǧi: animal spirit, animal interiority

wamák'ašką: animal, animals (literally, 'things that move upon the earth')

wamák'ognaka: universe, cosmos, entire creation

wamáyąka yo/ye: behold me, look at me

wanáǧi: spirit, ghost, soul separated from the body (refers to unknown people's ghosts, not a particular person's spirit, which is naǧí)

wanáǧi ktépi: Bell's palsy (literally, 'ghost killed')

wanáǧi t'ac'ą́ku: Milky Way (literally, 'ghosts' road, spirits' road')

wanáǧi t'amák'oc'e: spirit world

wanáǧi t'awác'ipi: northern lights (literally, 'spirits' dance, ghosts' dance')

Wanáǧi T'ą́ka: Great Spirit (another name for Táku Šką́šką́)

wanáǧi wap'áȟta: spirit bundle, ghost bundle

wanáǧi wic'ót'i: ghost village, ghost camp

wanáǧi yuhápi: ghost-keeping ceremony

waníya: life, breath, life-breath, life-transformation process (literally, 'that which causes life'); spirit

waníyąpi: domesticated animal (literally, 'what is kept alive')
wápaha: lance, war standard
wap'íya: to renew, make anew, make over, repair, fix; to cure or treat people, to practice traditional medicine, act as a healer, be a medicine man, traditional doctor; a healer, medicine man, traditional doctor
wap'íyapi: a doctoring or healing ceremony
wasábglepi: effigy
wasé: sacred red earth paint, vermilion
wašícų: spirit, soul, interiority; medicine bundle, ceremonial bundle, sacred bundle; indwelling spirit helper (*wašícųpi* is the plural form)
wašícų t'ųká: stone spirit (a sacred stone imbued with or possessing nonhuman power, potency, or *t'ų́*); also may refer to a sacred stone bundle
waúyąpi: sacrifice, offering
wazílya: to smudge, incense
Wazíya: Old Man, the Cold, the mythical Wizard of the North
wąblí: eagle
wąblí gleská: spotted eagle
wąyą́ka: to see someone or something; to look at someone or something
Wé Hokšíla: Blood-Clot Boy
Wí: Sun

wic'ác'ehpi icáhtake šni: never having touched human flesh
wic'ánaǧi: human soul
wic'áp'ehį yužúpi: they pull out the human hair (a Lakota sorcery/witchcraft practice)
wic'áša: human male (*wic'ášapi* is the plural form)
wic'áša t'ápi: dead people
wic'áša wak'ą́: holy man, holy men
wic'óh'ą: ceremony, ritual, rite; activity, action, undertaking; custom, tradition, way of life, culture; power or ability to act, power to do mysterious things, nonhuman power
wic'óh'ą šíca: bad deed, crime
wic'óic'aǧe: the generations; life, growth, longevity
wic'óni: the totality of life-forms
wic'ózani: health, wellness
wic'út'e: death
wíyą: human female (*wíyąpi* is the plural form)
Wíyą Nųpápika: Double Woman, Double Women
wóak'ip'a: misfortune, tragedy
wóc'ekiye: prayer
wóec'ų: ceremony, ritual, rite; activity, action, doing, event, performance, undertaking, work; custom, tradition
wógluze: taboo, something sacred or forbidden, a spiritual taboo or ceremonial restriction
wóhpa/wóhpe: meteor

Wóȟpe: Beautiful Woman (sacred name for White Buffalo [Cow] Woman)
wóiglakapi: vow
wóitʼupʼe: a cause of wonder, awe, or amazement
wókakiže: suffering
wókiksuye: memory
wókuze: an observance or rule imposed by a spirit being
wókʼokipʼe: dangerous, fearful, scary
wókʼuže: sickness
wóle: vision seeker, lamenter
wónaǧi: spirit or interiority of an inanimate thing; spirit of food
wóniya: life, breath, life-breath, life-transformation process (literally, 'that which causes life'); spirit
Wóniya Tʼą́ka: Great Life (another name for Táku Škąšką́)
wóohola: respect, reverence
wópʼila: thanksgiving, thanks, gratitude, appreciation, gratefulness; a thanksgiving or appreciation ceremony
wópʼiye: medicine bundle, medicine bag, ceremonial bundle, sacred bundle, mystery sack (*wópʼiyepi* is the plural form)
wóslolye: knowledge
wóšnapi: sacrifice, offering
wótʼawe: war bundle, war medicine
wótʼeȟi: difficulty, trouble, hardship, misfortune, woe, tragedy
wótʼeȟika: difficulty, trouble, hardship, woe, a tragic event, sorrow caused by hardship, adversity
wótʼeȟila: taboo, something sacred or forbidden, a spiritual taboo or ceremonial restriction (literally, 'something loved or cherished')
wówaglece: an omen, a twitching
wówaȟtani: bad conduct, transgression or violation of a tribal law or custom or religious taboo, wrongdoing; sin
wówakʼą: sacredness; spiritual power, medicine, nonhuman power; something *wakʼą́*; indwelling spirit
wówašʼake: strength, power, energy
wówayazą: sickness
wówihąble: a vision or dream, a communication from a nonhuman person
wówištece: shame, dishonor, disgrace, embarrassment
wóyakapi: human histories that occurred within the historical memory of the tribe (a Lakota traditional narrative genre)
wóyuonihą: honor
wóyušʼįyaye: fear
yeyá: to send something; to shoot with something, to send something toward there (a bullet, arrow, projectile, medicine, potency, etc.)
Yumní: Whirlwind

yuónihą: to honor someone or something

yuwípi: doctoring or healing ceremony of binding medicine men (usually performed in the dark and for purposes of finding lost objects and the cause of sickness)

yuwį́tapi: to stroke or rub something with the hands

zaní: to be healthy, well, whole

zįtkála: bird (*zįtkálapi* is the plural form)

Zįtkála Oyáte: Bird Nation, Bird People, Bird Tribe

zuyá wak'ą́: sacred war leader, war prophet

zuzéca: snake (*zuzécapi* is the plural form)

NOTES

INTRODUCTION

1. The best general treatments of Sioux culture and history are the chapters relating to the Sioux in DeMallie (2001); Mekeel (1943); and Gibbon (2003). All ethnographic examples presented herein reflect Lakota perspectives unless otherwise noted. Despite a number of significant differences between Eastern and Western Sioux culture I have found the central tenets of traditional religious philosophy and essential elements of ritual practice to be quite consistent between the two groups. It is for this reason that I include some Eastern Sioux or Dakota material herein.
2. My usage of Lakota-language terms and phrases comes largely from my experience working with native-language speakers on various language-related projects and from in-depth study of Lakota and working with historical texts written in Lakota. I use Ella Deloria's orthography and have referenced the work of Eugene Buechel, S.J. (1970, 1939, 1978) as well as the *New Lakota Dictionary* (Lakota Language Consortium 2008). This book's glossary includes all the Lakota terms and phrases used herein.
3. For a detailed exploration of the relationship between the Lakotas and bison, see Posthumus (2016).
4. See Hobsbawm and Ranger (1983); Sahlins (1993, 1999). Bruce Kapferer (2008, 23n6) argues against simplistic explanations concerning "invention of tradition" theories of ritual, writing, "This is not always the case even though their personal, social and political import is achieved or reinvented in contemporaneity. But in this sense rites through their repetition are always being reinvented simultaneously with the attempt to make them continuous with what was practiced before. Ritual in the sense I am suggesting here is

both continuous and inventive. These are not necessarily contradictions or oppositions as appears to be the implication of some invention of tradition perspectives." Generally, Kapferer sees no contradiction in the fact that ritual is both dynamic and static, characterized by both change and stasis (see Kapferer 2008).

1. HALLOWELL, DESCOLA

1. The major collections of Hallowell's work are *Culture and Experience* (1955) and the posthumously published *Contributions to Anthropology: Selected Papers of A. Irving Hallowell* (1976). More recently, Jennifer Brown and Susan Elaine Gray have edited a definitive collection of Hallowell's work with introductions and commentary, titled *Contributions to Ojibwe Studies: Essays, 1934–1972* (Hallowell 2010). Contextualizing Hallowell's Boasian roots, Regna Darnell writes, "Like Boas, Hallowell moved from history to the psychology that would be the focus of his subsequent career. Only after the analyst had disentangled such *historical* contacts and intersections based on trait distributions would it be possible to turn to pattern integration, focusing on psychological reality for members of a culture" (Darnell 2001, 46; emphasis in original). Hallowell was strongly drawn to history throughout his entire career (Jennifer Brown, personal communication).
2. *Worldview* refers to the culturally constituted ways in which a particular people view the world, or "that outlook upon the universe that is characteristic of a people" (Redfield in Hallowell 1960, 19). The concept was developed by Robert Redfield (1952), Hallowell (1960, 1963), Clifford Geertz (1973), and Michael Kearney (1975, 1984), among others. Similar to cosmology, worldview encompasses notions of self, other, classification, relationship, causality, space, and time and the interrelations between these domains.
3. Hallowell used *other-than-human* while contemporary theorists tend to use *nonhuman*. I employ both terms interchangeably.
4. I realize that adopting a posthumanist position may at first glance seem to conflict with Hallowell's reputation as a humanist (see Nash 1977). I would argue that much of Hallowell's work had a posthumanist thrust before the term was popularized, largely through the so-called ontological turn. Again, we see that he was far ahead of his time, in particular, in his exploration of expanded worldviews and ontologies that extend subjectivity to nonhumans and expand the person category to include other-than-human beings (Hallowell 1960). These concerns are at the heart of many posthumanist approaches that seek to decenter the position of humans in the universe and explore the personhood and relationality of nonhumans in a multispecies world, incorporating nonhumans into the fold and the material realities of existence. The work of Hallowell's

student Melford Spiro (1987, 1–29) debunking the notion of a universal human nature is decidedly posthumanist in spirit.

5. Several academic journals have dedicated special issues to this topic, perhaps the most intriguing being the colloquia titled "The Ontological French Turn," edited by John Kelly, in *HAU: Journal of Ethnographic Theory* 4 (1) (Summer 2014).

6. In particular, Descola's *Beyond Nature and Culture* (2013a), Kohn's *How Forests Think: Toward an Anthropology beyond the Human* (2013), Viveiros de Castro's (1998, 2012) insights on perspectivism, and Ingold's (2000, 2004, 2006, 2011) influential phenomenology and notions of "being-(alive)-in-the-world" have been far-reaching and instructive.

7. Descola (2013b, 79) defines ontologies as "systems of distributions of properties among existing objects in the world, that in turn provide anchoring points for socio-cosmic forms of aggregation and conceptions of self and non-self" or as "contrastive qualities and beings detected in human surroundings and organized into systems" (Descola 2014b, 275).

8. Viveiros de Castro (1998, 478) likens *body* to Bourdieu's concept *habitus*: "'body' is not a synonym for distinctive substance or fixed shape; it is an assemblage of affects or ways of being that constitute a *habitus*. Between the formal subjectivity of souls and the substantial materiality of organisms there is an indeterminate plane which is occupied by the body as a bundle of affects and capacities and which is the origin of perspectives."

9. Hallowell does not actually use the terms *interiority* and *physicality*. Rather, he uses *soul* and *body* or the appropriate corresponding Ojibwe terms. Descola coined *interiority* and *physicality* in an attempt to utilize inclusive terms that would be applicable cross-culturally.

10. This explains the animist definition of a person as any life-form, human or nonhuman, "animate" or "inanimate," that has a subjectivity or perspective on the world and is capable of social interaction and, importantly, relationship. Hence, phenomenological experience is a key axis in animist ontologies.

11. Another foundational concept in the poststructuralist or perspectivist approach is Bruno Latour's (1991) term *collective*, borrowed and adapted by Descola to refer to "a way of assembling humans and non-humans in a network of specific relations, by contrast with the traditional notion of society, which only applies, strictly speaking, to the subset of human subjects, thus detached from the fabrics of the relations that they maintain with their non-human environment" (Descola 2013b, 85). In ontologically inflected anthropologies this concept is used more or less interchangeably with *tribe-species* to refer to networks or communities of persons. I employ both terms interchangeably as integral elements in the logic of my subsequent analysis of Lakota ontological dynamics.

12. Descola's discussion of transformation and the notion of physicality as clothing or envelope is closely tied to Viveiros de Castro's *perspectivism*, a conception "according to which the world is inhabited by different sorts of subjects or persons, human or nonhuman, which apprehend the world from distinct points of view" (Viveiros de Castro 1998, 469). As Ingold (2004, 56n5) explains, according to perspectivism, "To be a person is to assume a particular subject-position, and every person, respectively in their own sphere, will perceive the world in the same way—in the way that persons generally do. But what they see will be different, depending on the position or form they have taken up." In other words, humans, animals, spirits, the dead, meteorological phenomena, celestial bodies, plants, objects, and other life-forms see themselves as persons and are considered as such in animist ontologies. According to Viveiros de Castro, "Such a notion is virtually always associated with the idea that the manifest form of each species is a mere envelope (a 'clothing') which conceals an internal human form, usually only visible to the eyes of the particular species or to certain trans-specific beings such as shamans. This internal form is the 'soul' or 'spirit' of the animal: an intentionality or subjectivity formally identical to human consciousness, materializable, let us say, in a human bodily schema concealed behind an animal mask" (Viveiros de Castro 1998, 470–71). For Viveiros de Castro, perspectivism is in a sense a mirror image—"a somatic complement" (1998, 482)—in logical opposition to animism: American Indian ontologies simultaneously postulate metaphysical continuity (animism) and physical discontinuity (perspectivism). The "spirit or soul (here not an immaterial substance but rather a reflexive form) integrates," he explains, "while the body (not a material organism but a system of active affects) differentiates" (Viveiros de Castro 1998, 479). Viveiros de Castro's analysis here is in agreement with the orientation of Descolian animism as a similarity of interiority and dissimilarity of physicality.

However, it seems that Hallowell presaged this focus on perspective characteristic of the ontological turn and developed most fully by Viveiros de Castro. In his classic 1960 paper "Ojibwa Ontology, Behavior and World View" Hallowell describes the perspectival form of apprehending phenomena common among the Ojibwe people with whom he collaborated. As an example, Hallowell describes how a man unknowingly married a Thunder Bird woman and followed her to her home, spending time with her family:

> He finds himself brother-in-law to beings who are the "masters" of the duck hawks, sparrow hawks, and other species of this category of birds he has known on earth. He cannot relish the food eaten, since what the Thunder Birds call "beaver" are to him like the frogs and snakes on this earth (a

genuinely naturalistic touch since the sparrow hawk, for example, feeds on batrachians [frogs and toads] and reptiles). He goes hunting gigantic snakes with his male Thunder Bird relatives. Snakes of this class also exist on this earth, and the Thunder Birds are their inveterate enemies. (When there is lightning and thunder this is the prey the Thunder Birds are after.) (Hallowell 1960, 33; thank you to my colleague Ian Puppe for bringing this reference to my attention)

Clearly, Hallowell planted many of the seeds that would later blossom as foundational concepts in the ontological turn.

Kapferer (2014a) advises caution in reference to Descola's "New Wave" ontological approach. *Beyond Nature and Culture*, explains Kapferer, smacks of an underlying dogmatism. In the first place Descola asserts the primacy of interiority/identity over physicality/externality/ relation, but Kapferer's critical misgivings only begin there. Note that Viveiros de Castro apparently reverses Descola's privileging of interiority, writing, "The set of habits and processes that constitute bodies is precisely the location from which identity and difference emerge. . . . The human body therefore must appear as the prototypical social object . . . [and] the locus of confrontation between humanity and animality" (1998, 480). Kapferer argues that Descola's project is Eurocentric, dualistic, and selective in terms of the arbitrary—"virtually Frazerian" (2014a, 394)—selection of ethnographic exemplifications. Descola's schema has an ahistorical, static feel and his dualistic concepts trouble Kapferer, who counters that "a nondualist perspective is consistent with some of the poststructuralist ideology with which Descola aligns (e.g., Deleuze's [1993] discussion of the fold). . . . A nondualistic ground is capable of generating an ontological orientation of the comparative value that Descola intends. This has the advantage of avoiding Western individualist assumptions, which are maintained in Descola's decision" (2014a, 392). Kapferer characterizes Descola's ontological categorizations as "exclusionary," leading to "a homogenization of societies as of one type or another" (2014a, 396). Arguing for situated ontological dynamics negotiated through practice and interaction Kapferer asks, "Why cannot a number of different ontologies operate, if under specific situated circumstances, in the one overall context?" (2014a, 396).

Although Kapferer's critical commentary must be acknowledged, much of the criticism of Descola's project is unfounded. In Descola's defense, he refutes the notion that the interiority/physicality distinction is an ethnocentric projection of the Western opposition between mind and body, persuasively arguing that it is a universal distinction made by all cultures, albeit in their own fashions (Descola 2013a, 116–21). He writes, "Contrary to an opinion currently in fashion, binary oppositions are neither a Western invention nor fictions of structural anthropology but are very widely used by all peoples in plenty of circumstances, so it is not so much their form that should be questioned but rather the suggested universality of their content" (2013a, 121). Further, Descola does not argue for the primacy of interiority per se; rather, he equates interiority with the self and asserts that the physicality or form is the crucial ontological differentiator in animist societies (2013a, 129–35). Descola also notes that perhaps the most common ontological situation is "one of hybridity, where one mode of identification will slightly dominate over another one, resulting in a variety of complex combinations" (2014b, 277). Finally, in response to the accusation of ethnographic arbitrariness, Descola plainly acknowledges the fact that his scholarly model aims to generalize about human ontological orientations and hence runs the risk of sacrificing "the spicy unpredictability and the inventive proliferations of day-to-day situations in order to reach a higher level of intelligibility regarding the mainsprings of human behavior" (2013a, 115).

13. Hallowell's pioneering role in the development of phenomenological approaches in anthropology is acknowledged by Jack Katz and Thomas Csordas (2003) and Robert Desjarlais and C. Jason Throop (2011, 100), who characterize Hallowell's *Culture and Experience* (1955) as an "influential articulation of some key phenomenological insights from an anthropological perspective."

2. SITUATED ANIMISM

1. "There is no doubt that the Indian held medicine close to spiritual things," explains Charles Eastman, "but in this also he has been much misunderstood; in fact, everything that he held sacred is indiscriminately called 'medicine,' in the sense of mystery or magic" (1980, 74). Compare the Lakota conception of power to Keith Basso's description of power among the Western Apaches: "The term *diyi'* [power] refers to one or all of a set of abstract and invisible forces which are said to derive from certain classes of animals, plants, minerals, meteorological phenomena, and mythological figures within the Western Apache universe. Any of the various 'powers' may be 'acquired' by man, either by dreaming about the class of objects after which it is named . . . and/or by purchasing the chants, prayers, and ritual procedures which activate and control it from another person. Once acquired, a 'power' may be used for a variety of purposes" (1966, 150).

2. Nineteenth-century Lakota understandings of interiority are complex and will be discussed in detail later in the chapter. According to William Powers, "The universe is composed of a finite amount of energy; good and evil are thus two aspects of the same energy. . . . All supernatural beings and powers and all animate and inanimate objects have innate power manifested in the concept

of šicun [the t'ų́ of a wak'ą́].... Because the šicun of things is immortal, reincarnation is possible.... A sacred man becomes powerful through visions with the supernaturals. To increase power, he must accumulate the šicun of as many animate and inanimate objects as possible" (1982a, 51–52).

3. As anthropologist Paul Radin points out, "animism is not a religion at all; it is a philosophy. The belief in the general animation of nature has nothing to do with the supernatural" (1957, 198).

4. To be fair, we must remember that Descola openly acknowledges both the hybrid nature of ontologies in practice and the unfortunate loss of some ethnographic detail in exchange for the broad, significant generalizations and progress his schema makes.

5. For more on the Dakota War of 1862, see Carley (1976); Meyer (1967); and G. Anderson (1988).

6. In 1911 the Santee Dakota Eastman wrote, "The American Indian was an individualist in religion as in war. He had neither a national army nor an organized church. There was no priest to assume responsibility for another's soul" (C. Eastman 1980, 27). In 1944 the Yankton Sioux ethnographer and linguist Ella Deloria, who grew up on Standing Rock Reservation, wrote, "Dakota religious life was purely individual. There was nothing that all must do with reference to God, but only what each man felt as an inner compulsion that could not be denied" (E. Deloria 1998, 60). Discussing the Lakotas, DeMallie writes, "What was esoteric knowledge was not standardized as it was in many other tribes, but was individual. Each man possessed certain types of esoteric knowledge based on his own visions and sacred experiences. These might or might not be shared with other shamans in the sweat lodge. Thus there was no single tightly structured body of sacred knowledge to be carefully guarded" (DeMallie in Walker 1991, 26). Clearly, Sioux spirituality was and is an idiosyncratic, fluid, and diverse phenomenon based on subjective experience and practical adaptation, fueled by visions and dreams, and resistant to dogmatic or hegemonic creeds.

7. Vine Deloria refers to mitákuye oyás'į as the "Indian principle of interpretation/observation," calling it "a practical methodological tool for investigating the natural world and drawing conclusions about it that can serve as guides for understanding nature and living comfortably within it.... We observe the natural world by looking for relationships between various things in it.... This concept is simply the relativity concept as applied to a universe that people experience as alive and not as dead or inert" (1999, 34). This relational principle, as explained by Deloria, is similar to Descola's analogism, another ontological schema, and certain kabalistic systems of symbolic associations. Perhaps this aspect of Lakota ethnometaphysics exemplifies a hybrid form at the margins of animist and analogist ontologies (see also Wissler 1907c, 53).

8. *Makʽá* is sometimes used, but it carries more of the meaning of earth, dirt, or country, rather than nature as an impersonal, objectified domain.
9. This is not universally true, i.e., in the case of malevolent or antisocial spirit beings such as Íya (the Cannibal, Giant Eater), Iktómi (Trickster), etc., but it is a useful generalization nonetheless.
10. White Buffalo Woman, the mythical nonhuman mediator and bringer of the sacred pipe, is another important teacher of culture in many Sioux accounts (see Black Elk in Joseph Brown 1989, 3–9; Lone Man in Densmore 2001, 63–67; Left Heron in DeMallie 1994, 127).
11. Apparently this was a common motif among Siouan speakers of the plains and many other tribes (see V. Deloria 1999, 228; 2009, 130). Describing a parallel Winnebago creation story, Paul Radin writes, "According to Winnebago thinkers no beings had any permanent form originally. They were all a kind of *tertium quid*, neutral beings, that could at will transform themselves into human beings or spirit-animals. At one particular period in the history of the world they decided to use all their unlimited power of transformation to change themselves definitely either into animals or human beings. Since then animals have remained animals and human beings, human beings, except for those few human beings who still possess the power of transforming themselves, for short periods of time, into animals" (1953, 51).
12. Compare to the Lakota term for domesticated animal, *waníyąpi*, literally, 'what is kept alive'.
13. The term *oyáte* 'people, nation, tribe', DeMallie (2001, 799) writes, "carried a meaning of ethnic identity as Lakota (*lakʰóta*) as well as a general sense of political unity based on common relationship. Each of the seven constituent [Lakota] groups recognized itself as a tribe, a level of social organization that was also called *oyáte*." William Powers (1982a, 33–36) mistakenly labels the nation-level division *tʽųwą́*. This term, a stem meaning 'village' or 'town', indicates a more strictly geo-local division and is used to identify villages and village sites.
14. Beliefs concerning the chiefs of nonhuman collectives in some ways parallel those concerning the nonhuman "masters" or "owners" of the different species of game and fur-bearing animals common among many North American tribes (see Hallowell 1955, 120, 145, 160, 163, 168).
15. A comparable enmity existed between the Thunder Birds and Water Spirits in Ojibwe culture, further evidence of Sioux-Ojibwe historical connections and hybridities (see Hallowell 1960, 33; Vecsey 1983).
16. These parallels are likely the result of a similarity of bedrock traditions across native North America and a long-documented history of interaction and exchange, sometimes friendly and sometimes hostile, between the Sioux and the Ojibwes. For more on Sioux-Ojibwe relations and hybridities, see G. Anderson

(1980); DeMallie (2006); Désveaux and Fornel (2009); and Hickerson (1988). For an alternate analysis of Sioux notions of personhood, see Detwiler (1992).

17. Paul Radin (1914) argues that there is no convincing evidence for an impersonal force in native North America comparable to the Austronesian *mana* concept, but that all explanations of causality and events are in personalistic terms (see also Hallowell 1966, 274). Descola (2013a, 370–71) argues that where animism is influenced by analogism, an ontological orientation characterized by a dissimilarity of both interiority and physicality, personal nonhuman spirits tend to become more impersonal and fluid. This scenario exemplifies hybrid ontologies in the Descolian framework.

18. In terms of its mediating function between subjectivity and objectivity, agency and structure, Hallowell's notion of self is similar to Bourdieu's notion of habitus (see Bourdieu 1977; Bourdieu and Wacquant 1992).

19. Thanks to my colleague Nicco La Mattina for bringing the connection between personhood and Dasein to my attention.

20. I am currently exploring the possibility that multiple ontologies operated simultaneously and/or situationally within Lakota society, particularly animism and analogism, which posits dissimilar interiorities and dissimilar physicalities.

21. For an earlier, more detailed discussion of Lakota conceptions of human interiority, see Posthumus (2015, 82–140).

22. As in general the traditional Sioux seemed little concerned with an afterlife, there is little agreement as to whether the Sioux believed in reincarnation as the term is used in English. Belief in the immortality of the interiority—or certain aspects of it—was apparently much more widespread than any belief in reincarnation per se. According to Chased By Bears, a Santee-Yanktonai man who spoke with Frances Densmore in the early 1900s,

> It is the general belief of the Indians that after a man dies his spirit is somewhere on the earth or in the sky, we do not know exactly where, but we are sure that his spirit still lives. Sometimes people have agreed together that if it were found possible for spirits to speak to men, they would make themselves known to their friends after they died, but they never came to speak to us again, unless, perhaps, in our sleeping dreams. So it is with Wakaŋ'taŋka. We believe that he is everywhere, yet he is to us as the spirits of our friends, whose voices we can not [sic] hear. (Chased By Bears in Densmore 2001, 96)

23. Linguistically the suffix *-la* differentiates *nağí* from *nağíla*. This suffix may act as a diminutive, indicating feelings of affection or the small size of the noun it is affixed to, or it may act as an auxiliary verbal suffix, indicating that something is regarded or considered in a certain way. In this case *nağíla* would mean something that is regarded or considered as a spirit, soul, or interiority.

3. THE LIVING ROCK

1. This is particularly evident in Sioux beliefs and practices associated with medicine or ceremonial bundles (šicų́ or wašícų).
2. Beede's early twentieth-century Northern Lakota interlocutors gave the form "taku niun chickchistina" (*táku ní ų́ cikcístįna*, literally, 'little things that are alive or living'), which they translated as 'little living things' or 'little living persons' (Beede 1912). In this term the stem is *ų́* 'to be, exist, live', from which is formed *ní ų́* 'to be alive, to be living'.
3. In 1914 Finger, an aged Oglala ritualist, claimed that practitioners symbolically understood the Rock and Thunder Bird as one. Some believe that Iktómi is in fact the offspring of Íyą and Wakíyą (Finger in Walker 1917, 82, 154). Illustrating the contrasting dynamic of destruction/death/predation and protection/life/gift, Gideon Pond (1889, 230) writes, "From the Wakinyan god, the Dakotas have received their war implements (spear and tomahawk), and many of those pigments which, if properly applied, will shield them from the weapons of their enemies."
4. On sacred stones, see Densmore (2001); Tyon in Walker (1991, 153–55); V. Deloria (2009, 92–98); and Powers (1982b, 11–18).
5. By "God" here is meant a nonhuman spirit person. Walker and his interlocutors chose some problematic terms to use in their translations of Lakota concepts (see DeMallie's introduction in Walker 1991).
6. The best study of the sweat lodge ceremony is Bucko (1998). For Black Elk's account of the ritual, see Black Elk in Joseph Brown (1989, 31–43). Traditionally men and women both participated in sweats, albeit separately, although it is likely that men engaged in sweats more frequently. Today it is common for men and women to sweat together or separately depending on the context and preference of the participants and religious practitioner.
7. Joseph Brown (1989, 5n6) understands *grandfather* in a different sense.
8. There is some indication of a belief in master spirits or controlling spirits of game animals among the Sioux. This belief was common among the Ojibwes and more ancient circumpolar ancestral tribes and is tied to the notion of tribes-species. Lynd, for instance, writes of a "general Dakota belief that each *class* of animals or objects of a like kind, possesses a peculiar guardian divinity, which is the mother archetype" (1889, 155; emphasis in original).
9. Illustrating the inherent individualism and idiosyncrasy of Sioux belief and ritual, Lynd writes,

> No one deity is held by them all as a superior object of worship. Some deem one thing or deity as *iyotan wakan*, or the supreme object of worship, whilst others reject this and substitute a different one as the main god. Thus, those

Dakota who belong to the Medicine Dance, esteem Unktehi as the greatest divinity. The western tribes neglect that deity, and pay their main devotion to Tunkan (*Inyan*), the Stone God, or *Lingam*. As a result of these differences of worship, an *apparent* skepticism arises on the ancient divinities among them, whilst a *real* skepticism exists as to their intrusive forms of religion. (1889, 159; emphasis in original)

Later, however, Lynd (168) lists Tʿuká or Íyą among the most popular spirits worshiped by the Dakotas, writing, "All Sioux agree in saying that the *Tunkan* is the main recipient of their prayers. . . . They pray to that and the spirit of the buffalo almost entirely" (174).

10. See DeMallie (1978) for a biography of Bushotter. These accounts illustrate the great continuity in terms of the basic assumptions underlying Sioux belief and ritual across tribal divisions. Fletcher notes a similar practice among the Santees. Buffalo dreamers placed a buffalo head on a mellowed-earth altar, painted it red and blue, and tied swan down to it. Then the pipe was ceremonially filled and offered to the adorned and consecrated buffalo head. The dreamer then addressed the head using kinship terms: "Grandfather! Venerable man! Your children have made this feast for you. May the food thus taken cause them to live, and bring them good fortune" (Fletcher 1887a, 282n4).

11. The tʿú 'emitted spiritual potency or essence, emitted interiority' of Wóȟpe or Ptesą́wį (White Buffalo Woman), the great intermediary between humans and nonhumans, is in the smoke from the pipe and sweetgrass. Recall that the smoke from the pipe is believed to carry the prayers and wishes of the people to the spirits, acting as an intermediary, much like Ptesą́wį herself (Walker 1991, 95).

12. In all interaction with relatives, whether human or nonhuman, it was proper to use kin terms instead of personal names for both address and reference. This practice functioned to bolster proper behavior among individuals, deemphasizing individuality and reminding them of their responsibilities and obligations to the social group (DeMallie 1994, 131; V. Deloria 2009, 146).

13. Lamenting, singing, and other forms of audible incantation, invocation, and evocation are believed to consecrate and infuse people, objects, and actions with potency. Language and the audible word have a performative magicality, a classificatory and constituting efficacy and potency comparable to J. L. Austin's (1962) notion of performative speech acts and Robert Segal's (1999, 2004) notion of word magic, based on the work of Ernst Cassirer, Jane Harrison, and S. H. Hooke. Other aesthetic dynamics, such as painting, adornment, and the plastic arts, also carry performative magical weight. So, for instance, if a pipe is to be smoked ceremonially, one should sing a sacred song or "pray" while

he is preparing the smoking material (Sword in Walker 1991, 75). Through this action, the filled pipe is consecrated to a particular purpose, and the various powers or potencies (interiorities) contained in and represented by it are activated and made present or manifested.

14. It will become apparent that this belief in the continuity between interiority and hair or feathers holds true also in regard to human hair. As a distinctive element of a given physicality, in many ways hair, fur, or feathers define individuals and collectives, illustrating the continuity between interiority and physicality.

15. This is why the ghost keeper should not run, go swimming, make any violent movements, shake blankets or clothing, or in any way disturb the air during his tenure in the ghost-keeping ceremony. This also explains why the ghost bundle could not be brought outside on windy or stormy days (see Fletcher 1887c).

16. As wacʻékiya may also be understood as ceremonially offering or smoking the pipe, this too often plays a critical role in establishing a ritual frame and enabling relationship and intersubjective interspecies communication. In reference to the hu̧ká 'making of relatives' ceremony, Walker writes, "As the younger man smoked the pipe, the Conductor removed the skull from the stone that supported it, placed a splotch of red paint on the stone, and then said, 'We will smoke with the Rock.' He took the pipe and blew smoke from it against the stone. He then gave the pipe to the younger man who also blew smoke on the stone. While he was doing so the Conductor said, 'You have smoked with the Rock and He will make you strong so that you will not quickly grow weary'" (1917, 137; see also Walker 1991, 233).

17. This exploration of Sioux ritual dynamics is in no way meant to be exhaustive. I am currently working on a more comprehensive project exploring Sioux ritual dynamics in greater detail.

4. PERSONS AND TRANSFORMATION

1. See Posthumus (2015, 218–31) for more on the distinction between innate or obtained power and acquired or attained power. Deloria's distinction is comparable to Basso's (1970, 40–42) distinction between the two ways to acquire power among the Cibecue Apache: "power finds you" vs. "you find power."

2. The Lakota stem is ų́šika or ų́šila 'to seek aid, help; to be poor, pitiful, destitute, helpless, needy, miserable'. According to Ella Deloria (n.d.c, 66), the reflexive term ų́ši icʼícʻaǧa 'to humble oneself, make oneself poor' idiomatically means "to humiliate oneself hoping thereby to be pitied or to invoke another's good will." See also Fletcher (1887d, 274n21).

3. Hallowell (1960, 28) also recognizes the inadequacy of the natural/supernatural dichotomy in analyses of American Indian cultures. On the tenuous nature of this dichotomy, see Hultkrantz (1983); Morrison (1992); and Saler (1977).

4. Descola basically relies on the same human/nonhuman polarity in *Beyond Nature and Culture*, as pointed out by Viveiros de Castro (2014, 81n39).

5. SPIRITS AND GHOSTS

1. There appears to be little semantic distinction between *nağí* and the related term *wanáği*. Good Seat insists that a wanáği is a nağí 'spirit' that has once been associated with a human physicality. So perhaps the distinction is between human and nonhuman: that a wanáği is a human nağí as opposed to a nonhuman nağí. The distinction may also lie in the difference between definite and indefinite as indicated by the prefix *wa-*, an indefinite object marker. Nağí is a definite spirit associated with a particular interiority and physicality, while wanáği is an indefinite, unknown interiority no longer associated (physically, at least) with a particular physicality. Richard Two Dogs, an influential contemporary Oglala ritual practitioner, explained to me that nağí is the type of spirit that all things have. It may refer to one's own spirit or to a specific spirit. Wanáği, on the other hand, is a spirit in a more general, abstract, or unknown sense. The important distinction appears to be between definite and indefinite and the fact that only a human spirit would be considered or referred to as wanáği, meaning a spirit that was once associated with a particular human physicality that is no longer associated with that body and now exists external from and unassociated with its original vessel (Posthumus 2008–17). Walker's interlocutors explained to him that "*Wanagi* is the name of ghosts. They are like shadows. They cannot be felt but they can be seen and heard" (Walker 1991, 106).
2. Significantly, Ojibwe beliefs concerning death and afterlife parallel those of the Sioux. For instance, the journey to the spirit world took four days and involved various trials, the principal obstacle being a swift river spanned by a log-like snake that the person had to cross. The Ojibwe spirit world, like that of the Sioux, was located either in the west or the south and was peopled by both human and nonhuman persons. It was a happy place where the people feasted and danced joyfully, creating the northern lights (see Hallowell 1955, 151–71; Vecsey 1983, 62–65). According to Vecsey, and similar to Sioux opinions, "The Ojibwe did not worry about their destiny after death. They anticipated no punishment in the afterworld for misdeeds committed during life; rather, they enforced their morality through disease sanctions. Sins found their punishment in the present life, not the next" (1983, 64).
3. Ghosts, like other nonhuman persons in Lakota cosmology, are easily offended (variant forms of the stem *šiglá*) and often resort to pouting (*wac'įk'o*), much like humans do. Describing the mysterious nonhuman origins of twins, Dorsey (1889a, 158) writes, "As they are not human beings, they must be treated very politely and tenderly, lest they should become offended and die in order to

return to Twin-land." Táku Škąšką was a particularly passionate and capricious nonhuman spirit person whose favor was difficult to retain. Likened to a whimsical child, Táku Škąšką was very easily offended by the slightest misstep, breach of taboo, or neglect of a vow. This belief also extended to *wicʻáša wakʻą* 'holy men', powerful magico-medico-ritual practitioners believed to be of nonhuman origin who were like the spirits in many ways and so feared and revered accordingly. Great pains were taken to avoid offending these individuals, as they had the power to heal or harm and could inflict misfortune, sickness, death, and other obstacles to life movement upon those who displeased them. In fact, much sickness was attributed to offending persons, whether human or nonhuman, and much Sioux belief and ritual centered on dynamics of propitiating spirits to avoid offending them or on purification and removing the ill effects caused by offended spirits. Offending others was considered a form of bad conduct subject to a disease sanction, which enforced and reinforced Sioux morality (see G. Pond 1889, 231, 242–47; M. Eastman 1995, 19, 27–28, 55–57; Walker 1991, 25, 45, 75, 82, 85, 89, 114, 170, 206; V. Deloria 2009, 159).

4. See Wallis and Wallis (1953) on Canadian Dakota disease theory and conceptions of the intergenerational transmission of negative energy among relatives as a cause of sickness.

5. The notion of contagious magic has its origins in the flawed nineteenth-century social evolutionary theory of James G. Frazer. Following Wouter Hanegraaff, I understand all varieties of magic as being primarily grounded in a religious worldview, not a rationalist or scientific one. From this perspective, then, what has been termed contagious magic is based on a theory of symbolic correspondences defined by Hanegraaff (2003, 361) as "the assumption that the world has been created in such a way that resemblances (whether formal or structural) are the reflection of real connections."

6. According to Gideon Pond (1889, 236; emphasis in original), "A man who dances to the sun is expected to make a song of his own, which embodies the *god-communication* to him."

7. Compare to Tyon's discussion of Bone Keepers in Walker (1991, 161–63) and Ella Deloria's (1937) interviews with Edgar Fire Thunder and Asa Ten Fingers.

6. LAKOTA MYTHOLOGY

1. Deleuze's notion of a plane of immanence, virtuality existing or remaining within actuality rather than opposed or separate from it, offers a practical opposition to transcendence or that which is beyond or outside. All of the many and varied possibilities of human existence are inherent in the plane of immanence (Deleuze and Guattari 1987, 1994; Deleuze 2001). Deleuze's opposition to transcendence dovetails with Vine Deloria's opposition to the

term as applied to American Indian belief: transcendence, writes Deloria, is "a particularly inadequate word . . . to describe a psychological process. The word implies reaching another level of reality, one with more substance than that previously experienced. In the North American Indian tradition such generalities can certainly not be used with any degree of accuracy because individuals do not transcend themselves, they simply learn additional things about the single reality that confronts them" (1999, 23–24).

2. The oral performance of mythology also provided the foundation and inspiration for human-nonhuman interaction and relationship in dreams and visions and ritual (cf. Hallowell 1966, 279n23). There is a mutually influential and reinforcing relationship between the realms of myth, dreams and visions, and ceremony. Vine Deloria discusses the connections between dream and myth motifs, writing, "Mythological motifs are certainly useful as central themes of dream expression. . . . It is, therefore, the images in dreams (rather than any dream narrative) that have a similarity to mythological motifs; the motifs themselves are only inferred from the appearance of familiar symbols that have other connections with already conscious and objective themes. Presumably these images were once unconscious, and when they appear they initiate or help to sustain religious and mythological interpretations and explanations of human experience" (2009, 171–72).

3. Ohúkaką are separate from *wóyakapi*, another important traditional narrative genre conceptualized as human histories that occurred within the historical memory of the tribe (see Jahner 1992; Jahner in Walker 2006, vii–40).

4. Marco Pasi (2011, 127) describes a similar process among practitioners of Western esotericism, writing, "When occultists offered new interpretations of occult practices, for the most part they were trying to make these practices understandable and acceptable to modern audiences." This process may be compared to the rationalizations of Deloria's and Hallowell's consultants and corresponds to what Olav Hammer (2001, 42–45) describes as "discursive strategies" within Western esotericism. In the Western esoteric tradition these discursive strategies for the rationalization of spiritual experience, phenomena, and practice have alternated between the poles of naturalization (objective, scientific, brain-based explanations) and psychologization (subjective, mental, mind- or consciousness-based explanations).

5. See, for example, Ingold (2004, 28–31). Hallowell makes a similar argument against anthropomorphism in his denouncement of the natural/supernatural dichotomy in relation to Ojibwe culture and worldview: "It would be an error to say that the Ojibwe 'personify' natural objects. This would imply that, at some point, the sun was first perceived as an inanimate, material thing. There is, of course, no evidence for this. The same conclusion applies over the whole area of

their cognitive orientation toward the objects of their world" (Hallowell 1960, 29). As we have seen, Descola prefers the term *anthropogenicism*. Descolian animism is anthropogenic "in that it derives from humans all that is necessary to make it possible for nonhumans to be treated as humans" (Descola 2013a, 258).

6. As noted above, a comparable enmity existed between Thunder Birds and Water Spirits in Ojibwe culture (see Hallowell 1960, 33; Vecsey 1983, 74–75).

7. LAKOTA DREAMS AND VISIONS

1. On the significance of the voice and calling in dreams and visions, see Vine Deloria (2009, 153–66).

2. However, as there was a sacred injunction against revealing one's vision, only the faster's medicine man or mentor was told of his vision in great detail. Violating this rule meant weakening or losing the powers exchanged in the vision (see Black Elk in DeMallie 1984; Neihardt 1991). A parallel belief was common among the Berens River Ojibwes (see Jennifer Brown 2006).

3. According to Descola, "Animals (and the spirits who act as their representatives) generally adopt a human appearance when they want to establish a relationship with humans" (Descola 2013b, 81).

4. Deloria (in Bushotter 1887–88, story 199) notes that it is not clear from the Lakota if this passage means that "the doctor wishes for the assistance of the bear-spirit residing within him; or, it may mean the bear-spirit within, seeing the doctor is not succeeding, chooses to help him." This discrepancy illustrates the significance of human-nonhuman relationships, ritual transformation, and the ambiguity of the distinction between human and nonhuman spirit power: the man ritually becomes (áya) the bear, as the bear ritually becomes the man, illustrating the convergence of interiorities at work.

5. Charles Eastman also notes this aspect of Sioux ritual in his discussion of the wak'ą wac'ípi (medicine lodge), which "originated among the Algonquin tribe, and extended gradually throughout its branches, finally affecting the Sioux of the Mississippi Valley" (1980, 64). Of the medicine lodge ritual he writes, "The whole performance was clearly symbolic of death and resurrection" (1980, 73). Eastman (1980, 60–61) also discusses figurative death in relation to the sun dance of the Eastern Sioux, and the ritual drama of life and death is clearly played out in the yuwípi ceremony as well (Posthumus 2008–17).

6. On the connections between Sioux healing practices and psychotherapy or depth psychology, see Vine Deloria (2009).

7. Note that in a Lakota text dictated to Ivan Stars by Brave Dog in July 1915 a ritual practitioner treats a man who is c'ąyą́ka 'heartsick, groaning or moaning in pain' (Buechel 1978, 207). Clearly psychological, emotional, or spiritual

ailments are types of symbolic illness considered to be within the purview of Sioux ritual specialists.

8. *Waȟtáni* was used by missionaries to express the Christian notion of sin.
9. I am currently preparing a manuscript that explores traditional Lakota ethnomedicine and disease theory in greater detail, connecting historical notions of intergenerational sickness caused by bad conduct to the modern notion of historical trauma.
10. Wallis and Wallis list the two reserves as "Sioux Village, on the outskirts of Portage La Prairie, and Oak River, near Griswold" (1953, 431). Today these reserves are known as Long Plain and Sioux Valley, respectively, and consist mostly of Sisseton, Wahpeton, and Mdewakanton people.
11. Hallowell notes that the Berens River Ojibwes held similar beliefs vis-à-vis women's blood but that Ojibwe men apparently did consider it unclean or polluting (Jennifer Brown, personal communication).
12. For a similar account of Dakota healing practices, see Mary Eastman (1995, 19).
13. Hallowell recorded parallel Ojibwe views on the torture of animals as bad conduct (see Berens 2009).

8. LAKOTA RITUAL

1. Commenting on Nurit Bird-David's now-classic article "'Animism' Revisited: Personhood, Environment, and Relational Epistemology," Alan Sandstrom (in Bird-David 1999, S85) insightfully notes that in hunter-gatherer cultures "to relate is to know and . . . to bring to life is to impersonate. Following this principle, and depending on the context, animals may be turned into mere objects, into people, or into divinities. And when natural kinds or natural forces are 'made alive' as persons, people relate to them and communicate and socialize with them exactly as if they were fellow human beings." This notion of impersonation as bringing to life is particularly relevant to the various types of *wak'ą́ kága* 'sacred impersonations or [re]enactments'.
2. Nineteenth-century Lakotas also approached the spirits in order to acquire power that would give them success in hunting, horse raiding, warfare, and love; power to diagnose, treat, and cure the sick; in accordance with vows made, obliging individuals to perform various ritual actions and observe various taboos; and in general to appeal for the maintenance and continuation of individual and collective life movement (that the people may live).
3. Recall that prayer (wac'ékiya) is a multivocal ritual dynamic and symbol encompassing many meanings, including 'to pray', 'to cry or weep to or for', 'to call on someone for aid', and 'to address someone using a kin term' (Dorsey 1894, 435–36; E. Deloria 1998, 28–29; DeMallie 1987, 30–31; 2001, 807). DeMallie

writes, "Thus the act of prayer was an invocation of relationship, begging the spirit beings—often with cries and tears—to live up to the kindness and generosity expected of a good relative. Sacrifice, of objects or of physical suffering, frequently accompanied prayer" (2001, 807). Wacʻékiya is tied to the evocation of pity, essential to enlisting aid and securing power, knowledge, or medicine from nonhuman persons. The necessity of establishing proper relationship is essential not only between humans, but also between human and nonhuman persons, giving an individual status with both the spirits and his fellow humans. Wacʻékiya is also used in reference to any ceremonial smoking of a pipe (E. Deloria 1998, 28–29).

4. According to Kapferer, "The virtuality of rite can be regarded as critical to what I have referred to as its *techné*. It is not a modeling of lived processes (as is indicated in some ritual analyses) but a method for entering within life's vital processes and adjusting its dynamics. By entering within the particular dynamics of life by means of the virtuality of ritual, ritualists engage with positioning and structurating processes that are otherwise impossible to address in the tempo and dynamics of ordinary lived processes as these are lived at the surface" (2010, 245).

5. Kapferer writes, "I do not oppose dynamics to statics, for what appears to be static, repetitive, or unchanging in ritual is nonetheless a product of the particular dynamics of its action, which has the capacity to effect changes in the experience of participants, as well as within the wider social and political contexts in which rituals are enacted. Overall, the concern with the dynamics of ritual is with the organizing or structurating practices or techniques through which it intervenes pragmatically (often constitutively) in lived experience" (2006a, 507).

6. The spirit world may be productively compared to the astral plane of Western esoteric traditions: an intermediate or inner plane of experience or reality, a "virtual reality," which is psychological in nature but no less an experiential reality. While the spirit world exists on a different level of reality, it is intimately connected to and permeates the human world or actuality. It is a separate but connected subtle plane or alternate reality wherein the things of the imagination are real and symbolism and symbolic correspondences abound (cf. Hanegraaff 2003, 368, 370–71; Luhrmann 1989, 276–79).

7. For alternative approaches to the Plains vision quest, see Lee Irwin (1994a, 1994b) and David Martínez (2004a, 2004b).

8. Kinship terminology also indexed these qualitative power differentials. Nonhuman spirit persons were linguistically integrated in the kinship terminology, referred to as grandfathers and grandmothers. When spirits directly addressed humans they used kinship terminology as well, often referring to them as "my

grandchild" (Fletcher 1887a, 276n1; E. Deloria 1998, 52; G. Pond 1889, 219; cf. Hallowell 1955, 181). An interesting idea for future research would be an exploration of kinship terms as indexing degrees of power. Humans, for instance, used respect terms (grandfather and grandmother) in reference to nonhuman persons, which also served to index generational differences and behavioral expectations. In mythology, the trickster figure Iktomi constantly addresses others as "my younger brother," placing them in a subordinate position and indicating their lesser degree of power (see E. Deloria 2006).

9. Due to their increased capacity for transformation, among other factors, the spirits of deceased humans were considered more powerful than living humans and hence more like nonhuman spirit persons (cf. Hallowell 1955, 180).

10. This is also tied to isolation or separation as an important ritual dynamic.

11. Berens River Ojibwe leader William Berens (2009) also emphasized the power of mind in his discussions with Hallowell.

12. Transformation is an indexical attribute of the person category. In mythology, dreams, and visions nonhumans often appeared in human form, while humans could assume various nonhuman forms. Recall that, according to Descola, "Animals (and the spirits who act as their representatives) generally adopt a human appearance when they want to establish a relationship with humans" (2013b, 81). In ritual, especially doctoring and sorcery, humans often assumed nonhuman forms. For instance, a shaman could *become* (áya) a bear by donning the hide or skin (há) of a bear in a ritual convergence of physicalities. In all cases the interiority was the essential and persisting attribute of the person class, but psychic continuity permitted movement across physical discontinuities (see Kohn 2015, 317). Because of this capacity for transformation, common in animist frameworks, no sharp line can be drawn between human and nonhuman on the basis of outward form or physicality (see Hallowell 1955, 179).

13. According to Wissler (1905, 262),

> It is well to note that while the elk is taken as the incarnation of the power over females, the real elk is regarded only as the recipient of such power. The power itself is conceived of in the nature of an abstraction similar to our conception of force. The fact that the elk seems to act in conformity with the laws governing this power is taken as evidence of its existence. Then the idea of the Indian is that the elk possesses the knowledge necessary to the working of the power. Thus a mythical, or hypothetical elk, becomes the teacher of man.

14. According to Jennifer Brown, such an explicit public performance of a vision was not an Ojibwe custom; a man's dream helpers and the nature of his vision

could be deduced only from observing his performative acts—as when Fair Wind spoke with Thunder Birds (personal communication).
15. Naming also figures prominently here. Fletcher writes, "A name implies relationship, and consequently protection; favor and influence are claimed from the source of the name" (1887b, 295n14). Naming is a generative, creative act (see Powers 1986).
16. Recall that, according to DeMallie and Lavenda (1977, 164), in order to be operative wakʻą́ energy or power requires a locus or vessel. Apparently this characteristic also applies to a šicų́.
17. Compare the contents of Jaw's war medicine bundle (in Densmore 2001, 389) to Sword's description of the contents of an Oglala Bear medicine bundle (in Walker 1991, 93).
18. Recall that Vine Deloria was fascinated by the connections between Lakota ethnometaphysics and Jungian psychoanalytic theory, as evidenced by his posthumously published book on the subject (V. Deloria 2009; see also V. Deloria 1999, 227–28). However, Deloria (2009, 36–42) was critical of Lévy-Bruhl's notion of participation mystique, largely because of its social evolutionary connotations. But, much like the concept of animism, if we can move beyond the value judgments of past scholarship tied to social evolutionary ideas these concepts can be used productively.
19. Apparently there was a semantic connection between looking at/beholding and identification (see Sword 1938).

9. THE DYNAMICS OF LIFE MOVEMENT

1. Ní 'life, breath, vitality' is a central concept in nineteenth-century Lakota disease theory, healing, and ritual (see Posthumus 2015, 162–76).
2. This is similar to Vine Deloria's notion of maturity as the ultimate goal of human existence in the American Indian context (see V. Deloria 1999, 13–14).
3. Ingold also utilizes the analogy of the trail or road in his discussion of animist ontologies. Life, he writes, is "a trail of movement or growth. Every such trail traces a relation. . . . a trail *along* which life is lived" (Ingold 2006, 13).
4. On disenchantment, secularization, and "New Age" religious traditions, see Hanegraaff (1996, 2000, 2003).

REFERENCES

Amiotte, Arthur. 1982. "Our Other Selves: The Lakota Dream Experience." *Parabola: Myth and the Quest for Meaning* 7 (2): 26–32.
Anderson, Gary Clayton. 1980. "Early Dakota Migration and Intertribal War: A Revision." *Western Historical Quarterly* 11 (1): 17–36.
———. 1988. *Through Dakota Eyes: Narrative Accounts of the Minnesota Indian War of 1862*. St. Paul: Minnesota Historical Society Press.
Anderson, Jeffrey D. 2001. *The Four Hills of Life: Northern Arapaho Knowledge and Life Movement*. Studies in the Anthropology of North American Indians. Lincoln: University of Nebraska Press.
Ansell-Pearson, Keith. 2005. "The Reality of the Virtual: Bergson and Deleuze." *MLN* 120 (5): 1112–27.
Austin, J. L. 1962. *How to Do Things with Words*. The William James Lectures, 1955. Cambridge MA: Harvard University Press.
Bad Heart Bull, Amos, and Helen H. Blish. 1967. *A Pictographic History of the Oglala Sioux*. Lincoln: University of Nebraska Press.
Basso, Keith H. 1966. "The Gift of Changing Woman." In *Bulletin of the Bureau of American Ethnology*, 196. Washington DC: Smithsonian Institution.
———. 1970. *The Cibecue Apache. Case Studies in Cultural Anthropology*. New York: Holt, Rinehart and Winston.
Beckwith, Martha Warren. 1930. "Mythology of the Oglala Dakota." *Journal of American Folklore* 43 (170): 339–442.
Beckwith, Paul Edmond. 1889. "Notes on Customs of the Dakotahs." In *Smithsonian Institution Annual Report for the Year 1886*, 245–57. Washington DC: U.S. Government Printing Office.

Beede, Aaron McGaffey. 1912. Journals and letters. Orin G. Libby Manuscript Collection, University of North Dakota, Grand Forks.

Berens, William. 2009. *Memories, Myths and Dreams of an Ojibwe Leader*. Edited by Jennifer S. H. Brown and Susan Elaine Gray. Montreal: McGill-Queen's University Press.

Bessire, Lucas, and David Bond. 2014. "Ontological Anthropology and the Deferral of Critique." *American Ethnologist* 41 (3): 440–56.

Bird-David, Nurit. 1999. "'Animism' Revisited: Personhood, Environment, and Relational Epistemology." *Current Anthropology* 40 (S1): S67–S91.

Black, Mary B. 1977. "Ojibwa Taxonomy and Percept Ambiguity." *Ethos* 5 (1): 90–118.

Bourdieu, Pierre. 1977. *Outline of a Theory of Practice*. Cambridge Studies in Social Anthropology, 16. Cambridge: Cambridge University Press.

Bourdieu, Pierre, and Loïc J. D. Wacquant. 1992. *An Invitation to Reflexive Sociology*. Chicago: University of Chicago Press.

Braun, Sebastian, ed. 2013. *Transforming Ethnohistories: Narrative, Meaning, and Community*. Norman: University of Oklahoma Press.

Brightman, Robert Alain. 1993. *Grateful Prey: Rock Cree Human-Animal Relationships*. Berkeley: University of California Press.

Brown, Jennifer S. H. 2006. "Fields of Dreams: Revisiting A. I. Hallowell and the Berens River Ojibwe." In *New Perspectives on Native North America: Cultures, Histories, and Representations*, edited by Sergei A. Kan and Pauline T. Strong, 17–41. Lincoln: University of Nebraska Press.

Brown, Joseph Epes, ed. 1989. *The Sacred Pipe: Black Elk's Account of the Seven Rites of the Oglala Sioux*. Norman: University of Oklahoma Press.

———. 1997. *Animals of the Soul: Sacred Animals of the Oglala Sioux*. Rockport MA: Element.

———. 2007. *The Spiritual Legacy of the American Indian: Commemorative Edition with Letters While Living with Black Elk*. Edited by Marina Brown Weatherly, Elenita Brown, and Michael Oren Fitzgerald. Bloomington IN: World Wisdom.

Bucko, Raymond A. 1998. *The Lakota Ritual of the Sweat Lodge: History and Contemporary Practice*. Studies in the Anthropology of North American Indians. Lincoln: University of Nebraska Press.

———. 2006. "Night Thoughts and Night Sweats, Ethnohistory and Ethnohumor: The Quaker Shaker Meets the Lakota Sweat Lodge." In *New Perspectives on Native North America: Cultures, Histories, and Representations*, edited by Sergei A. Kan and Pauline T. Strong, 162–84. Lincoln: University of Nebraska Press.

Buechel, Eugene. 1939. *A Grammar of Lakota: The Language of the Teton Sioux Indians*. Saint Francis SD: St. Francis Mission.

———. 1970. *A Dictionary of the Teton Dakota Sioux Language*. Edited by Paul Manhart. Pine Ridge SD: Red Cloud Indian School.

———. 1978. *Lakota Tales and Texts*. Edited by Paul Manhart. Pine Ridge SD: Red Cloud Indian School.

Bushotter, George. 1887–88. Lakota texts by George Bushotter; interlinear translations by James Owen Dorsey, aided by George Bushotter and John Bruyier. Manuscript No. 4800/103(1–3). Dorsey Papers, National Anthropological Archives, Smithsonian Institution, Washington DC.

Carley, Kenneth. 1976. *The Sioux Uprising of 1862*. St. Paul: Minnesota Historical Society Press.

Catlin, George. 1973. *Letters and Notes on the Manners, Customs, and Conditions of the North American Indians; Written during Eight Years' Travel (1832–1839) amongst the Wildest Tribes of Indians in North America*. New York: Dover.

Clark, W. P. 1982. *The Indian Sign Language*. Lincoln: University of Nebraska Press.

Cunfer, Geoff, and Bill Waiser, eds. 2016. *Bison and People on the North American Great Plains: A Deep Environmental History*. Connecting the Greater West. College Station: Texas A&M University Press.

Curtis, Edward S. 1908. *The North American Indian*. Vol. 3. Reprint, New York: Johnson Reprint.

Daniels, Robert E. 1970. "Cultural Identities among the Oglala Sioux." In *The Modern Sioux: Social Systems and Reservation Culture*, edited by Ethel Nurge, 198–245. Lincoln: University of Nebraska Press.

Darnell, Regna. 2001. *Invisible Genealogies: A History of Americanist Anthropology*. Critical Studies in the History of Anthropology Series. Lincoln: University of Nebraska Press.

———. 2006. "Keeping the Faith: A Legacy of Native American Ethnography, Ethnohistory, and Psychology." In *New Perspectives on Native North America: Cultures, Histories, and Representations*, edited by Sergei A. Kan and Pauline T. Strong, 3–16. Lincoln: University of Nebraska Press.

Deleuze, Gilles. 1988. *Bergsonism*. New York: Zone Books.

———. 1993. *The Fold: Leibniz and the Baroque*. Minneapolis: University of Minnesota Press.

———. 2001. *Pure Immanence: Essays on a Life*. New York: Zone Books.

Deleuze, Gilles, and Félix Guattari. 1987. *A Thousand Plateaus: Capitalism and Schizophrenia*. Minneapolis: University of Minnesota Press.

———. 1994. *What Is Philosophy? European Perspectives*. New York: Columbia University Press.

Deloria, Ella Cara. 1927. Correspondence with Franz Boas. MS 31. Boas Collection, American Philosophical Library, Philadelphia.

———. 1932. *Dakota Texts.* Publications of the American Ethnological Society, vol. 14. New York: G. E. Stechert, agents.

———. 1937. "Dakota Commentary on Walker's Legends." MS 30(x8a.5). Boas Collection, American Philosophical Library, Philadelphia.

———. 1998. *Speaking of Indians.* Lincoln: University of Nebraska Press.

———. 2006. *Dakota Texts.* Bison Books ed. Lincoln: University of Nebraska Press.

———. N.d.a. "Alpha. Buffalo Ceremony." Dakota Indian Foundation, Chamberlain SD.

———. N.d.b. "Dakota Ceremonies." Dakota Indian Foundation, Chamberlain SD.

———. N.d.c. "Dakota Ethnographic Notes." Dakota Indian Foundation, Chamberlain SD.

———. N.d.d. "Double Women Ceremony." Dakota Indian Foundation, Chamberlain SD.

———. N.d.e. "Gamma. Religion." Dakota Indian Foundation, Chamberlain SD.

———. N.d.f. "Ghost Keeping." Dakota Indian Foundation, Chamberlain SD.

———. N.d.g. "Rites and Ceremonies of the Teton." Dakota Indian Foundation, Chamberlain SD.

———. N.d.h. "Wakan Practices." Dakota Indian Foundation, Chamberlain SD.

Deloria, Vine. 1973. *God Is Red.* New York: Grosset & Dunlap.

———. 1999. *Spirit and Reason: The Vine Deloria, Jr., Reader.* Edited by Barbara Deloria, Kristen Foehner, and Samuel Scinta. Golden CO: Fulcrum.

———. 2009. *C. G. Jung and the Sioux Traditions: Dreams, Visions, Nature and the Primitive.* Edited by Philip J. Deloria and Jerome S. Bernstein. New Orleans: Spring Journal Books.

———. 2012. *The Metaphysics of Modern Existence.* Golden CO: Fulcrum.

DeMallie, Raymond J. 1976. "Appendix 3: Nicollet's Notes on the Dakota." In *Joseph N. Nicollet on the Plains and Prairies: The Expeditions of 1838–39 with Journals, Letters, and Notes on the Dakota Indians,* edited by Edmund C. Bray and Martha Coleman Bray, 250–81. St. Paul: Minnesota Historical Society Press.

———. 1978. "George Bushotter: The First Lakota Ethnographer." In *American Indian Intellectuals,* edited by Margot Liberty, 91–102. 1976 American Ethnological Society Proceedings. St. Paul: West.

———. 1982. "The Lakota Ghost Dance: An Ethnohistorical Account." *Pacific Historical Review* 51 (4): 385–405.

———. 1984. *The Sixth Grandfather: Black Elk's Teachings Given to John G. Neihardt.* Lincoln: University of Nebraska Press.

———. 1987. "Lakota Belief and Ritual in the Nineteenth Century." In *Sioux Indian Religion: Tradition and Innovation,* edited by Raymond J. DeMallie and Douglas R. Parks, 25–43. Norman: University of Oklahoma Press.

———. 1991. "Lakota Traditionalism: History and Symbol." In *Native North American Interaction Patterns*, edited by Regna Darnell and Michael K. Foster, 2–21. Ottawa: Canadian Museum of Civilization.

———. 1993. "'These Have No Ears': Narrative and the Ethnohistorical Method." *Ethnohistory* 40 (4): 515–38.

———. 1994. "Kinship and Biology in Sioux Culture." In *North American Indian Anthropology: Essays on Society and Culture*, edited by Raymond J. DeMallie and Alfonso Ortiz, 125–46. Norman: University of Oklahoma Press.

———. 1998. "Kinship: The Foundation for Native American Society." In *Studying Native America: Problems and Prospects*, edited by Russell Thornton, 306–56. Madison: University of Wisconsin Press.

———. 2001. *Handbook of North American Indians*. Vol. 13, *Plains*, edited by Raymond J. DeMallie. Washington DC: Smithsonian Institution.

———. 2006. "The Sioux at the Time of European Contact: An Ethnohistorical Problem." In *New Perspectives on Native North America: Cultures, Histories, and Representations*, edited by Sergei A. Kan and Pauline T. Strong, 239–60. Lincoln: University of Nebraska Press.

DeMallie, Raymond J., and Robert H. Lavenda. 1977. "Wakan: Plains Siouan Concepts of Power." In *The Anthropology of Power: Ethnographic Studies from Asia, Oceania, and the New World*, edited by Raymond D. Fogelson and Richard N. Adams, 153–65. Studies in Anthropology. New York: Academic Press.

DeMallie, Raymond J., and Douglas R. Parks, eds. 1987. *Sioux Indian Religion: Tradition and Innovation*. Norman: University of Oklahoma Press.

Densmore, Frances. 2001. *Teton Sioux Music and Culture*. Lincoln: University of Nebraska Press.

Descola, Philippe. 2013a. *Beyond Nature and Culture*. Translated by Janet Lloyd. Chicago: University of Chicago Press.

———. 2013b. "Beyond Nature and Culture." In *The Handbook of Contemporary Animism*, edited by Graham Harvey, 77–91. Durham, UK: Acumen.

———. 2014a. "All Too Human (Still): A Comment on Eduardo Kohn's *How Forests Think*." *HAU: Journal of Ethnographic Theory* 4 (2): 267–73.

———. 2014b. "Modes of Being and Forms of Predication." *HAU: Journal of Ethnographic Theory* 4 (1): 271–80.

Desjarlais, Robert, and C. Jason Throop. 2011. "Phenomenological Approaches in Anthropology." *Annual Review of Anthropology* 40 (1): 87–102.

Désveaux, Emmanuel, and Michel De Fornel. 2009. "From Ojibwa to Dakota: Toward a Typology of Semantic Transformations in American Indian Languages." *Anthropological Linguistics* 51 (2): 95–129.

Detwiler, Fritz. 1992. "'All My Relatives': Persons in Oglala Religion." *Religion* 22 (3): 235-46.
Dorsey, J. Owen. 1889a. "Teton Folk-Lore." *American Anthropologist* 2 (2): 143-58.
———. 1889b. "Teton Folk-Lore Notes." *Journal of American Folklore* 2 (5): 133-39.
———. 1894. "A Study of Siouan Cults." In *11th Annual Report of the Bureau of [American] Ethnology [for] 1889-90*, 351-544. Washington: Smithsonian Institution.
Douglas, Mary. 1966. *Purity and Danger: An Analysis of Concepts of Pollution and Taboo*. London: Routledge & Paul.
———. 1970. *Natural Symbols: Explorations in Cosmology*. New York: Pantheon Books.
Eastman, Charles A. 1971. *Indian Boyhood*. New York: Dover.
———. 1980. *The Soul of the Indian: An Interpretation*. Lincoln: University of Nebraska Press.
———. 1991. *Indian Heroes and Great Chieftains*. Bison Books ed. Lincoln: University of Nebraska Press.
Eastman, Mary H. 1995. *Dahcotah; or, Life and Legends of the Sioux around Fort Snelling*. Afton MN: Afton Historical Society Press.
Evans-Pritchard, E. E. 1965. *Theories of Primitive Religion*. Sir D. Owen Evans Lectures, 1962. Oxford: Clarendon Press.
Farnell, Brenda M. 1995. *Do You See What I Mean?: Plains Indian Sign Talk and the Embodiment of Action*. Austin: University of Texas Press.
Feinberg, Richard. 1981. "What Is Polynesian Kinship All About?" *Ethnology* 20 (2): 115-31.
———. 2011. *Anuta Polynesian Lifeways for the 21st Century*. Kent OH: Kent State University Press.
Fletcher, Alice C. 1887a. "The Elk Mystery Festival. Ogallala Sioux." In *16th Report of the Peabody Museum of American Archaeology and Ethnology, Harvard University, 1882*, 276-88. Cambridge MA.
———. 1887b. "The Religious Ceremony of the Four Winds or Quarters, as Observed by the Santee Sioux." In *16th Report of the Peabody Museum of American Archaeology and Ethnology, Harvard University, 1882*, 289-95. Cambridge MA.
———. 1887c. "The Shadow or Ghost Lodge: A Ceremony of the Ogallala Sioux." In *16th Report of the Peabody Museum of American Archaeology and Ethnology, Harvard University, 1882*, 296-307. Cambridge MA.
———. 1887d. "The White Buffalo Festival of the Uncpapas." In *16th Report of the Peabody Museum of American Archaeology and Ethnology, Harvard University, 1882*, 260-75. Cambridge MA.
———. 1897. "Notes on Certain Beliefs Concerning Will Power among the Siouan Tribes." *Science* 5 (113): 331-34.
Foster, Morris W. 1991. *Being Comanche: A Social History of an American Indian Community*. Tucson: University of Arizona Press.

Fugle, Eugene. 1966. "The Nature and Function of the Lakota Night Cults." *(W. H. Over) Museum News* (University of South Dakota) 27 (3–4): 1–38.

Geertz, Clifford. 1973. *The Interpretation of Cultures: Selected Essays*. New York: Basic Books.

Gibbon, Guy E. 2003. *The Sioux: The Dakota and Lakota Nations*. The Peoples of America. Malden MA: Blackwell.

Gingrich, André, and Richard G. Fox, eds. 2002. *Anthropology, by Comparison*. New York: Routledge.

Graeber, David. 2015. "Radical Alterity Is Just Another Way of Saying 'reality': A Reply to Eduardo Viveiros de Castro." *HAU: Journal of Ethnographic Theory* 5 (2): 1–41.

Greene, Shane. 2009. *Customizing Indigeneity: Paths to a Visionary Politics in Peru*. Stanford CA: Stanford University Press.

Greenwood, Susan. 2005. *The Nature of Magic: An Anthropology of Consciousness*. Oxford: Berg.

Grobsmith, Elizabeth S. 1974. "*Wakúza*: Uses of Yuwipi Medicine Power in Contemporary Teton Dakota Culture." *Plains Anthropologist* 19 (64): 129–33.

———. 1981. *Lakota of the Rosebud: A Contemporary Ethnography*. Case Studies in Cultural Anthropology. New York: Holt, Rinehart and Winston.

Hall, Edward T. 1959. *The Silent Language*. New York: Anchor Books.

Hallowell, A. Irving. 1934. "Some Empirical Aspects of Northern Saulteaux Religion." *American Anthropologist* 36 (3): 389–404.

———. 1955. *Culture and Experience*. Publications of the Philadelphia Anthropological Society, vol. 4. Philadelphia: University of Pennsylvania Press.

———. 1958. "Ojibwa Metaphysics of Being and the Perception of Persons." In *Person Perception and Interpersonal Behavior*, edited by Renato Tagiuri and Luigi Petrullo, 63–85. Stanford CA: Stanford University Press.

———. 1960. "Ojibwa Ontology, Behavior and World View." In *Culture in History: Essays in Honor of Paul Radin*, edited by Stanley Diamond, 19–52. New York: Columbia University Press.

———. 1963. "Ojibwa World View and Disease." *Man's Image in Medicine and Anthropology* (4): 258–315.

———. 1966. "The Role of Dreams in Ojibwa Culture." In *The Dream and Human Societies*, edited by Gustave E. von Grunebaum and Roger Caillois, 267–92. Berkeley: University of California Press.

———. 1976. *Contributions to Anthropology: Selected Papers of A. Irving Hallowell*. Chicago: University of Chicago Press.

———. 2010. *Contributions to Ojibwe Studies: Essays, 1934–1972*. Edited by Jennifer S. H. Brown and Susan Elaine Gray. Critical Studies in the History of Anthropology. Lincoln: University of Nebraska Press.

Hammer, Olav. 2001. *Claiming Knowledge: Strategies of Epistemology from Theosophy to the New Age*. Numen Book Series. Studies in the History of Religions, vol. 90. Leiden: Brill.

Hanegraaff, Wouter J. 1996. *New Age Religion and Western Culture: Esotericism in the Mirror of Secular Thought*. Studies in the History of Religions, vol. 72. New York: E. J. Brill.

———. 2000. "New Age Religion and Secularization." *Numen* 47 (3): 288–312.

———. 2003. "How Magic Survived the Disenchantment of the World." *Religion* 33 (4): 357–80.

———. 2015. "From Imagination to Reality: An Introduction to Esotericism and the Occult." In *Hilma Af Klint: The Art of Seeing the Invisible*, edited by Kurt Almqvist and Louise Belfrage, 59–71. Stockholm: Axel and Margaret Ax: son Johnson Foundation.

Harvey, Graham. 2005. *Animism: Respecting the Living World*. London: Hurst.

———, ed. 2013. *The Handbook of Contemporary Animism*. Durham, UK: Acumen.

Heidegger, Martin. 1962. *Being and Time*. New York: Harper.

Henare, Amiria, Martin Holbraad, and Sari Wastell, eds. 2007. *Thinking through Things: Theorising Artefacts Ethnographically*. London: Routledge.

Hickerson, Harold. 1988. *The Chippewa and Their Neighbors: A Study in Ethnohistory*. Prospect Heights IL: Waveland Press.

Hobsbawm, Eric J., and Terence O. Ranger, eds. 1983. *The Invention of Tradition*. Past and Present Publications. Cambridge: Cambridge University Press.

Hodder, Ian. 2011. "Human-Thing Entanglement: Towards an Integrated Archaeological Perspective." *Journal of the Royal Anthropological Institute* 17 (1): 154–77.

———. 2012. *Entangled: An Archaeology of the Relationships between Humans and Things*. Malden MA: Wiley-Blackwell.

———. 2014. "The Entanglements of Humans and Things: A Long-Term View." *New Literary History* 45 (1): 19–36.

Howe, Oscar. 2004. *Oscar Howe, Artist*. Vermillion: University of South Dakota.

Hultkrantz, Åke. 1983. "The Concept of the Supernatural in Primal Religion." *History of Religions* 22 (3): 231–53.

Ingold, Tim. 1997. "Life beyond the Edge of Nature? Or, the Mirage of Society." In *The Mark of the Social: Discovery or Invention?*, edited by John D. Greenwood, 231–52. Lanham MD: Rowman & Littlefield.

———. 2000. *The Perception of the Environment: Essays on Livelihood, Dwelling and Skill*. New York: Routledge.

———. 2004. "A Circumpolar Night's Dream." In *Figured Worlds: Ontological Obstacles in Intercultural Relations*, edited by J. R. Clammer, Sylvie Poirier, and Eric Schwimmer, 25–57. Toronto: University of Toronto Press.

———. 2006. "Rethinking the Animate, Re-animating Thought." *Ethnos: Journal of Anthropology* 71 (1): 9–20.

———. 2011. *Being Alive: Essays on Movement, Knowledge and Description*. New York: Routledge.

Irwin, Lee. 1994a. *The Dream Seekers: Native American Visionary Traditions of the Great Plains*. The Civilization of the American Indian Series, vol. 213. Norman: University of Oklahoma Press.

———. 1994b. "Dreams, Theory, and Culture: The Plains Vision Quest Paradigm." *American Indian Quarterly* 18 (2): 229–45.

Jahner, Elaine A. 1992. "Transitional Narratives and Cultural Continuity." *Boundary 2* 19 (3): 148–79.

Jensen, Casper Bruun. 2013. "Two Forms of the Outside: Castaneda, Blanchot, Ontology." *HAU: Journal of Ethnographic Theory* 3 (3): 309–35.

Jung, C. G. 1959. *The Basic Writings of C. G. Jung*. Edited by Violet S. De Laszlo. The Modern Library of the World's Best Books, 300. New York: Random House.

———. 1971. *Psychological Types*. Edited by R. F. C. Hull and Gerhard Adler. Translated by H. G. Baynes. Bollingen Series, 20. Princeton NJ: Princeton University Press.

Kapferer, Bruce. 1979. "Mind, Self, and Other in Demonic Illness: The Negation and Reconstruction of Self." *American Ethnologist* 6 (1): 110–33.

———. 2002. "Introduction: Outside All Reason: Magic, Sorcery and Epistemology in Anthropology." *Social Analysis: The International Journal of Social and Cultural Practice* 46 (3): 1–30.

———. 2004. "Ritual Dynamics and Virtual Practice: Beyond Representation and Meaning." *Social Analysis: The International Journal of Social and Cultural Practice* 48 (2): 35–54.

———. 2006a. "Dynamics." In *Theorizing Rituals: Issues, Topics, Approaches, Concepts*, edited by Jens Kreinath, Jan Snoek, and Michael Strausberg, 507–22. Boston: Brill Academic.

———. 2006b. "Virtuality." In *Theorizing Rituals: Issues, Topics, Approaches, Concepts*, edited by Jens Kreinath, Jan Snoek, and Michael Strausberg, 671–84. Boston: Brill Academic.

———. 2008. "Beyond Symbolic Representation: Victor Turner and Variations on the Themes of Ritual Process and Liminality." *Suomen Antropologi: The Journal of the Finnish Anthropological Society* 33 (4): 5–25.

———. 2010. "Beyond Ritual as Performance: Towards Ritual as Dynamics and Virtuality." *Paragrana Internationale Zeitschrift Für Historische Anthropologie* 19 (2): 231–49.

———. 2012. *Legends of People, Myths of State: Violence, Intolerance, and Political Culture in Sri Lanka and Australia*. Smithsonian Series in Ethnographic Inquiry. New York: Berghahn Books.

———. 2013a. "Montage and Time: Deleuze, Cinema, and a Buddhist Sorcery Rite." In *Transcultural Montage*, edited by Christian Suhr and Rane Willerslev, 20–39. New York: Berghahn Books.

———. 2013b. "Ritual Practice and Anthropological Theory." *Religion and Society: Advances in Research* 4 (1): 3–11.

———. 2014a. "Back to the Future: Descola's Neostructuralism." *HAU: Journal of Ethnographic Theory* 4 (3): 389–400.

———. 2014b. *2001 and Counting: Kubrick, Nietzsche, and Anthropology*. Paradigm, 45. Chicago: Prickly Paradigm Press.

Katz, Jack, and Thomas J. Csordas. 2003. "Phenomenological Ethnography in Sociology and Anthropology." *Ethnography* 4 (3): 275–88.

Kearney, Michael. 1975. "World View Theory and Study." *Annual Review of Anthropology* 4 (1): 247–70.

———. 1984. *World View*. Chandler & Sharp Publications in Anthropology and Related Fields. Novato CA: Chandler & Sharp.

Kelly, John D. 2014. "Introduction: The Ontological Turn in French Philosophical Anthropology." *HAU: Journal of Ethnographic Theory* 4 (1): 259–69.

Kohn, Eduardo. 2013. *How Forests Think: Toward an Anthropology beyond the Human*. Berkeley: University of California Press.

———. 2015. "Anthropology of Ontologies." *Annual Review of Anthropology* 44 (1): 311–27.

Lakota Language Consortium. 2008. *New Lakota Dictionary: Lakȟótiyapi-English, English-Lakȟótiyapi and Incorporating the Dakota Dialects of Yankton-Yanktonai & Santee-Sisseton*. Bloomington IN: Lakota Language Consortium.

Lame Deer, John (Fire), and Richard Erdoes. 1972. *Lame Deer, Seeker of Visions*. New York: Simon and Schuster.

Langer, Susanne K. 1953. *Feeling and Form: A Theory of Art*. New York: Charles Scribner's Sons.

———. 1957. *Philosophy in a New Key: A Study in the Symbolism of Reason, Rite, and Art*. Cambridge MA: Harvard University Press.

Latour, Bruno. 1991. *Nous n'avons jamais été modernes: Essai d'anthropologie symétrique*. Collection L'armillaire. Paris: La Découverte.

———. 1993. *We Have Never Been Modern*. Cambridge MA: Harvard University Press.

Lévi-Strauss, Claude. 1963. *Structural Anthropology*. New York: Basic Books.

Lévy-Bruhl, Lucien. 1926. *How Natives Think*. Translated by Lilian A. Clare. London: G. Allen & Unwin.

Lewis, Meriwether, and William Clark. 2002. *The Definitive Journals of Lewis and Clark*. Vol. 3. Edited by Gary E. Moulton Lincoln: University of Nebraska Press.

Luhrmann, T. M. 1989. *Persuasions of the Witch's Craft: Ritual Magic in Contemporary England*. Cambridge MA: Harvard University Press.

Lynd, James W. 1889. "The Religion of the Dakotas." In *Collections of the Minnesota Historical Society* 2: 150–74.

Lyons, Scott Richard. 2011. "Actually Existing Indian Nations: Modernity, Diversity, and the Future of Native American Studies." *American Indian Quarterly* 35 (3): 294–312.

Martínez, David. 2004a. "The Soul of the Indian: Lakota Philosophy and the Vision Quest." *Wicazo Sa Review* 19 (2): 79–104.

———. 2004b. "What the Eyes Alone Cannot See: Lakota Phenomenology and the Vision Quest." In *Imaginatio Creatrix: The Pivotal Force of the Genesis/Ontopoiesis of Human Life and Reality*, edited by Anna-Teresa Tymieniecka, 319–61. Analecta Husserliana, 83. Dordrecht, Netherlands: Springer.

McFatridge, Arthur E. 1937. "Among the Indians: A Study of the Habits, Customs and Characteristics of the Ogallallas, 1898–1905." University of South Dakota Archives and Special Collections, Vermillion.

Mekeel, H. Scudder. 1943. *A Short History of the Teton-Dakota*. Bismarck: State Historical Society of North Dakota.

Meyer, Roy Willard. 1967. *History of the Santee Sioux*. Lincoln: University of Nebraska Press.

Morrison, Kenneth M. 1992. "Beyond the Supernatural: Language and Religious Action." *Religion* 22 (3): 201–5.

Nash, Dennison. 1977. "Hallowell in American Anthropology." *Ethos* 5 (1): 3–12.

Neihardt, John G. 1991. *When the Tree Flowered: The Story of Eagle Voice, a Sioux Indian*. Lincoln: University of Nebraska Press.

———. 2008. *Black Elk Speaks: Being the Life Story of a Holy Man of the Oglala Sioux*. Excelsior Editions. Albany NY: State University of New York Press.

Neill, Edward D. 1872. "Dakota Land and Dakota Life." In *Collections of the Minnesota Historical Society* 1: 254–94.

———. 1890. "Memoir of the Sioux: A Manuscript in the French Archives, Now First Printed, with Introduction and Notes." *Contributions to the Department of History, Literature and Political Science* (Macalester College), 1st ser., (1): 223–40. St. Paul MN.

Pasi, Marco. 2011. "Varieties of Magical Experience: Aleister Crowley's Views on Occult Practice." *Magic, Ritual, and Witchcraft* 6 (2): 123–62.

Pflüg, Melissa A. 1996. "'Pimadaziwin': Contemporary Rituals in Odawa Community." *American Indian Quarterly* 20 (3/4): 489–513.

Pond, Gideon H. 1889. "Dakota Superstitions and Gods." In *Collections of the Minnesota Historical Society* 2: 215–55.

Pond, Samuel W. 1908. "The Dakotas or Sioux in Minnesota as They Were in 1834." In *Collections of the Minnesota Historical Society* 12: 320–501.

Posthumus, David C. 2008–17. Fieldwork interviews and personal communications.

———. 2015. "Transmitting Sacred Knowledge: Aspects of Historical and Contemporary Oglala Lakota Belief and Ritual." PhD diss., Indiana University.

———. 2016. "A Lakota View of *Pté Oyáte* (Buffalo Nation)." In *Bison and People on the North American Great Plains: A Deep Environmental History*, edited by Geoff Cunfer and Bill Waiser, 278–310. Connecting the Greater West. College Station: Texas A&M University Press.

Powers, William K. 1982a. *Oglala Religion*. Lincoln: University of Nebraska Press.

———. 1982b. *Yuwipi: Vision and Experience in Oglala Ritual*. Lincoln: University of Nebraska Press.

———. 1986. *Sacred Language: The Nature of Supernatural Discourse in Lakota*. Civilization of the American Indian Series, 179. Norman: University of Oklahoma Press.

Radcliffe-Brown, A. R. 1952. *Structure and Function in Primitive Society: Essays and Addresses*. Glencoe IL: Free Press.

Radin, Paul. 1914. "Religion of the North American Indians." *Journal of American Folklore* 27 (106): 335–73.

———. 1953. *The World of Primitive Man*. New York: Henry Schuman.

———. 1957. *Primitive Religion: Its Nature and Origin*. New York: Dover.

Radisson, Pierre Esprit. 1961. *The Explorations of Pierre Esprit Radisson: From the Original Manuscript in the Bodleian Library and the British Museum*. Edited by Arthur T. Adams. Minneapolis: Ross & Haines.

Rappaport, Roy A. 2000. *Ritual and Religion in the Making of Humanity*. Cambridge Studies in Social and Cultural Anthropology, 110. Cambridge: Cambridge University Press.

Redfield, Robert. 1952. "The Primitive World View." *Proceedings of the American Philosophical Society* 96 (1): 30–36.

Rice, Julian. 1998. *Before the Great Spirit: The Many Faces of Sioux Spirituality*. Albuquerque: University of New Mexico Press.

Riggs, Stephen Return. 1869. *Tah-Koo Wah-Kan; or, The Gospel among the Dakotas*. Boston: Congregational Pub. Society.

———. 1880. "The Theogony of the Sioux." *American Antiquarian* 2 (4): 265–70.

———. 1883. "Mythology of the Dakotas." *American Antiquarian* (5): 147–49.

———. 1893. *Dakota Grammar, Texts, and Ethnography*. Washington DC: Government Printing Office.

———. 1992. *A Dakota-English Dictionary*. Edited by James Owen Dorsey. St. Paul: Minnesota Historical Society Press.

Sage, Rufus B. 1857. *Rocky Mountain Life; or, Startling Scenes and Perilous Adventures in the Far West, during an Expedition of Three Years*. Boston: Wentworth.

Sahlins, Marshall. 1993. "Goodbye to Tristes Tropes: Ethnography in the Context of Modern World History." *Journal of Modern History* 65 (1): 1–25.

———. 1999. "Two or Three Things That I Know about Culture." *Journal of the Royal Anthropological Institute* 5 (3): 399–421.

———. 2013. *What Kinship Is—and Is Not*. Chicago: University of Chicago Press.

Saler, Benson. 1977. "Supernatural as a Western Category." *Ethos* 5 (1): 31–53.

Schneider, David M. 1969. "Kinship, Nationality and Religion in American Culture: Toward a Definition of Kinship." In *Forms of Symbolic Action*, edited by Robert F. Spencer, 116–25. Proceedings of the 1969 Annual Spring Meeting of the American Ethnological Society. Seattle: University of Washington Press.

Scott, Colin. 1989. "Knowledge Construction among the Cree Hunters: Metaphors and Literal Understanding." *Journal de la Société des Américanistes* 75 (1): 193–208.

———. 2006. "Spirit and Practical Knowledge in the Person of the Bear among Wemindji Cree Hunters." *Ethnos: Journal of Anthropology* 71 (1): 51–66.

———. 2013. "Ontology and Ethics in Cree Hunting: Animism, Totemism, and Practical Knowledge." In *The Handbook of Contemporary Animism*, edited by Graham Harvey, 159–66. Durham, UK: Acumen.

Scott, Michael W. 2013. "The Anthropology of Ontology (Religious Science?)." *Journal of the Royal Anthropological Institute* 19 (4): 859–72.

Segal, Robert Alan. 1999. *Theorizing about Myth*. Amherst: University of Massachusetts Press.

———. 2004. *Myth: A Very Short Introduction*. Very Short Introductions, 111. Oxford: Oxford University Press.

Shils, Edward. 1981. *Tradition*. Chicago: University of Chicago Press.

Smart, Ninian. 1987. *Religion and the Western Mind*. Albany: State University of New York Press.

Spiro, Melford E. 1976. "Alfred Irving Hallowell, 1892–1974." *American Anthropologist*, n.s., 78 (3): 608–11.

———. 1987. *Culture and Human Nature: Theoretical Papers of Melford E. Spiro*. Edited by Benjamin Kilborne and L. L. Langness. Chicago: University of Chicago Press.

Standing Bear, Luther. 2006a. *Land of the Spotted Eagle*. Lincoln: University of Nebraska Press.

———. 2006b. *My Indian Boyhood*. Lincoln: University of Nebraska Press.

Sword, George. 1938. Dakota Texts from the Sword Manuscripts. Translated by Ella Cara Deloria. x8a.18. Boas Collection. American Philosophical Library, Philadelphia.

Tabeau, Pierre Antoine. 1939. *Tabeau's Narrative of Loisel's Expedition to the Upper Missouri*. American Exploration and Travel Series, vol. 3. Norman: University of Oklahoma Press.

Tambiah, Stanley Jeyaraja. 1990. *Magic, Science, Religion, and the Scope of Rationality*. The Henry Lewis Morgan Lectures, 1981. Cambridge: Cambridge University Press.

Thompson, Evan, and Dan Zahavi. 2007. "Philosophical Issues: Phenomenology." In *Cambridge Handbook of Consciousness*, edited by Philip David Zelazo, Morris Moscovitch, and Evan Thompson, 67–88. Cambridge: Cambridge University Press.

Throop, C. Jason, and Keith M. Murphy. 2002. "Bourdieu and Phenomenology A Critical Assessment." *Anthropological Theory* 2 (2): 185–207.

Tomasello, Michael. 1999. "The Human Adaptation for Culture." *Annual Review of Anthropology* 28: 509–29.

———. 2000. "Culture and Cognitive Development." *Current Directions in Psychological Science* 9 (2): 37–40.

———. 2014. *A Natural History of Human Thinking*. Cambridge MA: Harvard University Press.

Tylor, Edward B. 1871. *Primitive Culture: Researches into the Development of Mythology, Philosophy, Religion, Art, and Custom*. London: J. Murray.

Vecsey, Christopher. 1983. *Traditional Ojibwa Religion and Its Historical Changes*. Memoirs of the American Philosophical Society, vol. 152. Philadelphia: American Philosophical Society.

Vestal, Stanley. 1984. *Warpath: The True Story of the Fighting Sioux Told in a Biography of Chief White Bull*. Lincoln: University of Nebraska Press.

Viveiros de Castro, Eduardo. 1998. "Cosmological Deixis and Amerindian Perspectivism." *Journal of the Royal Anthropological Institute* 4 (3): 469–88.

———. 2012. "Cosmological Perspectivism in Amazonia and Elsewhere." *HAU: Masterclass Series* 1 (0): 45–168.

———. 2014. *Cannibal Metaphysics: For a Post-structural Anthropology*. Edited by Peter Skafish. Minneapolis: Univocal.

Walker, J. R. 1917. "The Sun Dance and Other Ceremonies of the Oglala Division of the Teton Dakota." In *American Museum of Natural History Anthropological Papers* 16 (2): 51–221.

———. 1982. *Lakota Society*. Edited by Raymond J. DeMallie. Lincoln: University of Nebraska Press.

———. 1991. *Lakota Belief and Ritual*. Edited by Raymond J. DeMallie and Elaine A. Jahner. Lincoln: University of Nebraska Press.

———. 2006. *Lakota Myth*. Edited by Elaine A. Jahner. Lincoln: University of Nebraska Press.

Wallis, Ruth Sawtell, and Wilson D. Wallis. 1953. "The Sins of the Fathers: Concept of Disease among the Canadian Dakota." *Southwestern Journal of Anthropology* 9 (4): 431–35.

Wedel, Mildred Mott. 1974. "Le Sueur and the Dakota Sioux." In *Aspects of Upper Great Lakes Anthropology: Papers in Honor of Lloyd A. Wilford*, edited by Elden

Johnson, 157–71. Minnesota Prehistoric Archaeology Series, 11. St. Paul: Minnesota Historical Society.

White, Richard. 1978. "The Winning of the West: The Expansion of the Western Sioux in the Eighteenth and Nineteenth Centuries." *Journal of American History* 65(2): 319–43.

White Hat, Albert. 1999. *Reading and Writing the Lakota Language = Lakȟota Iyapi Uṉ Wowapi Nahaṉ Yawapi*. Edited by Jael Kampfe. Salt Lake City: University of Utah Press.

———. 2012. *Life's Journey—Zuya: Oral Teachings from Rosebud*. Edited by John Cunningham. Salt Lake City: University of Utah Press.

Willerslev, Rane. 2007. *Soul Hunters: Hunting, Animism, and Personhood among the Siberian Yukaghirs*. Berkeley: University of California Press.

———. 2013. "Taking Animism Seriously, but Perhaps Not Too Seriously?" *Religion and Society: Advances in Research* 4 (1): 41–57.

Williamson, T. S. 1869. "Dakota Medicine." In *Tah-Koo Wah-Kan; or, The Gospel among the Dakotas*, 435–50. Boston: Congregational Pub. Society.

Wissler, Clark. 1905. "The Whirlwind and the Elk in the Mythology of the Dakota." *Journal of American Folklore* 18 (71): 257–68.

———. 1907a. "Some Dakota Myths. I." *Journal of American Folklore* 20 (77): 121–31.

———. 1907b. "Some Dakota Myths. II." *Journal of American Folklore* 20 (78): 195–206.

———. 1907c. "Some Protective Designs of the Dakota." In *American Museum of Natural History Anthropological Papers* 1 (2): 19–53.

———. 1912. "Societies and Ceremonial Associations in the Oglala Division of the Teton-Dakota." *Anthropological Papers of the American Museum of Natural History* 11 (1): 1–99.

INDEX

Alphabetization in the index treats oral and nasal vowels as well as aspirated and unaspirated stops as distinct letters.

adoption, 6, 151, 187, 222
akíc'ita, 55, 101, 221
ak'íp'a, 160, 221
altar, 78, 81–82, 90, 118, 166, 178–80, 222, 224, 226, 241n10
Amiotte, Arthur (Oglala Lakota), ix, 66–67
animals, 14–15, 32, 42, 46–47, 51, 53, 62, 70, 77, 85, 101, 118, 127, 130, 173, 177–78, 189, 194–95, 210, 227–28, 234n12, 238n11, 238n12; and animal ceremonialism, 106, 109, 132, 155, 162, 175, 198, 208; and animism, 21, 24, 27–28, 58; bear, 55–56, 96, 107, 126–27, 149–50, 190–92, 222–23, 246n4, 249n12, 250n17; beaver, 56, 194, 198, 202, 234n12; bison, 4, 7–8, 50, 52, 55–56, 81–82, 90, 94–95, 101, 105, 107, 115–16, 127, 129, 133–34, 150, 182, 189, 193, 224–25, 231n3, 241n9, 241n10; and ceremonial bundles, 194–95, 198, 201–2; as collectives, 50, 62, 132, 143, 164–65; coyote, 76, 128, 129; deer, 56, 107, 165, 190, 224; dog, 81, 82, 191; in dreams and visions, 95, 105–6, 136–37, 140, 143–45, 149–50, 152, 179, 181, 187–88; duck, 205; elk, 52, 55, 101, 105–7, 127, 144, 166, 187, 190, 205, 222, 249n13; horse, 4, 8, 94–95, 107, 224; and kinship, 15, 52, 105–6, 143, 155, 165; mole, 56, 76, 226; offending spirits of, 109, 155; as offering or sacrifice, 87; as persons, 35, 39, 43, 48, 56, 60, 71–72, 106, 123, 129; and sickness, 153, 157, 161–64, 247n13; Sioux classification of, 47; in Sioux mythology, 50–53, 129, 132–33; snake, 56, 152, 163–64, 166–67, 230, 234n12; as spirit masters of game species, 55, 94, 105, 107, 127, 186–87,

267

animals (*continued*)
    234n12, 238n14, 240n8; and transformation, 28, 93–95, 101–2, 129, 143, 189–90, 246n3, 247n1, 249n12; turtle, 95, 110; wolf, 76, 107, 127, 132–33, 150, 198, 205, 224. See also *wamákʻašką*
animism: new, 20, 23–25, 48, 72; as ontology, 92, 95–96, 216, 219; and personhood, 233n10, 234n12, 247n1; and phenomenology, 30–32; and Philippe Descola, 10–11, 14–17, 24–26, 29, 40–41, 44, 246n5; as philosophy, 237n3; site-specific or situated, 38–41, 57, 60; and social evolutionary theory, 24, 39–40, 74–75; and transformation, 189–90, 249n12; and Willerslev's dilemma, 111
Anų́gite, 107–8, 127, 152, 221
Arikaras, 8
asníya, 147, 221
áya, 191, 221, 246n4, 249n12

Bad Bear (Oglala Lakota), 151
bad conduct, 109, 115–16, 138, 152–53, 155–64, 168, 169, 197, 208, 229, 244n3, 247n9, 247n13. See also disease theory; *wówaȟtani*
Bad Wound (Oglala Lakota), 51
bear. See *under* animals
beaver. See *under* animals
Beckwith, Paul, 84–85
Beede, Aaron McGaffey, 44, 56, 96–97, 185–86, 207, 209–12, 240n2
birds, 15, 32, 47–48, 51–52, 55–56, 93, 105–6, 137, 140, 179, 181, 192, 201–2, 210, 230, 234n12; cormorant, 192–93, 222; crow, 199, 205; eagle, 55–56, 107, 194–95, 198–200, 228; and eagle down, 36, 81, 90; hawk, 192, 205, 234n12; spotted eagle, 55, 228

bison. See *under* animals
Black Elk (Oglala Lakota), 1, 3, 52, 86; and *Black Elk Speaks* (Neihardt), 12; and hunting, 175; and ritual, 161, 178, 240n6; and visions, 95, 138, 173, 175, 177, 181, 246n2
Black Elk, Nicholas. See Black Elk (Oglala Lakota)
Black Elk Speaks (Neihardt), 3, 12, 171
blessings, 23, 41, 42, 65, 90, 99, 104, 207, 208
Blish, Helen, 188
Blood-Clot Boy, 127–28, 228
blotáhųka, 203, 221. See also war: prophet
Bone Keepers, 244n7
Brave Buffalo (Standing Rock Sioux), 105, 136, 144
Brave Dog (Oglala Lakota), 246n7
Brown, Joseph Epes, 21, 72, 92, 138, 175, 178, 181–82, 240n7
Brulé Sioux, 163. See also Lakota Sioux
Bucko, Raymond, x, 214
Buechel, Eugene, 231n2
buffalo. See animals: bison
Buffalo Bull (spirit master of bison), 55, 107, 127. See also Tʻatʻą́ka
buffalo calf pipe, 37, 81, 129, 133–34, 144, 221, 238n10
Bushotter, George (Lakota), 51, 83, 149–50, 154, 190, 241n10

Catches, Peter, Sr. (Oglala Lakota), 3
Catlin, George, 121, 191–92, 202
cedar, 79, 87, 117
Chased By Bears (Santee-Yanktonai Sioux), 239n22
Cheyennes, 23
chiefs, 5, 6, 52, 55, 127, 209, 222, 238n14
confession, 153

268 INDEX

conjuring, 177–78. *See also* sorcery; witchcraft
coyote. *See under* animals
Crazy Buffalo, 127, 221. *See also* Gnaškíyą
Crazy Horse (Lakota), 1, 171, 179
crow. *See under* birds
Crow Dog, Leonard (Brulé Lakota), 3
curse, 158–59
Curtis, Edward S., 146, 149, 153

cʻašt'ų́, 76, 221
cʻągléška wakʻą́, 38, 221
cʻąnáǧi, 70, 221
cʻąnų́pa iyáȟpeyapi, 88, 221
cʻąnų́pa wakʻą́, 37, 129, 221
cʻąté, 64, 221
cʻąté ištá, 181, 221
cʻątóžuha, 202, 221
cʻąyáka, 221, 246n7
cʻékiya, 49, 83, 86, 221
cʻéya, 86, 221

Dakota Sioux, 1, 5, 11, 16, 22, 47, 56, 78, 231n1; and animism, 38, 41; and belief and ritual, 83–85, 87, 89, 90, 107, 110–11, 117, 120, 137, 139, 153–54, 162, 184–85, 191–92, 202–3, 247n12; Canadian, 160–61, 244n4; and Dakota War of 1862, 41, 237n5; at Lac Qui Parle, 37, 41; in Minnesota Territory, 57, 75, 80, 81, 158, 175, 176, 201; and spirits, 197, 240n3, 240n8, 241n9; and war bundles, 198–200, 203
Dakota War of 1862, 41, 237n5
dance, 52, 80, 82, 84, 99, 107, 170, 171, 176, 189, 191–92
death: drama of, in ritual, 87, 153, 246n5; spirits as cause of, 153–54, 159, 160, 169, 244n3; spirits having no, 64, 127, 174, 178; and *šicų*, 66–69, 119, 148; as transformation, 27, 65–66, 114–16
deer. *See under* animals
Deleuze, Gilles, 16, 24, 103, 235n12, 244n1
Deloria, Ella C., 16; and belief and ritual, 78, 82, 84, 86, 90, 99, 100, 112, 115, 120–21, 144–46, 165, 180–82, 193–94, 237n6, 242n1, 244n7; and dreams and visions, 138, 142, 144–46, 150, 165, 166, 172, 175; and kinship, 37, 49, 54, 55, 86, 207, 218; and mythology, 124, 125–28, 144–46; orthography and language, 231n2, 242n2, 246n4; and transformation, 193–94, 244n7
Deloria, Vine, Jr., 17, 21; and animals, 51, 52, 60, 106, 164; and animism, 39–40, 46–48, 63, 92, 217; and belief and ritual, 32, 35, 36, 84–85, 135, 139, 178; and covenant, 216; and dreams and visions, 136–37, 139, 142, 245n2, 246n1; and experience and knowledge, 32, 58, 140, 146, 150; and kinship, 55, 79, 140, 237n7; and maturity and the moral universe, 25, 215, 250n2; and nature, 43; and personhood, 43–44; and psychotherapy and depth psychology, 246n6, 250n18; and representation, 210; and respect, 216; and the supernatural, 57; and transcendence, 244n1; and transformation, 93, 95, 212, 213
DeMallie, Raymond, x, 12, 231n1; and belief and ritual, 178, 184, 237n6; and dreams and visions, 95; and ethnohistory, 127; and gender and sexuality, 161; and George Bushotter, 241n10; and kinship, 54, 238n13, 247n3; and language, 6; and the supernatural, 43; and *wakʻą́*, 148–49, 250n16; and William K. Powers, 49–50

Densmore, Frances, 46, 94, 105–6, 136, 144, 200, 224, 239n22, 240n4

Descola, Philippe: and animism, 10–11, 15, 21, 22, 24, 25, 28, 40–41, 48, 214, 246n5; *Beyond Nature and Culture*, 10–11, 14, 21, 30, 43, 59, 233n6, 234n12, 243n4; and collectives, 45, 50, 52–53, 233n11; fourfold schema, 25–26, 40, 219; and interiority and physicality, 25–30, 38, 40, 48, 58, 61–63, 66, 72, 209, 233n9; and modes of identification, 16; and ontology, 233n7, 237n4, 237n7, 239n17; and participation, 204; and relational schemas, 16, 45, 106, 108; and self, 60; and transformation, 189–90, 234n12, 246n3, 249n12

De Smet, Pierre-Jean, 132

disease sanction, 152–54, 157–58, 162–64, 166, 168, 188, 197, 201, 208, 243n2, 244n3. *See also* bad conduct

disease theory, 96, 152–53, 156, 169, 244n4, 247n9, 250n1

dog. *See under* animals

Dorsey, James Owen, 77, 86, 99–100, 117, 130–32, 184, 190–91, 203, 243n3

dreams, 221, 222, 229; Brave Buffalo's, 105; and calling, 246n1; and ceremonial bundles, 197; and dreamers, 77, 136–37, 141, 142, 145, 149, 150, 171, 186–87, 190–91, 205, 222, 241n10; and dream world, 70; individual nature of, 9; and interiority, 26, 175; and kinship, 77; and knowledge/power, 32, 58, 236n1; and music, 205; and ritual, 171–72, 184, 188, 245n2; and the self, 61, 69; and the Sioux, 136–67, 237n6; and Thunder Birds, 130; and transformation, 28–29, 94, 96, 102, 249n12. *See also* vision quest

duck. *See under* animals

eagle. *See under* birds

Eastman, Charles (Santee Dakota), 38, 47, 154, 155, 172, 202, 236n1, 237n6, 246n5

elk. *See under* animals

feasts, 80, 115, 118, 119, 122, 132, 241n10, 243n2; Dakota raw fish, 90, 112, 191–93; mystery or sacred, 77, 87, 227

Fire Thunder, Edgar, 128, 244n7

Fletcher, Alice, 74, 81, 82, 85, 88, 89, 101, 118, 119, 162–63, 194, 241n10, 242n2, 250n15

Fools Crow, Frank (Oglala Lakota), 3

Fort Snelling, 80, 153

Four Brothers or Four Winds, 82, 101, 107, 113, 127, 130, 225

four legged, 47, 56, 222

ghost-keeping ceremony, 74, 118, 119, 121, 163, 203, 226, 227, 242n15

ghosts, 64–66, 69, 103–22, 127, 174, 178, 223, 227, 243n1, 243n3. *See also wanáǧi*

Gnaškíyą, 108, 127, 152, 191, 221. *See also* Crazy Buffalo

Goldenweiser, Alexander, 19

Good Lance, Frank (Lakota), 3

good red road, 211, 217

Good Seat (Oglala Lakota), 36, 70, 75, 85, 117, 209, 243n1

grandfathers: in Lakota ceremonial life, 49, 77–79, 81, 87, 101, 125, 142, 199, 202, 225, 240n7, 241n10, 248n8; Ojibwe dream visitors as, 29, 79, 104, 207. *See also* kinship

Great Mystery, 15, 22, 36, 38, 42, 55, 65, 79, 199, 209, 227. *See also* Great Spirit; Wakan Tanka; Wakʼą́ Tʼą́ka

Great Spirit, 38, 65, 82, 97, 107, 181, 185, 209, 212, 227. *See also* Great

Mystery; Wakan Tanka; Wakʻą́ Tʻą́ka
Grobsmith, Elizabeth, 116, 154, 157–60, 164

há, 63, 141, 189, 221, 249n12
Hallowell, A. Irving: and animism, 21, 24, 27, 33, 72, 95, 214; background and works, 19–20, 214, 232n1, 232n4; and bad conduct, 109, 153, 156–58, 160, 169, 247n13; and "blessings," 99, 104; and dreams and visions, 137, 140–43; and the Four Winds, 130; and kinship, 249n8; and language, 35; and mythology, 79, 93, 123–24, 129, 245n2; and (Ojibwe) ontology, 16–17, 22, 24, 35, 59–60, 234n12, 247n11, 249n11; and personhood, 35, 41, 53, 62–63, 65–66, 104, 127, 130–31, 232n3, 233n9, 239n18; and perspectivism, 234n12; and phenomenology, 29–31, 125, 138, 140, 179, 236n13; and *pimadaziwin*, 23, 206–8; and rationalization, 126, 245n4; and rocks, 73–74; and spirit masters of game species, 238n14; and the "supernatural," 242n3, 245n5; and transformation, 98, 128, 174–75, 249n9; and worldview, 232n2
Harvey, Graham, 24, 25, 29
hąblé, 172, 221
hąblécʻeyapi, 143, 170, 172, 222. *See also* vision quest
hąblóglaka, 138, 144, 222
Hąwí, 127, 222
healing: and animals, 106, 149, 191; and covenant, 216; Dakota, 247n12; *lową́pi*, 223; and medicine men, 147, 244n3; and *ní* or life, 80, 250n1; and psychotherapy, 246n6; *pʻiyá*, 154, 164, 228; and stones, 77–78; *yuwípi*, 181, 230
health, 9, 23, 97, 121, 154, 156, 206, 208, 211–12, 215, 228, 230. *See also* wellness; *wicʻózani*
hécʻel lená oyáte kį nípi kte, 208, 222
He Dog (Oglala Lakota), 153, 155
heȟáka, 55, 107, 127, 222
Hé Kʻątʻúhu Sápewį, 166, 222
herbs and herbal medicines, 79, 95, 106, 145, 198, 200. *See also* medicine
Hé Tʻacʻą́nųpa Tʻokáhewį, 166, 222
heyókʻa, 130, 222
heyókʻa wózepi, 130, 222
hókawįȟ, 43, 222
holy men, 76, 118, 128, 135, 152, 160, 196, 200, 228, 244n3. *See also* medicine men
Horn Chips (Lakota), 3
horse. *See under* animals
hó ukʻíya, 139, 222
Hunkpapa Sioux, 14, 100, 166, 200, 224. *See also* Lakota Sioux
hunting: and animal ceremonialism, 106, 109, 155; and animism, 28, 31, 40, 46, 50, 52, 55, 72, 170, 247n1; and belief and ritual, 191–92, 247n2; bison, 4, 7, 8; and deer women, 144; and dreams and visions, 151, 180; and gender and sexuality, 161; and ghosts, 117, 119; hunter-gatherer, 5, 8, 11, 16, 22, 24, 50; and mythology, 235n12; and purification, 175; and stones, 88; and wolves, 133
Hunų́p, 127, 222
hunų́pa, 56, 222
hutópa, 56, 222
hųká, 89, 104–5, 222, 242n16

INDEX 271

huką́takuya, 104–5, 222
hų́tka ką́ǧa, 193, 222

ȟeyáta, 43, 222
ȟmų́ǧa wicʿáša, 128, 222
ȟmų́ǧa wį́yą, 128, 222

icʿą́ǧa, 62, 97, 222
identity: and belief and ritual, 168; and dreams and visions, 144; and ethnicity, 238n13; and hair, 120; and hunting, 175; and interiority and physicality, 11, 26–27, 44, 63, 69, 92–94, 138, 235n12; and movement, 53; and participation, 203–4; Sioux, 4, 13, 25; and sorcery/witchcraft, 96; and tradition, 214
ihą́bla, 143, 145, 150, 222
ihą́bla okʿólakicʿiye, 150, 222
ihą́blapi, 53, 103, 222
iȟpéyapi, 83, 222
ikcéka, 180, 222
Iktó/Ikto, 51, 128, 222. See also Iktómi/Iktomi
Iktómi/Iktomi, 50–51, 54, 75, 107–8, 126–27, 129, 152, 222, 238n9, 240n3, 249n8. See also Iktó/Ikto
Ingold, Tim: and animism, 24, 31, 40, 72–74, 233n6; and engagement, 193; and Hallowell, 29, 74, 245n5; and movement, 53; and personhood, 60–61, 91, 212, 234n12; and phenomenology, 30–31; and the trail analogy, 250n3; and transformation, 94
iníhą, 37, 85, 222
inípi, 173, 180, 184–85, 222
ítqhą matʿó cʿįcála kį hécʿa wą hiyú, 150, 222
ité yuwį́tapi, 86, 203, 222

itʿą́cʿą, 55, 222
Íya, 47, 94, 108, 126, 127, 128, 152, 222, 238n9
iyótą wakʿą́, 222, 240n9

Íyą, 75, 77, 79–80, 82–83, 127, 222, 223, 240n3, 241n9
Íyą Hokšíla, 127, 222,
íyą tʿaníya, 79, 83, 223

James Bay Crees, 24

ką́ǧa, 138–39, 165, 188, 190–91, 193, 223, 227, 247n1. See also wakʿą́ ką́ǧa
ką́ǧapi, 122, 223
kaǧí, 85, 223
kinship: and animism, 28, 48–50, 62, 72, 80, 143, 218; and belief and ritual, 4, 174, 189, 204, 214–16; and dreams and visions, 138; and mitákuye oyásʾį, 14, 15, 42–43; and mythology, 132; and pipe, 134–35; and sickness, 161; and Sioux culture and identity, 4, 6, 37, 49–51, 54–56, 86, 104–5, 140, 206–8; terms, 78, 87, 125, 142, 221, 225, 226, 241n10, 248n8
Kit Fox society, 199
Kohn, Eduardo, 10, 24, 25, 59, 144, 233n6

kʿokípʿa, 37, 85, 223
kʿolá, 104–5, 223
kʿolátakuya, 104, 223

-la, 223, 239n23
Lakota language, 12–13, 15, 35, 42–43, 101, 231n2, 242n2, 246n4, 246n7
Lakota Language Project, 12–13
Lakota Sioux: animals, 46–48, 51, 53, 62, 152, 238n12; and animism, 11,

21–22, 25, 40, 57, 60, 75, 218, 237n7, 239n20; belief, 96, 169, 237n6; and bison, 52, 231n3; collectives, 46–48, 49–50, 54, 56–57, 62; disease theory, 152–67, 169, 247n9, 250n1; divisions and organization of, 1; dreams and visions, 95–96, 104, 136–67, 172; early accounts of, 8; ethnography, 33, 231n1; Four Winds or Four Directions, 107, 130; ghosts, 114–22, 243n3; hair, 119–21; health and wellness, 208; identity, 13, 214, 238n13; individualism, 41; kinship, 15, 34–37, 43, 49–50, 54, 108, 125, 174, 208; *Lakʿól wicʿóȟ'ą*, 80, 223; life-transformation process, 23, 97; medicine men, 13, 141, 148, 175, 210; *mitákuye oyás'į*, 14, 22, 208; mythology, 50–53, 75–76, 124–35, 222, 224, 229; and nature, 9, 42–43; ontology, 5, 8, 14–15, 20–22, 25, 34, 59, 233n11; origins of, 5–6; personhood, 42, 53, 58, 60–73, 92, 106, 236n2, 239n21; phenomenology, 31–32; power, 236n1, 247n2; prayer, 84, 86, 99; and psychoanalytic theory, 250n18; relational ontology, 35, 208; religion of, 1, 3–5, 8–9, 12–15, 213–14; ritual, 89, 99, 141, 168–205, 210; spirits, 107–14, 240n5, 247n2; spirit world, 93, 141, 195; stones, 77, 79, 83; and the supernatural, 43; support of, ix, 12–13; *šicų́*, 66–68; territory of, 2, 4; tradition, 213–14; *wakʿą́*, 36–37, 42, 97–98; war, 131, 197–201; *Wóniya*, 208–11; worldview of, 42–43, 113, 143. *See also* Teton Sioux

Lakʿól wicʿóȟ'ą, 80, 134, 223

Lakʿóta, 56, 108, 223

Lame Deer, John Fire (Lakota), 3, 23, 105, 171

language: and anthropology, 23, 25, 35, 241n13; and belief and ritual, 4, 48–49, 51, 55, 62, 70–71, 81, 213; body, 125; Sioux, 6, 12–13, 15–16, 35, 42, 45, 231n2; and tradition, 214; and war bundles, 198

Left Heron (Lakota), 238n10

lekší, 13, 223

Le Sueur, Pierre-Charles, 8

life movement, 23, 65–67, 80, 85, 106, 109, 117–18, 134, 146, 160, 205–16, 244n3, 247n2

life-transformation process, 23, 61, 69, 97, 212–13, 227, 229. *See also wóniya*

lightning, 76, 93, 94, 130, 138, 176, 227, 235n12

Little Crow (Dakota), 41

Little Moon (Hunkpapa Lakota), 100–101, 165–68

Little Wound (Oglala Lakota), 36, 49, 80, 89, 102, 131, 209

Lone Horn (Minneconjou Lakota), 121

lowápi, 138, 223

Lynd, James W., 41, 73, 82, 83, 107, 111–12, 185, 198, 201, 202, 240n8, 240n9

makʿá, 108, 127, 223, 238n8

manítu, 43, 223

matʿó, 55, 56, 107, 108, 127, 223

matʿó hotʿúpi, 191, 202, 223

matʿó káǧa, 191, 223

McFatridge, Arthur E., 152–53, 155–56, 158

medicine: bad, 95, 120, 146, 157, 168; as "blessings," 207; bundles, 21, 35, 58, 176, 195–202, 228, 229, 240n1, 250n17; and dreams and visions, 171–73, 179; and ghosts, 117–18;

medicine (*continued*)
    as power/knowledge, 36, 76,
    95, 104–5, 125, 128–29, 135, 139,
    142–43, 146–48, 150, 165, 173,
    194, 229; practices, 153, 156; and
    prayer, 248n3; *pʿežúta*, 136, 143, 145,
    149–50, 187, 191, 224; and religion,
    236n1; and spirits, 62, 76–77, 109,
    132, 145, 165, 188–89; *wakʿą́*, 227.
    See also blessings; *pʿežúta*
medicine men, 12, 13; and belief and
    ritual, 49, 76–77, 111, 147–48, 152,
    154, 158, 164, 175, 179; and collectives, 55; and dreams and visions,
    136, 138, 167, 180, 246n2; *wapʿíya*,
    228; and war, 199; *yuwípi*, 230. *See also* shamans
Mesteth, Wilmer "Stampede," ix, 3
metamorphosis, 28–29, 91–96, 98, 123,
    126, 128. *See also* transformation
missionaries, 84, 107–8, 209, 247n8
Missouri River, 4, 7–8, 202
mitákuye oyásʾį, 14, 22, 41–42, 56, 62,
    80, 204–5, 208, 215, 219, 223, 237n7
mitʿáwašicų, 175, 223
mní wicʿóni, 218, 223
mole. *See under* animals
Moves Camp, Richard (Lakota), 3

nağí, 62, 64–71, 96, 114, 140–41, 144,
    209, 223, 227, 239n23, 243n1
nağíla, 64, 68, 70–71, 87, 162, 223,
    239n23
nağípi, 70, 131, 223
nağípila, 68, 223
nasúla, 186, 223
Navajos, 23
Neihardt, John G., 12, 171
ní, 47, 62, 64–65, 68–70, 73, 104, 114,
    119, 223, 250n1

Nicollet, Joseph N., 7
ní ų́, 223, 240n2
niyá, 47, 62, 64–66, 68, 69, 73, 76, 78,
    114, 119, 209, 212, 223
niyápi, 68, 223
No Flesh (Oglala Lakota), 5, 64, 152–53,
    162, 197

ó, 176, 223
Oglala Sioux: belief and ritual, 13–15,
    38, 77, 98, 112, 118, 127, 135, 151,
    162–63, 178; ceremonial bundles,
    195, 250n17; collaboration with, 13–
    15; and dreams and visions, 144, 151;
    and James R. Walker, 67, 68, 75,
    76, 97, 129, 161, 196, 200–201, 209;
    mythology, 124; origins of, 6; and
    Pine Ridge Reservation, 1, 72; and
    wakʿą́, 92. *See also* Lakota Sioux
ohóla, 37, 85, 118, 223
ohų́kaką, 53, 103, 125–28, 223, 245n3
oícʿağe, 54, 224
Okícʿize-tʿàwa, 200, 224
ókiya, 118, 224
ómakiya ye/yo, 90, 224
onámahʾų we/wo, 90, 224
oníya, 47, 224
oral tradition, 94, 116, 125, 171, 222
oų́cʿağe, 63, 224
oų́ye, 64, 224
ową́gkağapi, 179, 224
ową́ka, 81, 118, 179, 224
oyáte, 42–44, 54–56, 62, 123, 127–33, 150–
    51, 186, 206, 208, 210, 224, 238n13

-pi, 176, 224
Pine Ridge Reservation, 1–3, 12–15, 38,
    68–72, 95, 118, 144, 151, 175, 201
pipe: and belief and ritual, 180, 185,
    199–201, 204, 242n16; and kinship,

62, 80–81, 86, 133–35, 206; offering of, 87–88, 117, 155, 178, 221, 226, 241n10, 241n13, 248n3; sacred, 37–38, 41, 54–55, 129, 133–35, 144, 221, 238n10, 241n11

Plenty Wolf, George (Oglala Lakota), 68

Pond, Gideon, 57, 85, 88, 111, 162, 175, 176, 192, 200–201, 203, 240n3, 244n6

Pond, Samuel, 75, 78, 81, 87, 110–11, 117, 137, 158, 162, 191

Powers, William, 48–50, 57, 67–70, 76–77, 80, 98, 147, 153–54, 157, 236n2, 238n13, 240n4

prayer: and belief and ritual, 67, 74, 99–100, 110–12, 117, 145, 150, 155, 171, 187–89, 193, 199, 203, 236n1, 241n9; and ceremonial bundles, 196; and hunting, 175; and pipe smoke, 55, 81, 133–34, 241n11; study of, 13; wacʻékiya, 49, 83–89, 170, 181, 221, 228, 247n3. See also wacʻékiya

pté hí pahpá, 193, 224

ptéȟcakapi, 56, 224

Pté Oyáte, 55, 129, 224

Ptesáwį, 38, 81, 99, 107, 108, 129, 133–35, 144, 197, 224, 241n11. See also White Buffalo Woman

p'ó, 83, 224

pʻežúta, 136, 143, 145, 150, 187, 191, 224. See also medicine

pʻežúta waštéšte yuhá, 150, 224

pʻiyá, 129, 147, 164, 224

Radisson, Pierre-Esprit, 7–8

Red Cloud (Oglala Lakota), 1, 68, 197

Red Cloud Indian School, x, 12

regalia, 139, 188, 199

reincarnation, 67, 70, 237n2, 239n22

relatedness, 37, 49, 108, 123, 135, 215. See also kinship

Rice, Julian, 108

Ringing Shield (Oglala Lakota), 5, 80, 109, 113, 173, 180, 201

Rock Crees, 24

rocks: and animism, 15, 35, 39, 58, 73–84; and belief and ritual, 13, 88–91, 100, 113, 127, 176–78, 210, 222, 223, 225, 240n3, 242n16; and bison, 52; and personhood, 21, 44, 72; and prayer, 242n16

Rosebud Reservation, 37, 67, 153, 159–60

sacred bundles: and animism, 21, 35, 58, 195–205, 225, 228, 229, 250n17; and ghost-keeping, 119–20, 122, 227, 242n15; and pipe, 133, 221; and stones, 77–78, 240n1; and tųwą́, 176

sacred clown, 222

sacred hoop, 38, 43, 134, 177, 221

sacred pipe, 37–38, 41, 62, 81, 129, 133–34, 144, 200, 221, 226, 238n10

sacred stones, 76–77, 149, 160, 204, 228, 240n4

sacred tree, 162

sage, 77, 79, 87, 149, 166

Sage, Rufus B., 163–64

Santee Sioux, 47, 150, 162, 237n6, 239n22, 241n10. See also Dakota Sioux

Scott, Colin, 24

Scott, Michael, 10

Seven Rabbits (Oglala Lakota), 147

shamans: and belief and ritual, 76–77, 95, 111, 144, 148–49, 151, 155, 168, 171, 195–96, 200; Lakota, 5, 52, 55, 109, 164, 175, 177–78, 181, 193, 202, 204, 212, 237n6; language of, 81; and transformation, 28, 189–90, 234n12, 249n12. See also holy men; medicine men

Shils, Edward, 214
sin, 111, 113, 153, 155, 158, 160–63, 226, 229, 243n2, 247n8. *See also* bad conduct
Sioux Indians. *See* Dakota Sioux; Lakota Sioux; Teton Sioux; Yanktonai Sioux; Yankton Sioux
Sitting Bull (Hunkpapa Lakota), 1, 3, 14–15, 94, 179
sįtésapela, 107, 224
sky, 15, 53, 65, 77, 80, 94, 105, 127, 197, 209, 225, 239n22
smudging, 87, 171, 176, 179, 204. See also *wazílya*
snake. *See under* animals
sorcery, 96, 120, 152, 156, 213, 228, 249n12. *See also* witchcraft
Spider, 50, 58, 75, 127, 129, 205, 222. *See also* Iktó/Ikto; Iktómi/Iktomi
spotted eagle. *See under* birds
Standing Bear, Luther (Oglala Lakota): and animals, 46, 51; and dreams and visions, 141, 171, 205; and kinship, 15, 48; and nature, 9, 42, 57; and war medicine, 199
Standing Bear, Stephen (Lakota), 183
Standing Rock Reservation, 46, 94, 105, 136, 166, 185, 224, 237n6
Star People, 94
Stars, Ivan (Lakota), 246n7
Stone Boy, 76, 94, 107, 127, 128, 222. *See also* Íyą Hokšíla
stones. *See* rocks
suffering, 99, 112, 113, 141, 157, 162, 169, 229, 248n3. See also *wókakiže*
sun dance, 4, 120, 134, 141, 162, 163, 171, 185, 246n5
Sun God, 156
sweetgrass, 79, 87, 241n11

Sword, George (Oglala Lakota), 3; on ceremonial bundles, 196, 197, 250n17; on disease, 152; on dreams and visions, 138, 165, 172, 179, 181, 185; on *nağí*, 70, 131; on *ní*, 65; on pipe, 38, 134–35, 199; on purification, 180; on shamans, 175; on *šicų́*, 66, 115; on taboo, 201; on *tųwá*, 176; on *t'ų́*, 68; on *wak'ą́*, 36, 131, 174, 209
šayápi, 83, 224
šicų́: acquired, 66–68, 169, 186–87; given, 64, 66–68, 71, 140, 151, 197; and spirit helpers or guardians, 64, 69, 76–77, 147–49, 186, 195–96, 201, 224, 237n2, 240n1, 250n16
šiglá, 224, 243n3
šiná wóųye, 89, 224
Šiyáka (Lakota), 46, 224. *See also* Teal Duck (Lakota)
šką́, 62, 65, 224, 225
šųgmánitut'ąka, 107, 127, 224
šų́kawak'ą, 107, 224

Tabeau, Pierre-Antoine, 8–9, 136, 152, 202
taboo, 109, 115, 119, 155, 160–64, 198, 201–2, 208, 225, 226, 228, 229, 244n3, 247n2. See also *wógluze*
táku, 62, 224
táku ní ų cikcístina, 225, 240n2
Táku Škąšką́: and birth, 53, 65–66, 148, 224; and movement, 53, 147; and *Ptesą́wį*, 81, 94; Sky, 105, 107, 127, 197, 209, 225; and stones, 75, 77, 78, 80, 225; as Wanáǧi T'ą́ka, 227; as whimsical, 244n3; as Wóniya T'ą́ka, 229
táku t'ókeca, 97, 225

táku wakʻą́, 85, 98, 107, 158, 176, 225
táku wínihą, 97, 225
takúye, 108, 225
tąyą́ úpi, 207, 225
Teal Duck (Lakota), 46, 224. See also Šiyáka (Lakota)
Teton Sioux, 1, 121. See also Lakota Sioux
thunder, 76, 93, 130, 132, 205, 226, 235n12
Thunder Bear (Oglala Lakota), 179
Thunder Birds: collective, 55, 226, 227; and destruction, 108; and dreams and visions, 94, 250n14; enmity with Ųktéȟi, 57, 238n15, 246n6; and interiority and physicality, 93; and kinship, 75, 105, 240n3; and lightning, 176; and mythology, 127, 130–32, 235n12. See also Wakíyą
Thunder dreamers, 150
Thunderers, 131, 132
tobacco, 79, 81, 82, 83, 84, 87, 118, 199, 221
Tobtób Kį, 68, 225. See also Wakan Tanka; Wakʻą́ Tʻą́ka
transformation: and animism, 16, 27–28, 62, 63, 102, 190, 234n12, 249n12; and death, 27, 66; and life-transformation process, 23, 34, 60–61, 69, 212–13, 227, 229; and mythology, 124, 128, 132, 134; and personhood, 62, 91–98, 178, 193, 206, 213, 249n12; and power, 174–75, 238n11, 249n9; and ritual, 76, 91, 104, 141, 188–91, 195, 246n4; and virtuality, 102, 104; and *wakʻą́*, 148. See also metamorphosis
Tunkan, 80, 83, 241n9. See also *tʻųką́*
turtle. See under animals

tųwą́, 93, 131, 169, 176, 201, 225, 227
Two Dogs, Richard (Oglala Lakota), ix, 3, 13, 243n1
Tyon, Thomas (Oglala Lakota), 38, 47, 65, 78, 79, 84, 114, 117–18, 191, 197, 199, 240n4, 244n7
tʼekínica, 150, 226

Tʻaté, 81, 105, 107, 127, 130, 225
Tʻatúye Tópa, 107, 127, 225
Tʻatʻą́ka, 55, 94, 105, 107, 108, 127, 225
tʻáwa, 198, 200, 224, 225
tʻawácʻį, 181, 184, 225
tʻawášicu, 77, 175, 225
tʻącʻą́, 63, 66, 96, 114, 141, 225
tʻeȟí, 160, 225
tʻiwáhe, 54, 115, 225
tʻiyópa, 178, 225
tʻiyóšpaye, 6, 54, 55, 115, 225
tʻóka, 108, 225
Tʻokáhe, 128, 225
tʻókeca, 97, 101, 225
tʻų́: and birth, 53, 212; and consecration, 201; as emitted potency, 71, 76, 147–48, 225, 228; and individuation, 68; and interiority, 87, 151; and Ptesą́wį, 81, 135, 241n11; and sickness, 169; and *šicų́*, 66, 237n2; and transformation, 97, 212; and *wakʻą́*, 98, 148, 195, 224
tʻųkášila, 78, 79, 87, 125, 202, 225
tʻųką́, 78, 80, 82, 225, 228, 241n9. See also Tunkan
tʻų́tʻųšni, 148, 225
tʻų́tʻųšniyą, 148, 225

ųcí, 79, 87, 125, 226
Ųktéȟi, 57, 94, 107, 127, 131, 152, 197, 200–201, 226

Uktéȟi Oyáte, 131, 226
ųmáni, 81, 118, 226
ųmašike, 174, 226
ų́ši ic'íc'aǧa, 226, 242n2
ų́šika, 112, 174, 226, 242n2
ų́šila, 85–86, 112, 118, 174, 226, 242n2
ų́šimala ye/yo, 90, 174, 226

virtuality: and animism, 106; and dreams and visions, 138, 188–89; and mythology, 124, 129–30, 134; and ritual, 81, 134, 168, 170–71, 179, 183, 186, 188–89, 213, 248n4; theory of, 16, 103–4, 170, 244n1; and transformation, 193
vision quest: and animism, 170–75, 179; and kinship, 143; and medicine, 165; and medicine men, 147–48; and nonhuman grandfathers, 79; and participation, 203; and the Plains, 4, 248n7; and spirit, 141, 182–83, 186, 221, 222; and transformation, 96; and virtuality, 210
visions. See dreams
Viveiros de Castro, Eduardo: and animism, 27, 28, 72, 243n4; and death, 65–66; and Hallowell, 29, 65–66; and interiority, 235n12; and mythology, 129; and the ontological turn, 24, 233n6; and perspectivism, 71, 97, 149, 234n12; and physicality, 189, 233n8, 234n12; and soul, 66
vow, 105, 155, 160, 202, 226, 229, 244n3, 247n2. See also wóiglakapi

wa-, 226, 243n1
waábleza, 184, 226
waálową, 181, 226
wac'ą́tkiyapi, 211, 226
wac'ékiya: as ceremonial appeal, 89–90, 118, 242n16; and kinship, 49, 54–55, 112; as prayer, 75, 84–97, 99, 181, 226, 247n3. See also prayer
wac'į́, 64, 84, 96, 171, 181, 184, 186, 226
wac'į́k'o, 226, 243n3
wahį́heyapi, 56, 226
wahúk'eza, 199, 226
waȟtáni, 160, 226, 247n8
waȟúpa, 56, 226
waíc'išpapi, 87, 226
wakáǧapi, 84, 226
Wakan Tanka: and animism, 15, 36; and dreams and visions, 138, 172; and imagination, 181; and kinship, 79, 97; offering to, 55; and Oscar Howe, 82; and ritual, 205; and taboo, 202; and wak'ą́, 65, 92, 131, 209, 212. See also Tobtób Kį; Wak'ą́ T'ą́ka
Waką́ka, 127, 226
wakíc'aǧapi, 119, 226
wakį́ȟtani, 118, 226
Wakíyą, 55, 57, 75, 82, 93, 105, 107, 108, 127, 130–32, 176, 226, 227, 240n3. See also Thunder Birds
Wakíyą hot'úpi, 93, 226
Wakíyą Oyáte, 131, 227
wakíyą tųwápi, 93, 176, 227
wakúza, 154, 159–60, 164, 227. See also bad conduct
wak'ą́: as central religious concept, 36–37; and ceremonial bundles, 195–96, 198–99, 201, 204; as dangerous, 116, 162; and dreams and visions, 143, 145–51, 172; and kinship, 49; and language, 55; and life, 211, 213; as mysterious, 107, 142, 166, 178, 208; and personhood, 62, 64; and power, 63, 129, 133, 145–49, 161, 179, 187, 194, 209; as sacred, 42, 80–82, 86, 88, 100, 162, 180; and sickness, 162,

164, 169, 208; and spirits, 66, 74, 80, 110–11, 113, 127–28, 139, 186, 224, 225, 227, 229; and stones, 74, 76; and transformation, 94, 97, 101, 193; and tųwápi, 176; and t'ų́, 71, 98, 237n2
wak'ą́ káǧa, 165, 227, 247n1
wak'ą́la, 85, 169, 227
wak'ą́lapi, 76, 227
Wak'ą́ T'ą́ka, 36, 38, 55, 84, 107, 152, 209, 225, 227. See also Tobtób Kį; Wakan Tanka
wak'ą́ wac'ípi, 120, 227, 246n5
wak'ą́yą, 101, 227
wak'úwa, 55, 227
Wallace, Anthony F. C., 30
Wallis, Ruth, 160–61, 244n4, 247n10
Wallis, Wilson, 160–61, 244n4, 247n10
walúta, 89, 227
wamák'anaǧi, 70, 118, 227
wamák'ašką, 53, 56, 62, 227. See also animals
wamák'ognaka, 35, 123, 227
wamáyąka ye/yo, 90, 227
wanáǧi, 114–17, 119, 121, 127, 174, 227, 243n1. See also ghosts
wanáǧi ktépi, 117, 227
wanáǧi t'ac'ą́ku, 114, 227
wanáǧi t'amák'oc'e, 114, 227
wanáǧi t'awác'ipi, 115, 227
Wanáǧi T'ą́ka, 65, 209, 227
wanáǧi wap'áȟta, 119, 227
wanáǧi wic'ót'i, 115, 227
wanáǧi yuhápi, 119, 227
waníya, 65, 227
waníyąpi, 228, 238n12
wápaha, 199, 228
wap'íya, 147, 154, 164, 168, 228
wap'íyapi, 164, 228
war: and animism, 28, 50; and collectives, 55–57, 131–32; Dakota, 41, 237n5, 237n6; and dreams and visions, 151, 240n3, 247n2; and gender and sexuality, 161–62; and ghosts, 119; Lakota, 52; prophet, 203–4, 221, 230; and stones, 75, 77, 88; and warriors, 1, 89, 94, 147, 149, 161–62, 180, 192, 197–204, 221, 250n17; and wolves, 133, 150. See also war bundle; war medicine
war bundle, 197–201, 229, 250n17. See also war; war medicine
war medicine, 197, 199–200, 229, 250n17. See also war; war bundle
wasábglepi, 84, 228
wasé, 81, 100, 200, 228
wasicun, 77, 147, 195–97. See also wašícų
wašícų, 77, 147, 149–50, 172, 174, 187, 195–97, 202, 228, 240n1. See also wasicun
wašícų t'ųká, 77, 228
waúyąpi, 87, 112, 198, 228
wazílya, 87, 117, 118, 228. See also smudging
Wazíya, 126, 127, 228
wąblí, 107, 228
wąblí gleška, 55, 228
wąyąka, 165, 228
Wé Hokšíla, 127, 228
wellness, 147, 152, 168, 208, 228. See also health; wic'ózani
Whirlwind, 127, 229,
White Buffalo Woman, 38, 81, 94, 107, 129, 133–34, 144, 224, 229, 238n10, 241n11. See also Ptesą́wį
White Bull, Joseph (Minneconjou Lakota), 94
White Clay, 38, 70
White Hat, Albert (Sicangu Lakota), 37, 49, 55, 62, 67, 80, 174

White-Plume-Boy, 128
Wí, 105, 127, 156, 228
wicʻácʻeȟpi icáȟtake šni, 180, 228
wicʻápʻehį yužúpi, 120, 228
wicʻáša, 56, 228
wicʻáša tʼápi, 114, 228
wicʻáša wakʻą́, 128, 228, 244n3. See also medicine men; holy men
wicʻóȟʼą, 53, 80, 99, 103, 112, 134, 223, 227, 228
wicʻóȟʼą šíca, 109, 228. See also bad conduct
wicʻóicʻaǧe, 212, 228
wicʻóni, 67, 70, 141, 218, 223, 226, 228
wicʻózani, 23, 208, 212, 228. See also health; wellness
Willerslev, Rane, 24, 30–31, 40–41, 72, 111
Wissler, Clark, 53, 193, 237n7, 249n13
witchcraft, 96, 120, 228. See also sorcery
wíyą, 56, 228. See also women
Wíyą Nųpápika, 108, 127, 228
wóakʼipʻa, 109, 118, 160, 169, 228
wócʻekiye, 84, 228. See also prayer
wóecʻų, 53, 103, 112, 227, 228
wógluze, 155, 198, 228. See also taboo
wóȟpa/wóȟpe, 80, 228
Wóȟpe, 80, 81, 129, 197, 228, 229, 241n11. See also Ptesą́wį; White Buffalo Woman
wóiglakapi, 155, 229. See also vow
wóitʻųpʻe, 37, 85, 229
wókakiže, 112, 169, 229
wókiksuye, 62, 229
wókųze, 154, 229
wókʻokipʻe, 37, 85, 195, 229
wókʻuže, 109, 169, 229
wóle, 181, 229

wolf. See under animals
women: and dreams and visions, 137, 142, 144, 173; and effigies, 121–22; and friendship, 105; and hair, 120; and menstruation, 162, 184, 247n11; and meteors, 80; and ritual, 240n6
wónaǧi, 70, 118, 229
wóniya, 23, 39, 44, 47, 56, 208–9, 211–13, 229. See also life-transformation process
Wóniya Tʻą́ka, 65, 229
wóohola, 37, 109, 170, 229
wópʼila, 112, 229
wópʼiye, 202, 229
wóslolye, 95, 136, 143, 165, 229
wóšnapi, 87, 112, 198, 229
wótʻawe, 197–99, 229. See also war bundle; war medicine
wótʻeȟi, 109, 118, 160, 164, 229
wótʻeȟika, 118, 169, 229
wótʻéȟila, 155, 201, 229. See also taboo
Wounded Knee, 151
wówaglece, 164, 229
wówaȟtani, 109, 138, 155, 164, 229
wówakʻą, 77, 149, 187, 229
wówašʼake, 64, 95, 136, 143, 145, 187, 229
wówayazą, 109, 169, 229
wówihąble, 172, 229
wówištece, 50, 229
wóyakapi, 229, 245n3
wóyuonihą, 37, 229
wóyušʼįyaye, 37, 229

Yanktonai Sioux, 1, 5, 22, 82, 239n22
Yankton Sioux, 1, 5, 16, 22, 49, 122, 144, 237n6
yatápika, 78, 225
yeyá, 176, 229

Yumní, 127, 229
yuónihą, 37, 85, 109, 118, 170, 229, 230
yuwípi, 4, 77–79, 111, 141, 160, 171–72, 177–78, 181, 182, 225, 230, 246n5
yuwį́tapi, 86, 88, 203, 222, 230

zaní, 212, 230. *See also* health; wellness
zįtkála, 56, 230. *See also* birds
Zįtkála Oyáte, 55, 230
zuyá wakʼą́, 198, 230. *See also* war
zuzéca, 56, 230

In the New Visions in Native American
and Indigenous Studies series

*Ojibwe Stories from the Upper
Berens River: A. Irving Hallowell and
Adam Bigmouth in Conversation*
Edited and with an introduction
by Jennifer S. H. Brown

*Ute Land Religion in the
American West, 1879–2009*
Brandi Denison

*Blood Will Tell: Native Americans
and Assimilation Policy*
Katherine Ellinghaus

*Ecology and Ethnogenesis: An
Environmental History of the Wind
River Shoshones, 1000–1868*
Adam R. Hodge

*Of One Mind and Of One Government:
The Rise and Fall of the Creek
Nation in the Early Republic*
Kevin Kokomoor

*Invisible Reality: Storytellers,
Storytakers, and the Supernatural
World of the Blackfeet*
Rosalyn R. LaPier

*Indigenous Lanaguages and
the Promise of Archives*
Edited by Adrianna Link, Abigail
Shelton, and Patrick Spero

*Life of the Indigenous Mind:
Vine Deloria Jr. and the Birth
of the Red Power Movement*
David Martínez

*Everywhen: Australia and the
Language of Deep History*
Ann McGrath, Laura Rademaker,
and Jakelin Troy

*All My Relatives: Exploring Lakota
Ontology, Belief, and Ritual*
David C. Posthumus

*Standing Up to Colonial Power:
The Lives of Henry Roe and
Elizabeth Bender Cloud*
Renya K. Ramirez

*Walking to Magdalena: Personhood
and Place in Tohono O'odham
Songs, Sticks, and Stories*
Seth Schermerhorn

To order or obtain more information on these or other University of Nebraska Press titles, visit nebraskapress.unl.edu.